Reorienting Accounting Education: Reports on the Environment, Professoriate, and Curriculum of Accounting

Joseph J. Schultz, Jr.
Editor

Marcos F. Massoud
Jay M. Smith
Associate Editors

Library of Congress Catalog Card Number 89-081150
ISBN 0-86539-072-X
Printed in the United States of America

American Accounting Association
5717 Bessie Drive
Sarasota, Florida 34233

CONTENTS

FOREWORD

In 1986 when then-President Ray Sommerfeld commenced the appointment of individuals to the Committees whose reports are reflected herein, it was hoped that the product of those committees would provide information useful in establishing a profile of the environment, curriculum and the professorial community which comprise the educational establishment of our discipline. The follow-up committee appointed by President Bill Beaver synthesized the prior committee materials so that their usefulness in policy development would be enhanced.

This monograph provides evidence of trends to be studied, understood, and addressed during a period of transition toward a graduate entry educational standard for the accounting profession. The completed reports build upon the basic structure of the Report of the Bedford Committee (Committee on the Future Structure, Content, and Scope of Accounting Education). They provide information which sets that report in perspective and which should be of interest to anyone who is seeking to gain a better understanding of the contemporary content and process of accountancy education.

The completion of this study coincides with the initiation of the work of the Association's Accounting Education Change Commission which has been established to assist in achieving a goal of serving the public interest through improving the educational process which prepares accountants. The Commission will draw its guidance from both the Bedford Committee Report and the recent report of the managing partners of major public practice firms, *Perspectives on Education: Capabilities for Success in the Accounting Profession* (April 1989).

The efforts of Professor Schultz; the co-editors, Professors Smith and Massoud; and the Committee members are appreciated and gratefully acknowledged.

Gary John Previts
Director of Education
American Accounting Association
Rocky River, Ohio
July 1989

PREFACE

This collection of committee reports represents the culmination of an important effort on the part of many dedicated accounting educators and practitioners. Dating from Doyle Williams' establishment of the AAA Committee on the Future Structure, Content, and Scope of Accounting Education, this effort has spanned nearly five years. Three of the reports contained in this document were made possible by the foresight and understanding supplied by Ray Sommerfeld who appointed the committees during his term as AAA President. The summary report at the beginning of this collection is due to Bill Beaver's desire to see closure on these projects during his office as AAA President. The recent support from the senior partners of the Big Eight firms and the responsive action by the AAA Executive Committee assure that the opportunity for progress will continue. We have now entered an action stage.

I would be remiss if I failed to thank the many people who have contributed to this monograph. Gary Previts, the AAA Director of Education, deserves primary credit as he has provided support and guidance throughout. Gerhard Mueller, AAA President, has nurtured the project to assure its completion. John Simmons, AAA President-Elect, also merits credit for his encouraging remarks and dedication to this monograph that meant more than he can appreciate. As well, the timely and helpful assistance of the project's Research Advisory Committee is recognized. This group was chaired by Jan Williams, University of Tennessee. He was joined by Don Madden, University of Kentucky and Kent St. Pierre, James Madison University.

Marc Massoud and Jay Smith, my associate editors, have done yeoman duty on the initial formulation of their reports and in assisting me in the production stage. JaNoel Lowe has patiently taught me much about editing. Finally, I speak for Marc, Jay, and myself when I thank the nearly 30 committee members who helped us so very much and the many fine educators and practitioners who gave their valuable time to share their insights and opinions.

Joseph J. Schultz, Jr.
Tempe, Arizona
June 1989

PREFACE

REORIENTING ACCOUNTING EDUCATION: REPORTS ON THE ENVIRONMENT, PROFESSORIATE, AND CURRICULUM OF ACCOUNTING

Editor's Note: The committee reports contained in this monograph were submitted to the American Accounting Association Executive Committee during Summer 1987 and Spring 1988. Each committee was formed expressly to assist understanding the circumstances concerning, and making suggestions with respect to, implementing the Bedford Committee report. Since the reports were filed, the Executive Committee and the senior partners of the Big Eight accounting firms have reviewed them and taken action to support many of the ideas and suggestions contained in the reports. In this quote from a memorandum from AAA President Gerhard G. Mueller dated January 1989, he notes that the Executive Committee:

1. Has endorsed postbaccalaureate accounting education as a reasonable expectation,
2. Has endorsed the Bedford Committee Report,
3. Disavows the superiority of any single avenue of educational preparation, and
4. Has committed itself to leadership in bringing about appropriate changes in accounting education programs (Mueller, 1989).

In April 1989, the Big Eight senior partners issued *Perspectives on Education: Capabilities for Success in the Accounting Profession* (Arthur Andersen & Co. et al., 1989). The publication acknowledged a concern about "the quality and number of the accounting graduates available to the public accounting profession" and supported efforts by the AICPA and the Bedford Committee and its follow-up groups. The position piece recognized the Bedford Committee report, the essence of which is described shortly, as providing an "excellent foundation for the future of accounting education, including curriculum content, the teaching process and faculty responsibilities." The focus was on the "capabilities needed by the profession that should be developed by the educational process." It accepted the proposition that curriculum development and teaching methodology to reach these needs should be primarily academia's responsibility. Also, the paper pledged up to $4 million of support over the next five years contingent that the funds be used "effectively and in a timely way for the design and implementation of innovative curricula, new teaching methods and supporting materials that will equip graduates . . . for success. . . ." The paper challenged the AAA to exercise leadership in bringing about this implementation.

As this publication goes to press, the AAA has assumed a leadership role and has begun formation of a committee to forge change in accounting education. The chairman of that committee will be Doyle Williams who, as President of the AAA, established and charged the Bedford Committee. Some of the other significant issues that arose subsequent to the issuance of the original reports are included in the first report, which summarizes all the reports and relates them to the Bedford Committee report.

FOLLOW-UP COMMITTEE ON THE FUTURE STRUCTURE, CONTENT, AND SCOPE OF ACCOUNTING EDUCATION 1987-88

Joseph J. Schultz, Jr.
Chairman
Arizona State University

David R. Campbell
Case Western Reserve University

Charles G. Carpenter
Miami University

James W. Deitrick
University of Texas at Austin

Don Dupont
Arthur Andersen & Co.

Thomas W. Lin
University of Southern California

Marcos F. Massoud
Claremont McKenna College

Mohamed Onsi
Syracuse University

Jane T. Rubin
American Assembly of
Collegiate Schools of Business

Douglas Snowball
University of Florida

Miklos A. Vasarhelyi
AT & T Bell Labs and
Columbia University

REPORT OF THE FOLLOW-UP COMMITTEE ON THE FUTURE STRUCTURE, CONTENT, AND SCOPE OF ACCOUNTING EDUCATION 1987-88*

This report represents the culmination of two AAA committees: the Professorial Environment Committee established by then President Ray Sommerfeld for the 1986–87 year and the Follow-Up Committee on the Future Structure, Content, and Scope of Accounting Education established by President William Beaver for the 1987–88 year. The charge to the Professorial Environment Committee was as follows:

To document, in as much detail as possible, how the professorial environment of the accounting professor has changed during the past 25 years so that we might better anticipate the significance of these factors on the near-term implementation issues inherent in the 1986 Report on the Future Structure, Content, and Scope of Accounting Education (AAA, 1986).

---

*Prescribing implementation guidance for the future course of accounting education is an awesome and humbling task. Consequently, most of this document should be viewed as describing and recommending an array of options to be considered in achieving the views set forth by the Future Structure, Content, and Scope of Accounting Education Committee.

I am indebted to Ray Sommerfeld, who, while President of the American Accounting Association, asked me to chair the Professorial Environment Committee. Also I thank his successor, William H. Beaver, who allowed me to continue as chair of a new committee, the Follow-Up Committee, until the first task was completed, and extended the scope to consolidate several other matters.

Both committees identified trends that began nearly 25 years ago and are expected to continue through the mid–1990s. The committees contrasted those trends with the direction recommended by the original future committee and proposed intervention where needed to accomplish those recommendations. The first part of the report contains a summary of the Professorial Environment Committee findings and addresses the implementation charge.

The extent to which this report has merit is attributable to the fine committee members and to several others who played major roles. Dave Campbell acted effectively as a co-chairman of the Committee and assumed responsibility for the "external" section of the Professorial Committee report. He was ably assisted by several on the 1986–87 Committee. Don Dupont provided tremendous assistance, supplying data on fund-raising and hiring trends that would not otherwise have been obtainable. Miklos Vasarheyli gave us insight on the future of technology that we could not have secured (or understood). Doug Snowball researched and wrote the section dealing with trends in higher education and produced the idea for the schematic in Exhibit 1.

As to the "internal" part of the Professorial Committee report, I relied most heavily on Jan Meade (at the time my graduate assistant) to help me formulate the overall plan, develop much of the instrumentation, coordinate the mailing, and assist with the editing. Jane Rubin researched and drafted the portion on the AACSB effect and helped us keep our perspective. Tom Lin contributed significantly throughout and in the final preparation. Shyam Sunder helped to conceptualize our task and to develop a part of the questionnaire. Chuck Carpenter kept our focus on the material issues, thus preventing us from wandering into pure triviality. Miklos Vasarheyli amplified our notions on how technology may assist in accounting education. Jim Dietrick, Marc Massoud, and Mohamed Onsi joined us for the Follow-Up Committee and brought needed perspective to our effort. Inder Khurana, my graduate assistant, brought the massive data base to its knees through determined and effective effort. Finally, Barbara Bennett typed the questionnaires, manuscript, and tables and struggled through numerous drafts, and Susan Hendershot helped with the editing.

Again, I thank these people but recognize that responsibility for errors or lack of clarity rests with me.

Joseph J. Schultz, Jr.
Tempe, Arizona
March 1988

The Committee on the Future Structure, Content, and Scope of Accounting Education was chaired by Norton M. Bedford and was composed of distinguished accountants from education, public accounting, industry, and government. After two years of study (1984 to 1986), the Committee concluded that the existing structure of accounting education "required major reorientation" before the year 2000. The Committee's recommendations included having colleges and universities approach accounting education "as an information development and distribution function for economic decision making" and placing that emphasis on "learning to learn as the primary classroom objective." The Committee's most comprehensive concern that accounting education should provide the foundation for a broad education was the basis for 28 recommendations. These 28 recommendations and findings from the follow up committees are summarized in Exhibit 2 of our report. Various articles related to the report and other aspects of the future of accounting and the necessary education appear in *Issues in Accounting Education* (AAA, 1986) and the *Journal of Accountancy* (Bedford and Shenkir, 1987; Mednick, 1988).

In addition to the Professorial Environment Committee, President Sommerfeld established two other committees in 1986-87 to develop matter relevant to implement the Futures Committee's report. One, the Future Structure Follow-Up Committee of 1986-87, was charged to determine the extent to which accountants supported the recommendations of the Futures Committee and to implement those suggestions.The other, the Changes in Accounting Education Committee, was charged to document significant changes in accounting education over the past 25 years that may present difficulties in implementing the Futures Committee recommendations. This committee dealt primarily with issues involving the accounting curriculum and the use of different teaching methods.

The 1987-88 Future Structure Follow-Up Committee, constituted by President Beaver, was charged to revisit the Futures Committee report; combine the findings and recommendations of the three committees established by Sommerfeld; and make recommendations regarding implementation. Because the five committees involved in this report may prove confusing, they will be referred to as follows:

- •Futures Committee (Committee on the Future Structure, Content, and Scope of Accounting Education), existed for 1984–85 and 1985–86, chaired by N. M. Bedford (This committee's report is often referred to as the "Bedford Committee report.")
- •Changes Committee (Committee on Changes in Accounting Education), existed for 1986–87, chaired by J. M. Smith
- •Professorial Committee (Professorial Environment Committee), existed for 1986–87, chaired by J. J. Schultz, Jr.
- •Follow-Up I (Follow-Up Committee on the Future Structure, Content, and Scope of Accounting Education), existed for 1986–87, chaired by M. F. Massoud
- •Follow-Up II (Follow-Up Committee on the Future Structure, Content, and Scope of Accounting Education), existed for 1987–88, chaired by J. J. Schultz, Jr.

Because of the expansive scope of the combined charges, the first section of this report presents the summary and conclusions of the Professorial Committee; reviews the recommendations of the Futures Committee and relates the findings of the three 1986–87 committees to those recommendations; and proposes ways to implement the recommendations in view of conclusions from the findings of the various committees. The report presents the completed report of the Professorial Committee, which provides substantial supporting data for the summary and conclusions set forth immediately. Reports of the Changes Committee and the Follow-Up Committee are included in their entirely later in this volume.

THE PROFESSORIAL COMMITTEE

In addition to the charge noted, President Sommerfeld asked members of the Committee to document changes in the following areas over the past 25 years and to anticipate their impact on near-term implementation of the recommendations of the Futures Committee (AAA, 1986):

1. Professorial competence in relative and absolute terms.
2. The promotion and tenure process and criteria.
3. The requirements for terminal degree.
4. The extent of specialization.

Also, we were encouraged to review other factors (e.g., salary compression), which we deemed relevant to both the professorial environment and near-term implementation. Our overall strategy in approaching the charge was to

1. Consider the trends over the past 25 years and project these trends to 1995 (the "near-term" future alluded to by the Futures Committee—AAA, 1986).
2. Anticipate the extent to which these trends would militate for or against implementation of the recommendations.
3. Propose intervention strategies, if needed, to assist in implementation.
4. Report to the Executive Committee of the American Accounting Association for its ultimate disposition of the report.

TOPICAL OVERVIEW

Exhibit 1 depicts a representation of the professorial environment that generally underlaid our study. Clearly, a major part of this environment falls outside the university. Thus some of our effort addressed changes in this external environment, particularly as related to the practice of accounting. The second part of our study considered changes at the macro level for higher education generally. The third part of our study focused on changes internal to the university that more directly affect the accounting professor. Some of the changes in this section emanated from outside the university (e.g., private funding, accreditation standards) but were so directly related to the accounting professorial environment that we included them in this part of the study. This last part directly addressed the forces identified by President Sommerfeld.

The first part of our study, which dealt with external environmental factors, tracked trends in and influences of (1) the growth of accounting practice and education; (2) macroeconomic factors relevant to this growth; (3) international forces contributing to change; (4) social awareness of accountants' roles both by U.S. society and by members of our profession; (5) increased litigation; (6) the growth of technical standards; (7) the changes in the scope of services provided by public accounting firms; and (8) technological innovation. The second part of our study scrutinized *general* trends in higher education involving students, institutions, faculty, and financing. With regard to student trends, we examined patterns of enrollment, level (undergraduate versus graduate), gender, race, age, attendance status, admission scores, student attitudes and values, and academic and career interests. To a limited extent, we related these general patterns to trends with accounting students and graduates. The final part of our study examined more specific factors within the university that have changed with regard to the individual accounting professor and the components of the university environment. At the *individual* level we investigated trends in competence, allocation of time, job satisfaction, and specialization. Specific factors measured and the methodology employed are discussed thoroughly in the full Professorial Report, which follows this summary report. In part, the findings are based on a survey of accounting faculty divided on the basis of their start-dates (early 1960s, early 1970s, and early 1980s) and whether their program offers a doctoral concentration in accounting.

SUMMARY AND CONCLUSIONS

The growth in demand for accounting education and the 1969 AACSB accreditation requirement that a minimum proportion of accounting faculty have doctoral degrees result primarily from direct factors driving change in the accounting professorial environment over the past quarter of a century. External conditions (e.g., techno-

EXHIBIT 1
INTERFACE BETWEEN EXTERNAL
AND PROFESSORIAL ENVIRONMENT

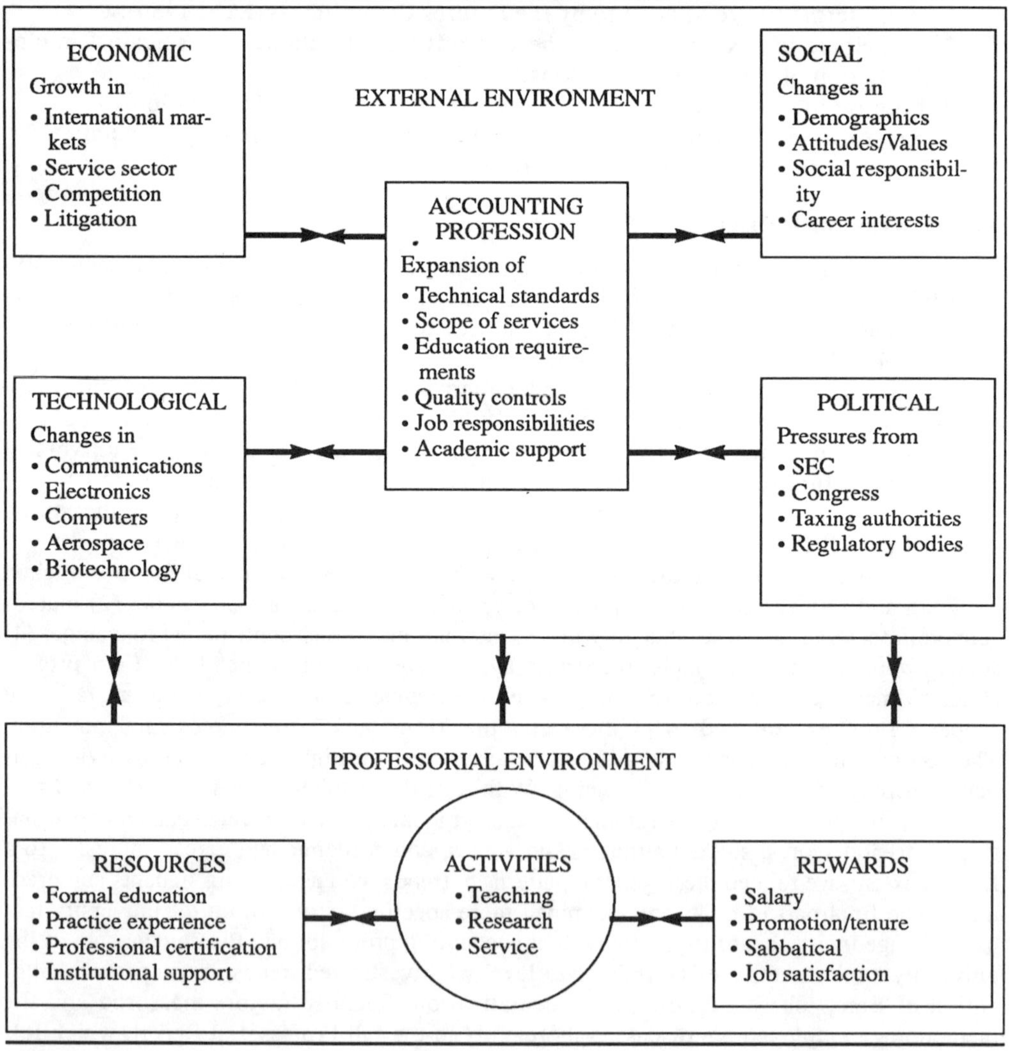

logical change, economic growth) beyond the control of accounting practice or education have driven and augmented these factors. Profound change has resulted in the professionalization of accounting faculty separate from accounting practice. That is, the common body of knowledge for the two differ sharply, and many of their interests and several important goals and values differ.

The growth in the demand for accounting education over the past 25 years constitutes the single greatest factor affecting the accounting professorial environment. During this period the total number of college students increased 150 percent; the number of accounting degrees, 400 percent. Because the relationship between student and faculty population tends to be proportional, the opportunities for new members to enter the accounting professorial profession have been exceptional due to this growth alone.

The 1969 AACSB doctoral degree requirement has contributed very significantly to this opportunity and to the change in the body of knowledge among accounting faculty. The timing of the changed requirement from a master's degree coupled with a CPA certificate to a doctoral degree has proved critical.

At the outset of the "Sputnik era" and just before the "baby boomers" embarked on their university education, studies by Pierson (1959) and Gordon and Howell (1959) levied serious criticism at business education. Concommitant with that criticism came increased demand and heightened concern about scientific/mathematical training, widespread availability of computers, and increased funding for graduate education and research. Although formal experimentation/study was present to a limited extent in accounting near the beginning of this era (e.g., Stedry, 1960; Dyckman, 1964A, 1964B), the major change occurred in the late 1960s (e.g., Beaver, 1968; Ball and Brown, 1968). The effect of introducing sophisticated methodologies into accounting research on a pervasive basis had a marked effect on accounting doctoral programs. Of *all* doctoral degrees with an accounting emphasis, *two-thirds* have been awarded since 1971. During the past 20 years, the proportion of full-time accounting faculty to total accounting faculty has risen from 54 percent to 71 percent, thus introducing far more sophisticated research expertise into the accounting professorial environment.

Meteoric growth in the common body of technical and codified accounting knowledge coupled with the requirement for in-depth knowledge of these research methodologies and the rising demand for increased research output have significantly strained accounting faculty. Exacerbating this strain is the reluctance of both the practitioner and academic arms to take positive steps to increase the four years required for accounting education. Although the AICPA Council's 1969 position favoring a five-year requirement has served as early endorsement of added education, not until 1988 did the AICPA membership vote for a postbaccalaureate requirement to take effect for new members *after 2000* (AICPA, 1988). The American Accounting Association's Executive Committee, however, has endorsed the Futures Committee Report, which calls for graduate education as appropriate for obtaining a full university professional accounting education. Also, as of June 1989, eight states had adopted some version of this "graduate equivalent" requirement lending more weight to an extended period for accounting education (Thomashower, 1989; Williams, 1989; AICPA and NASBA, 1987–88).

Implementation Concerns

Substantive implementation of the Futures Committee's 28 recommendations will prove to be a major challenge. Because we believe the weight of our findings tilt toward the challenge, we initially identified those conditions from both the external and internal environments to the university that threaten implementation. Between now and the mid-1990s (the checkpoint called for by the Futures Committee), increased complexity in computer application and codification related to external reporting, auditing, and taxation is likely. The conflicting pressures wrought by increased litigation and competition in public accounting do not seem likely to abate. The shift in orientation from the traditional focus of accounting and auditing to tax and management consulting in the public accounting sector threatens the public accounting financial support historically available almost exclusively to accounting academic units.

Student population in higher education peaked in 1983 and is expected to decline by 6 percent by the mid-1990s. Because the population of 18- to 22-year-olds in the United States is expected to decline by 25 percent during the decade ending in the mid-1990s, an influx of foreign, older, or graduate students will be necessary to hold such decline to 6 percent. Older students will more likely attend universities in urban as opposed to rural areas. The population increase of 18- to 22-year-olds beyond the mid-1990s will increasingly consist of minorities who are substantially underrepresented in higher education populations generally and especially in the more technical areas of business education (e.g., accounting and computer information systems). The number of faculty overall is expected to decrease by 12 percent in private schools and 9 percent in public schools in the decade ending in 1993.

When adjusted for inflation, higher education budgets have changed directly proportionally to increases in student populations. Over the past 15 years, state government has funded a larger proportion of these budgets; federal government, a smaller proportion; students, about the same proportion. Private contribution, especially that from business, has become much more important in recent years. Given the aging of U.S. society, the political strength of its older members, and the existing trend of federal budget deficits, higher education budgets are unlikely to secure any real increases from the federal sector between now and the mid-1990s. A real decrease seems more probable. Other sources of increased funding may also be difficult to secure.

As with the above factors, the measures that we made of changes in competence over time have mixed implications for implementing the Futures Committee Report recommendations. One source of mixed implications is increased research expertise. That is, extensive devotion to research *could* lead to the neglect of other matters, for example, curriculum development. Such development lies at the heart of the Committee's recommendations. Because the recommendations call for integration of accounting with broad organizational objectives to form a total information system, the decrease in full-time practice experience prior to becoming a full-time academic may also threaten implementation of the Futures Committee's recommendations. We note that among members in our three start-date groups, this experience has decreased (early 1960s—84 months, early 1970s—74, early 1980s—64) but not to the point of serious concern. Those starting in the doctoral-granting institutions in the early 1980s reported the lowest amount of experience, 47 months, that is consistent with a slightly decreasing emphasis on professional certification (early 1960s—72 percent certified, early 1970s—79, early 1980s—64). Clearly, the doctoral degree is now the entree to academic accounting as the proportion of accounting faculty with doctorates has increased from 31 percent 20 years ago to 57 percent currently.

Newer faculty spend more time on research than faculty who started their careers earlier. Faculty at doctoral-granting institutions spend more time on research than faculty at nondoctoral-granting institutions. Conversely, faculty at nondoctoral-granting schools spend more time on teaching and on outside remunerative activities. Probably due to different reward structures and the availability of research grant money, the divergence of the pattern between the faculty at the two types of institutions becomes more pronounced during the summer period.

In contrast to their peers who began their careers in the early 1960s, faculty starting in the early 1970s and 1980s derive less relative satisfaction from teaching and more from research. This pattern holds even when satisfaction from the early phases of their careers is compared.

Extensive specialization in a limited number of business functions may prove damaging to the integrative type of knowledge needed for accounting education as envisioned by the Futures Committee. Although our results showed a tendency toward increasing specialization (concentration) in teaching and practice experience areas by newer faculty, these trends do not appear to pose a significant threat to the goal of broader education as recommended by the Futures Committee. In examining the AAA's sectional membership data, however, we noted a very sharp decline in overall practitioner AAA membership, which may signal at least a perceived lack of relevance of AAA activities to practitioners. Such a trend does not bode well for increased future private support.

Decreased faculty-student contact outside of class over the past 25 years received the strongest unfavorable rating by our respondents. The rating deviated little across start-date groups or types of institutions. Our respondents also expressed substantial concern about the increased use of multiple choice questions and increased class sizes (including megasections) in the accounting educational process. The use of megasections, especially in the first principles course, is gaining relatively wide use because it allows for some gains in efficiency while normally assuring student contact with a full-time faculty member. It is noteworthy that AACSB accreditation standards count *all* the student credit hours taught in this format as taught by full-time faculty, although usually a substantial portion of actual class contact comes with part-time instructors, including graduate students. Our concern is twofold: the presence of large classes (including megasections) may require innovative approaches to implement the Committee's recommendations, and the use of megasections may be difficult to change in view of inertia and changing faculty reward structures and interests.

Perhaps the greatest concern to implementation of the Futures Committee's recommendations is the change in the faculty reward structure. Over the past 25 years, performance in research has grown in importance compared to performance in teaching. Performance in the service/administration area has remained at a somewhat nominal level. For the tenure decision at doctoral-granting schools, faculty respondents report an average weight for research of 66 percent; for teaching, 27 percent. For nondoctoral-granting schools, the reported weights are 47 percent and 42 percent, respectively. Our findings indicate an even stronger emphasis on research in this decision process by the mid-1990s. Furthermore, compensation decisions (i.e., raises) depend in part on market value in nearly every school. Market value in turn is principally determined by research productivity. For those currently seeking tenure, our respondents report an average success rate of 60 percent. They expect this rate to to fall to nearly half of that by the mid-1990s. Two outcomes seem likely. First, all faculty who wish to achieve relatively positive rewards will need to focus more heavily on research outputs as rewards are likely to become far more scarce (see earlier discussions on budget predictions and enrollment patterns). Second, administrators at all levels will be pressed for more resources to support research activity, thus limiting any amounts available for curriculum development. Based on our information, it appears that much of this control will remain with administrators at the college and university levels. And, although our data do not presently support a strong case for salary compression, the likely tight budget situation may well contribute to intensify this condition further. Publication in academic journals that typically involves time-consuming methodologies will continue to be valued far more than publication in even the most prestigious practitioner outlets.

Implementation Aids

To this point, our report may be viewed as indicating significant concerns about implementation of the Futures Committee's recommendations. Positive conditions for change based on data in our findings do, however, exist. Perhaps foremost among these is an extraordinarily talented group of accounting faculty who report more relative satisfaction from teaching than from any other endeavor. As a whole, our respondents report 52 percent of their relative job satisfaction from teaching as compared to 18 percent from research, the second highest rated source. At doctoral-granting schools, this spread narrows to 44 percent for teaching and 29 percent for research.

As compared to faculty of earlier times, faculty of today seem to have better training and understanding of how knowledge is formulated. They are well versed in challenging the soundness of the bases underlying ideas. This suggests a heightened level of intellectual curiosity. The relative lack of this very attribute seems to lie at the center of the current debate on the value of today's education. Increased emphasis in doctoral education in the areas of mathematical models, probability theory and application, decision processes, and experimental design contributes substantially to the ability to assess ideas critically. Application of these approaches holds the promise for increased student understanding of matters ranging from the integration of complex concepts to computer-based models that are already being used in practice. We believe that it is this intellectual curiosity, often associated with our best researchers, that led deans, who were surveyed, to report a strong positive correlation between good researchers and good teachers.

Even though faculty population in general is expected to decrease between now and the mid-1990s, accounting faculty positions will probably still remain attractive. Accounting faculty tend to earn about 15 percent more than faculty at large. New accounting faculty, however, earn nearly 40 percent more than new faculty generally; this premium does not include summer research support that is frequently available at amounts in excess of that for faculty in other areas. Also contributing to a positive forecast for accounting doctorates is the fact that only 57 percent of accounting faculty possess a doctoral degree.

Student population, clearly a concern in all academic areas, does not appear to be so serious in accounting. Our respondents ranked the increased quality of accounting students as having the second most favorable effect on accounting education over the past 25 years. Moreover, today's entering freshmen are far more interested in being well off financially than their counterparts two decades ago. Nearly 26 percent of all entering freshmen recently reported a desire to study business as compared to half that percentage 25 years ago. This trend seems likely to continue to the mid-1990s.

When considered simultaneously, several apparent trends seem to unfold into a pattern militating in favor of implementation. A reduction in the extent of the supply-demand imbalance for accounting faculty, considered in conjunction with the prospect of a stable or slightly decreasing student population, leads to favorable prospects for improved class sizes and reduced student-to-faculty ratios. Decreased teaching loads (typically 10 to 12 hours per week in 1967–68; currently, 6 to 9 hours) and a still relatively large number of different preparations per faculty (about five over the last three years, according to our respondents) offer a genuine opportunity for increased attention to teaching of the type recommended by the Committee. Greater attention to interactive learning and integrative approaches, reduced usage of multiple-choice questions, greater contact outside the classroom, and other matters of concern to the Committee and our respondents increase in their likelihood.

Availability of computers combined with accounting faculties' computer expertise offers the opportunity for significant gains in teaching efficiency. To the extent that computer-assisted instruction can be made available to help students practice problems outside the classroom, the goal of interactive learning both in and out of class can be enhanced. Other advancements that offer potential are CD-ROM storage and expert systems. When the first is endowed with key word-search capabilities, the process of bibliographic research may become so efficient that some of the current focus on learning rote details can be converted to an integrative experience. Expert systems offer the possibility of enhanced learning in developing judgment and decision-making skills that parallel realistic models.

Some aspects of the reward structure offer favorable potential for implementing the Futures Committee's recommendations. The huge increases in the donated amounts from the three large firm foundations surveyed in our study (1966—$100,000; 1976—$3,000,000; 1986—$10,000,000) indicate a willingness and an ability to support development of accounting education. If a program could be conceived and executed with the same apparent effectiveness of the Peat Marwick Foundation's Research Opportunities in Auditing program, implementation prospects should improve substantially. Summer periods, paid sabbaticals (available to 80 percent of our respondents), relatively unstructured time constraints during the regular academic year, and differential reward structures among accounting units offer the potential for maximizing progress by the mid-1990s.

Finally, in light of the recent AICPA vote on education for the year 2000, increased general concern about broader based education and related changes in state laws, it is expected that the movement toward a standard postbaccalaureate program with a broader base of studies, including liberal arts, will be received more favorably.

THE 1985-86 FUTURES COMMITTEE RECOMMENDATIONS AND THE 1986-87 COMMITTEE REPORTS

President Beaver asked the Follow-Up Committee II to analyze and synthesize the findings and conclusions reached by the three committees established by then President Sommerfeld as related to the Futures Committee's recommendations. A convenient method for such integration was to borrow the integrative framework already begun by Smith (1987). We label this Exhibit 2, which is organized to parallel the

EXHIBIT 2
THE SOMMERFELD COMMITTEES' FINDINGS
AND CONCLUSIONS RELATED TO
THE BEDFORD COMMITTEE'S RECOMMENDATIONS*

Number	Recommendations/Committees' Findings	25-Year trend
Scope and Content (Recommendations 1–7)		
1	**View accounting as broad information system.** Both practitioner and academic respondents strongly agree that accounting is a total information system and that it consists of multiple types of information. Educators believe that practice will continue its trend toward breadth. PROF: Clearly, change in practice environment is pervasive and dynamic. The scope of service in public accounting has changed and is likely to continue to at a rapid rate.	Little change
2	**Broad general education—avoid premature specialization.** Both agree—practitioners agree very strongly.	Negative (E)
3	**Expand liberal arts and sciences.** Both agree—practitioners strongly. Academics want many of the courses in this area specified rather than freely elected.	Negative (M)
4	**Accounting education—emphasize skills for life-long learning.** Both groups strongly agree.	Positive (M)
5	**Design learning objectives to help students learn, think, and be creative.** Both groups very strongly agree.	Little change
6	**Establish high expectations for students. Adjust curriculum to match professional skills, capacities, and knowledge needed.** Not addressed	Positive (M)
7	**Flexible accounting programs** Not addressed.	Negative (M)
Structure (Recommendations 8–10)		
8	**Broad educational accounting structure.**	Negative (M)
9	**Specialized education only at graduate level. Total time for accounting education, at least five years.** Two issues surveyed. Both groups agree relatively strongly that accounting education be at least five years. Considerable disagreement exists on whether specialized accounting should be taught only at the graduate level (about 50 percent against and 35 percent for).	Negative (E)

Note: The findings listed under each item is that of Follow-Up Committee I unless otherwise noted. Where the Professorial Committee has information that bears on the item, it is preceded by "PROF:." The far right column describes findings from the Changes Committee that dealt primarily with curriculum and textbook issues.
M = Moderately
E = Extensively
*Adapted directly from Exhibit 7 of Smith (1987).

EXHIBIT 2
(CONTINUED)

Number	Recommendations/Committees' Findings	25-Year trend
10	**Comparative advantage to determine type of specialization offered in academia.** Not addressed	Negative (M)
Faculty, Administrative, and Professional Concerns—The Teaching Process (Recommendations 11–13)		
11	**Design courses so students can be active, independent learners.** Both strongly agree. PROF: Decreased emphasis as indicated by time allocated to, reward for, and job satisfaction from teaching may make this difficult to realize. Faculty still cite satisfaction from teaching as major contributor to satisfaction. Deans and faculty both expect greater emphasis on research in the future. Tenure and promotion will be much harder to secure in the future.	Negative (M)
12	**Design learning technologies to increase faculty contact with students.** Educators only surveyed and only indirectly. Strongly agree that implementation will be difficult due to reward structure. Strongly agree that research is rewarded more than teaching, which in turn is rewarded much more than service. PROF: Respondents uniformly cited decreased student contact outside of class as greatest negative change in accounting education over the past 25 years. See comment under item 11.	Little change
13	**Change in textbooks to realize these objectives.** Not addressed PROF: See comments under item 11.	Little change
Faculty, Administrative, and Professional Concerns—Faculty Responsibilities ((Recommendations 14–15)		
14	**Faculty rewards should be broad.** Not addressed directly, although some findings in item 12 are related. PROF: See comments under 11.	Positive (E)
15	**Encourage basic and applied research.** Addressed indirectly. Both seem to agree that this is how research grants are allocated. PROF: Increased value placed on academic journal articles and decreased value placed on practitioner journals over time. Decreased practice experience of faculty may impair. Increased research competence of faculty may enhance academic research. Decreased practitioner membership may decrease interaction between academics and practitioners.	Positive (M)
Faculty, Administrative, and Professional Concerns — Administration (Recommendations 16–20)		
16	**High standards of admission to accounting programs.** Educators only surveyed. Strongly support need for more autonomy for admissions. See item 23 also. PROF: Increased quality of accounting students cited by respondents as major positive change over the past 25 years.	Positive (M)

EXHIBIT 2
(CONTINUED)

Number	Recommendations/Committees' Findings	25-Year trend
17	**Faculty involvement in introductory and intermediate. Increased student advisement.** Two issues: only educators surveyed. Agree with concept. Strongly doubt implementation due to cost concerns. PROF: Increased use of megasections in Principles in recent years. See comments under items 11 and 12.	Little change
18	**Resources for complementary programs.** Not addressed. PROF: Potential for serious financial strain among some colleges from present to mid-1990s. Strain may be widespread.	No information
Faculty, Administrative, and Professional Concerns — The Teaching Process (Recommendations 19–20)		
19	**Extend peer review of accounting programs by nonaccounting faculty, other accounting faculty, and practitioners.** Survey asked educators only for evaluation by other *accounting* faculty. Agree. PROF: AACSB plays a major role in influencing accounting education.	No information
20	**Encourage interaction among faculty members in accounting and liberal arts.** Not addressed.	No information
Faculty, Administrative, and Professional Concerns — Accreditation (Recommendations 21–24)		
21	**University action to encourage graduate study.** Not addressed. PROF: May come as a reaction to financial concerns (see comments under item 18) and due to encouragement of various nationally prominent committee recommendations for pushing technical education beyond basic education.	Positive (M)
22	**University action to emphasize use of arts, sciences, and humanities resources.** Not addressed. PROF: See comment under item 21.	No information
23	**University action to allow more autonomy to accounting programs.** Survey educators only. Agree. PROF: See comment under item 21. Control of tenure/promotion system and reward structure likely to become more centralized. Integrative nature of changes in practice seem to militate for closer ties to other areas taught in colleges of business.	Positive (M)
24	**Minimize procedural accounting in courses required for accreditation.**	Little change

EXHIBIT 2
(CONTINUED)

Number	Recommendations/Committees' Findings	25-Year trend
	Two issues surveyed, which related indirectly. Strongly agree that the CPA exam influences course content. There is disagreement that students' pass rate on CPA exam measures quality of program. Addressed indirectly in responses reported for item 25. PROF: Increase in codified knowledge over the past 25 years seen as having little effect on quality of accounting education by our respondents.	
Faculty, Administrative, and Professional Concerns —Professorial Examinations (Recommendation 25)		
25	**Base curricula on accounting practice and research and multidisciplinary research.** Agree, with practitioners agreeing more strongly than educators (6:1 versus 2:1). PROF: See comments under item 11.	Little change
Faculty, Administrative, and Professional Concerns — The Teaching Process (Recommendations 26-28)		
26	**Employers of entry-level accounting graduates should increase their understanding of the impact of their policies on differentiating between undergraduates and graduates.** Not addressed.	No assessment
27	**Institutions should consider reward structures that build diverse research faculty while respecting traditions of freedom and tenure.** Considerable concern over lack of autonomy and lack of reward of diversity. PROF: See comments under item 11.	No assessment
28	**Research funds directed to understanding economics of accounting education.** Not addressed. PROF: See comments under item 11.	No assessment

Futures Committee's recommendation as they related to various dimensions of the accounting educational process. The broad dimensions are clearly denoted preceding the pertinent recommendations, which have the same number as those in the Bedford Committee report. In addition to the conclusions noted in Exhibit 2, the Changes Committee (Smith, 1987) reported six factors that have a pervasive impact on, and that are essential to any analysis of, accounting education. These are the factors:

1. Textbook dependency.
2. Lack of faculty rewards.
3. CPA examination.
4. Accreditation requirements.
5. FASB, Congress, and SEC influence.
6. Business environment.

The Changes Committee's discussion of these six factors is summarized below and is supplemented by the other committees' reports.

Most accounting courses are textbook dependent. Radical departures from existing texts have generally resulted in failure, with few exceptions. Many undergraduate sections are taught by graduate students who rely very heavily on existing text material. Indeed, Follow-Up Committee I found that some of its faculty respondents expressed serious concern about teaching skills in which they had limited training (Massoud, 1987, p. 189). In recognition of this dilemma, the Committee recommended that the AAA develop a model curriculum with detailed courses and specific content and seriously consider presenting "workshops and seminars in learning theory, teaching methods, and classroom concepts" (Massoud, 1987, pp. 185 and 187).

Curriculum development and experimentation, which fall under the classification of teaching, are seldom rewarded to the same extent as research and publication. In addition to the formal reward system, the Committee concluded that grants and release time for curriculum development were in short supply compared to grants for research that may lead to refereed articles in academic publications. The Professorial Committee findings support the conclusion that research will continue gaining in importance relative to teaching through the mid-1990s. Follow-Up Committee I called for recognition of outstanding teaching on the same basis as outstanding research and publishing (Massoud, 1987, p. 187).

The timing and content of the CPA examination has a major and understandable impact on accounting education. The Change Committee advocates two modifications to disassociate the exam from university education. A movement of the exam to several weeks after typical graduation times and a curtailment of the publication of pass rates by university affiliation will help achieve this goal. Follow-Up Committee I makes similar recommendations (Massoud, 1987).

Accreditation requirements have "perhaps the greatest influence on overall curriculum. . ." (Smith, 1987, p. 172). In particular, in accounting the requirements have influenced systems, computers, and general business courses. They represent a deterrent to curriculum experimentation due to the emphasis on a broad status quo. Deans who control the AACSB are typically not close to the needs of the accounting profession. The Professorial Committee's findings support the notion that the AACSB accreditation requirements have had a profound effect on the accounting professorial environment. The Professorial Committee's findings are more positive. For example, the AACSB requirement limiting business course work in the degree program has contributed to students receiving a broad general education, and requirements for a doctoral degree have contributed to the extensive storehouse of human talent present among accounting faculty.

The FASB, Congress, and SEC have also influenced the accounting profession and the nature of the material taught in accounting programs. These agencies and the courts seem to have done more than any others to expand the common body of knowledge. This expansion in part provides the justification for added formal education. The Professorial Committee's findings support this conclusion. The Changes Committee recommended that "students should understand that accounting is a discipline that has significant impact on the economy both of our country and the world. Professors should broaden their courses to incorporate these influences wherever appropriate" (Smith, 1987, p. 173).

Most curricula in accounting master's programs recognize this influence and have kept their structures relatively broad, incorporating an appropriate number of nonaccounting courses. The Changes Committee recommended that all universities bear this in mind when considering changing their curricula. Follow-Up Committee I's findings support this notion with minor exception (i.e., based only on practitioner responses, in the near term, graduates possessing a master's degree with a specialization appear more likely to command entry positions than are generalists). Also, practitioner respondents indicated that persons with bachelor's degrees will continue to be hired to fill many positions.

The findings indicate a practical need for five-year accounting curricula to offer specialization tracks for students, at least initially. Follow-Up Committee I indirectly recognizes the economic dilemma of both the student and the employer in several of its recommendations. In essence, the Committee supports the continuation of a four-year program that could feed into a single fifth year for students. Also, it supports separate career tracks within accounting firms for those with bachelor's versus those with master's degrees. Finally, the Committee cites a need for the AAA to design, as specifically as possible, some model curricula to meet those needs.

Follow-Up Committee I reported several other findings as well. Both practitioners and educators believe that changing the structure of accounting education will be difficult. In addition to the implied problems noted, political issues encroaching on existing units' subject matter were specifically noted (e.g., that of management information systems units).

Another finding indicated that both educators and practitioners strongly support the proposition that "the accounting program [should] induce students to develop higher levels of professionalism, leadership and work ethic. . . ." Yet a slight preponderance of educators (the only audience surveyed on this item) accepts the proposition that "a student's ambition, work ethic, and leadership potential are derived from *within* rather than taught. . . ." (Massoud, 1987, p. 192). The practitioner group so strongly supported the first proposition (94 percent strongly agreed or agreed) that they attribute more influence to accounting programs and educators than educators realize or believe they have.

In addition to suggestions already noted, Follow-Up Committee I recommended that the AAA take a firm stand on the need for a five-year education in preparation for entry to the profession along with implementing guidelines and that doctoral students be required to take a teaching methods seminar. The Committee also recommended that all existing faculty be required to participate in a workshop on teaching methods and that young practitioners be exposed to these new methods.

OVERALL PROPOSALS FOR IMPLEMENTATION

The primary objective of Follow-Up Committee II was to investigate and suggest ways to implement the recommendations of the Futures Committee, *if* such recommendations were meritorious and practical. Because the Futures Committee viewed the mid-1990s as a check point, we selected 1995 as a target.

Based on the evidence, it was the consensus of the members of the Follow-Up II that the recommendations of the Futures Committee are realistic and appropriate. Support for change is overwhelming when potential costs and benefits are considered. The major impediments to such change include (1) other academics' understanding of accounting, (2) reward structure, (3) leadership, and (4) operational plan for implementation.

Academic accountants differ significantly from their associates in colleges of business and most of the rest of the university. The differences arise in part because accountants have long practiced as service agents for the public at large where the only product is information or the enhancement of information processing. In particular, the auditing function distinguishes public accounting because the SEC, as well as states, insist that auditors be licensed independent public accountants. Endowment of a franchise is peculiar among disciplines taught in business colleges and in much of the rest of the university. Also, the accountant involved in independent auditing is placed in a unique conflict role between the contractor and the public. Auditors, along with others involved in accounting, are subjected to a code of ethics that differs from other business graduates. The extensive body of rules (e.g., FASB Statements) passed to provide relevant information to serve the public interest also differentiates accountants from other close academic associates. Although the scope of public accounting practice has become more diverse, the traditional attest function will likely remain at the core of services that now includes consulting and tax. Corporate and government practice will probably also increase in importance.

These factors set accounting apart in both the academic and practice sectors from other business disciplines. They generate widespread support for a continuously updated curriculum aimed at preparing students to face the new and growing challenges society holds for accountants. We believe it is the unique nature of accounting that in part motivated faculty respondents to the Professorial Committee's survey to cite decreased student-faculty contact outside of class as having the greatest negative impact on the quality of accounting over the past 25 years. From our view the trend in the reward system unfortunately portends unfavorable consequences for faculty who choose to implement the recommendations and who become involved in student contact outside of class.

The reward structure for educators consists of performance in teaching, research, and service. Curriculum development most logically falls under teaching; organized interaction with students, under service. The increasing emphasis on research productivity indicates that more time will likely be devoted to that pursuit as compared to teaching or service. Therefore, the apparent future scarcity of funds at the university-wide level will likely make realizing all objectives increasingly difficult. Thus administrators will make choices in terms of what behavior can be rewarded. We believe that a primary objective of most administrators is to improve their units' standing within its peer group. In part because teaching and service are largely unobservable to members of the peer group consisting of educators located at other schools, research productivity will continue to be emphasized in allocating monetary rewards. Major commitments to curriculum development are imperiled without intervention.

Achieving effective national initiatives is inherently difficulty in academia due to geographic separation, different aspirations of universities and faculty, academic freedom, and so on. Coordination and assistance are the two types of leadership primarily needed to implement the Futures Committee recommendations.

Clearly, the findings of the three 1986–87 committees call for guidance in the areas of curriculum content, textbook development, assistance in integrating new technology, and help in learning new teaching skills and methods. We feel that the improved use of technology and the restructuring of the way accounting is taught can provide greater student-faculty contact while allowing adequate faculty time to address other reward areas.

PROPOSAL 1—EXECUTIVE COMMITTEE LEADERSHIP

The AAA Executive Committee should assume a leadership role. Although those outside accounting education are willing to help, none are as well qualified to represent accounting education as this committee. The Committee can provide the message that implementation is a worthwhile (essential) endeavor. Without a powerful champion, restructuring will not be realized by the mid-1990s.

In *Perspectives on Education: Capabilities for Success in the Accounting Profession*, the Big Eight accounting firms include this among the five recommendations needed to effect change (Arthur Andersen & Co. et al., 1989). Some specific leadership needs are embodied in the ensuing proposals.

PROPOSAL 2—ENDORSEMENT OF POSTBACCALAUREATE EDUCATION

The AAA Executive Committee should strongly and enthusiastically endorse a postbaccalaureate program for entry into the accounting profession. We believe that failure to endorse this may signal a lack of commitment to restructuring.

A postbaccalaureate program seems appropriate. Respondents (especially practitioners) strongly support the deferral of specialization. This deferral is consistent with the positions of prestigious national committees only indirectly related to accounting education (e.g., Carnegie Foundation, 1987, and the National Commission on Excellence in Education, 1983). Also, university enrollment patterns and financial conditions make broader and extended study a welcome option. Traditional four-year schools may especially embrace this type of program in view of enrollment patterns. Deans in general are likely to endorse changes leading to additional graduate enrollment. Although accounting faculty express concern about teaching specialized courses at the graduate level only, survey results indicate that faculty at nondoctoral-granting schools (those expressing the major concern) prepare an average of just over one graduate-level course every three years. Because graduate-level teaching in accounting is already widespread, incorporation of a required fifth year does not appear to constitute an onerous burden. As noted earlier, the AAA Executive Committee has endorsed the Bedford Committee Report and the position that postbaccalaureate education is a reasonable expectation for accounting education.

PROPOSAL 3—PRACTITIONER SUPPORT

Accounting foundations and other interested funding sources should agree to allocate a substantial, but reasonable, proportion of their available funds to restructuring. Without supplemental funds, we believe that it will be impossible to adjust the reward structure to provide the human capital necessary to accommodate the restructuring. We believe that the aggregate funds and the willingness to participate are available. (This is an informed opinion as our committee obtained direct input from representatives from several large-firm foundations.) The Professorial Committee findings indicate that three large accounting firms donated $10 million during 1985, excluding local office donations. Perhaps $25 million per year is available from all sources. Assuming stability, approximately $250 million in 1985 dollars can be expected over the next decade. Although much more detailed planning is needed, we believe that a reasonably minor allocation of this total to restructuring can accomplish the bulk of the change by the mid-1990s. Indeed, as their contribution to this effort, the Big Eight accounting firms have stated their support of "the development of stimulating and relevant curricula" with the commitment of up to $4 million over a five-year period (Arthur Andersen et al., 1989).

In addition to funding, large firms/foundations could provide substantial assistance by providing computer expertise, existing computer-assisted instruction (CAI) packages/courses and other new technological applications, existing research on the effectiveness of such approaches, in-house development facilities/capabilities, practitioners on temporary leave to teach or assist faculty involved in development, and various other innovative cooperative ventures.

PROPOSAL 4—ESTABLISHMENT OF A COORDINATING COMMITTEE

A coordinating committee of interested parties should be assembled to expedite implementation of the recommendations. Its principal goals should be to suggest common elements to be contained in the restructured curriculum and to design appropriate mechanisms for funding proposals.

Some commonality in the placement of the courses within the curriculum and the course content is strongly desirable based upon the findings of the Follow-Up Committee I. Although all courses may be affected, the lower-level courses seem to be especially important in serving as building blocks for further courses. In a world governed by efficiency, the coordinating committee would specify course content, but experimentation and discussion will likely be needed prior to such a detailed resolution. This committee should meet periodically (semiannually or annually) with the parties involved in actual curriculum development to facilitate understanding and communication.

The Committee may consist of parties representing the AAA, AACSB, AICPA, large-firm foundations, and perhaps others (FSA, NASBA, FEI, AGA, NAA). The AAA, AICPA, and large-firm foundations are obvious choices. The AACSB must be represented to provide a safe harbor exclusion for those institutions experimenting with new methods and to provide input from deans. Recall that the Changes Committee believed that the AACSB stifled innovation. The Professorial Environment Committee found that the AACSB has an unparalleled ability to effect change. With its long-standing commitment to an added year of education, experience with postbaccalaureate courses, and existing five-year structures in place (a nontrivial issue in terms of time required for implementation and in terms of sanction from others within the university), the FSA may play a vital role. NASBA may play a special role because much of the administration of the CPA exam is tied to this organization and because the nature and timing of the CPA exam seem to represent impediments to implementing restructuring.

In *Perspectives on Education* (Arthur Andersen & Co. et al., 1989), the Big Eight senior partners make it clear that "passing the CPA examination should not be the goal of accounting education. The focus should be on developing analytical and conceptual thinking—versus memorizing rapidly expanding professional standards."

NASBA and the Board of Examiners of the AICPA have reacted to the issues surrounding the nature of the CPA examination. NASBA has proposed a new format for the exam that includes evaluating writing skills on selected essay answers. The Board of Examiners has tentatively approved the format and the evaluation of writing skills beginning with the May 1994 examination (Flaherty, 1989).

PROPOSAL 5—GRANT APPLICATION CONTENT

Project proposals should be accepted on a holistic basis and on an individual or small group basis. The requests for support may be evaluated on the basis of their likelihood to contribute to efficient and timely implementation of the Futures Committee recommendations.

NATURE OF PROPOSALS

Holistic proposals encompassing the whole accounting unit and other relevant units within the university are a necessity if the course content is to be altered substantially and other related courses appropriately modified. Failure to provide this type of approach will likely result in cosmetic rather than substantive changes as called for by the Futures Committee. One very tentative example of how funding and other integration may effect timely change is reflected in Exhibit 3. Further refinement is definitely needed.

EXHIBIT 3

A BLUEPRINT FOR CHANGE*

The key to implementation is to involve whole programs in quasiexperimental testing of curricula from introductory principles through the postbaccalaureate courses. These would be implemented sequentially because it is presumed that course content would vary greatly from existing courses, rendering old prerequisites obsolete. A small number of schools is desirable initially to focus the available funds effectively and to provide for thorough analysis and communication. Grants would be awarded for five years to assure orderly development and to provide adequate incentive for faculty investing the time in the projects. Each year more schools would be added at a lower total grant because it would be presumed that existing materials would become more available. The following example shows how this program might work. (The amounts in this example were determined prior to the issuance of *Perspectives on Education*, Arthur Andersen et al., 1989.)

Date	
Summer 1989	Secure sponsors, announce program, and call for proposals.
11/30/89	Receive proposals.
12/15/89	Announce recipients (this may allow release time as early as Spring 1990). Approximately six schools in holistic program for a total of $2,400,000 over five years and expert release time. Individual projects (See ideas in Exhibit 4) of about $500,000 for year and another $100,000 for conferencing and dispersal of information.
Fall 90	**R** Introduce ACC I (4-semester credit hours, including lab). Accept second-round schools: eight at a total of $2,400,000, individual projects of $400,000, and $200,000 for conferencing, information dissemination, etc. Total schools involved equals 12.
Spring 91	**R** Introduce ACC II (4 hours including lab).
Fall 91	**R** Introduce External Reporting Systems I (FAS, Environment of Accounting, Not-for-profit, . . .) at first-round schools; introduce ACC I at second-round schools. Accept third-round schools: 12 at a total of $2,400,000 and individual projects at $300,000 for conferencing, information dissemination, etc. Total schools, 24.
Spring 92	**R** Introduce Internal Reporting Systems II.
Fall 92	**R** Introduce Decision Support Systems (DSS) I—Decision Analysis/Accounting Information Systems (AIS)/Documentation Aids. **R** External Reporting Systems II. Accept fourth-round schools: 20 at $2,400,000 and $600,000 for other. Total schools: 44.
Spring 93	**R** Data Integrity Systems (Internal Controls/Auditing). **R** Taxation.
Fall 93	**R** DSS II (Aimed to support management). Auditing Topics (Second auditing).

EXHIBIT 3
(CONTINUED)

	Various other elective courses (initially at least these would offer the opportunity for considerable specialization). Accept fifth-round schools: 30 at $2,400,000 and $600,000 for other. Total schools: 74.
Spring 94†	**R** Capstone (integrative problem solving directed to support management, AIS, tax, etc.). Taxation Topics (several different courses). External Reporting Topics (several different courses). AIS Topics (several different courses). International Topics. FIRST CLASS GRADUATES, perhaps 900 accountants.
Spring 95	SECOND CLASS GRADUATES, perhaps 2,100 accountants.
Spring 96	THIRD CLASS GRADUATES, perhaps 3,600 accountants.
Spring 97	FOURTH CLASS GRADUATES, perhaps 6,600 accountants.
Spring 98	FIFTH CLASS GRADUATES, perhaps 11,100 accountants.

*This schedule is *not* meant to be prescriptive but merely descriptive of a set of ideas to represent how a plan may work. Thus all parts of it should be read with that in mind. Courses preceded by an **R** are ideas for required courses and sequencing. It seems that introductory courses may well consist of 4 semester hours of credit, including a 3-hour lab—1 hour of credit—in which computer-assisted instruction (CAI) tools would be used to demonstrate/teach the concepts of elementary bookkeeping. Other courses may also be 4-credit hours with a lab to provide reasonable assurance of interactive learning experiences. All amounts are tentative. Specific schools should receive varying amounts based on the size of the student body and other relevant factors.

†By this time sufficient materials should be available through private enterprise forces to allow for wide dissemination. Also, it is likely that some schools that may not receive funding will make the transition to a five-year program as others come on line and the year 2000 approaches. Ongoing conferences, somewhat like those currently sponsored by the Management Accounting Section of the AAA, will prove extremely useful for information dissemination, teaching methodology, etc.

Individual projects are needed to involve outstanding educators located at institutions that are either unwilling to commit to a holistic approach or cannot be funded due to constraints. These experts may work on modular components of the program. A sample of these types of projects is provided in Exhibit 4.

ELEMENTS OF A PROPOSAL

Certain nuances/changes are inherent in any substantial restructuring. We believe that the following listing contains some of the elements that are likely to achieve the outcome envisioned by the Futures Committee and should be considered when evaluating proposals.

Textbook/Classroom Material Development

Widespread adoption of the restructuring cannot take place without these items. To what extent does the proposal envision development? Does the proposal contain innovative ideas to encourage development? For example, some initial sharing of royalties among the developer, his or her institution, and the funding agency established for nurturing the restructuring may occur. Eventually, it seems only appropriate that all royalties go to the developer.

EXHIBIT 4
POTENTIAL INDIVIDUAL PROJECTS

As noted, individual projects are those that may be implemented outside the scope of involvement by the whole accounting unit. These projects are needed due to the probable inability to fund all holistic proposals and the need to involve highly motivated and competent individuals at nonholistic schools. The items below represent a sample of ideas that may be considered by the coordinating committee. Some of these items are also applicable to faculties involved in a holistic approach.

1. Development of beginning accounting courses to introduce innovative methods and approaches to make students aware of general information about business disciplines along with specific information about accounting. Should not affect the manner in which subsequent courses are taught.
2. Development of beginning accounting courses using innovative approaches that also used the megasection lecture and breakout discussion format. The lecture/breakout format is increasingly used in accounting education, and it is generally more economical than competing approaches. It would have the added advantage of using graduate students as teaching assistants, which would aid them financially in completing their fifth year.
3. Development of textbook and course materials for the introductory courses by individual faculty.
4. Formation of teams to teach complex topics or unstructured approaches to accounting. Having two persons in the classroom simultaneously facilitates delivery of the unstructured approach and reduces the burden of knowledge and memory on a single instructor. The integrative intent of the recommendations would be more likely accomplished under this approach. Faculty could also team teach sequentially rather than simultaneously.
5. Use of a modular approach to allow students the freedom to concentrate on specific areas. This would be more applicable at the specialization level than at the general course level.
6. Emphasize communication skills in this environment. As the stress will be on how one reaches a solution as opposed to the solution reached, written explanations could be subjected to evaluative feedback concerning grammatical propriety, writing style, etc. Also, discussion of unstructured material in class should assist in augmenting oral skills.
7. Consider providing a practitioner to assist in teaching and/or developing new materials. This may provide more realism and free the academic to spend more time on development.
8. Development of screening exams to assist students in making the correct career choice would help the classroom environment in terms of homogeneity of motivation and ability. These exams could focus on aptitude for accounting, personality characteristics common to successful accountants, and interests generally found among successful accountants. An admission requirement may elicit greater students' dedication to the program once they are enrolled.
9. Study retention practices and success rates for the various examinations noted above. This would necessarily occur after the students leave the program.
10. Funnel private support to meritorious students entering their postbaccalaureate study. This would assist in gaining a critical mass of students needed to conduct the postbaccalaureate study and ease the financial strain.
11. Study different career tracks of those with master's degrees versus those with bachelor's degrees. This may encourage people to pursue the postbaccalaureate study and assist in retention.
12. Pursue studies that would yield insight into the economic viability of the restructured approach versus the traditional approach. Because hiring will continue at both degree levels, firms can contrast the benefits and costs of the two so far as they are concerned, and the individuals can also assess their personal cost versus their benefit. Universities can also quantify costs for a limited comparison. The first analysis is likely to provide the best evidence.
13. Establish AAA or other monetary award for best curriculum development relating to the restructuring.
14. Provide fund-raising expert to assist in filing grants to other agencies interested in integrating technology into the classroom. Or encourage collaboration with existing experts by providing automatic matching funds at some percentage.
15. When establishing fellowships or professorships, target some toward outstanding performance in the area of curriculum development related to the restructuring.
16. Consider ways to measure the quality of teaching and learning more accurately than by depending

EXHIBIT 4
(CONTINUED)

upon the CPA exam results. Consider alternatives. For example, have the firms who regularly keep performance records by university contribute anonymous "objective" data based on actual performance of individuals after employment. Relative quality of inputs may well need to be measured also.

17. Develop better teaching and curriculum development measurement tools. For example, assessment of students after several years. Students' opinions on how exercises assisted their learning. Questions aimed at students' professional development based on outside of class contact.
18. Provide for dissemination of knowledge. Consider funding faculty to attend such functions. Offer educational materials at cost initially.
19. Provide conferences for high-level university administrators to explain need for and approach to restructuring. Get input from them on major obstacles for implementation.
20. Provide a "roving expert" to assist with implementation of new methodology.

Integration of New Technology

This is a *critical* area that *must* be developed if the Future's Committee recommendations are to become a reality. This position is supported by the reality of the emphasis on research productivity in the reward stricture and by the inherent job satisfaction derived from research by faculty. New technology, *especially computer-assisted instruction (CAI),* offers the opportunity to move much of the rote learning of mechanical procedures currently covered during valuable classroom time to a laboratory or individual setting. Successful integration of new technology offers the promise of direct interaction between the student and the computer, direct interaction between the faculty member and the student on nonprocedural issues in the classroom, exposure to cases and data bases paralleling experiential settings, and the promise for adequate faculty time to devote to research pursuits. This area is so important that we present some ideas for consideration in Exhibit 5.

Upper-level Administrative Support

Because restructured programs will involve matters that transcend accounting units, upper-level administrators *must* support the development. As mentioned, existence of a five-year program already signals support and will expedite implementation significantly. Existence of a relatively large honors track may also signal support. However, other support may well be needed. Some (e.g., measurement of teaching performance during the experimental phase, matching) are noted below. A key signal, however, is that relevant upper-level administrators lend their explicit support to holistic proposals and to some individual proposals.

Comprehensive Faculty Support

Closely related to the previous element is the notion of uniform faculty support within the accounting unit. Diversity among academics, which is clearly provided for in the cherished traditions of academic freedom, mandates that accounting faculty reach a consensus on the program and that restructuring will involve virtually everyone and the content/approach of every course. Thus, an element of each holistic proposal should include an indication of the extent of faculty support.

EXHIBIT 5
POTENTIAL PROJECTS OR ISSUES RELATING TO APPLICATION OF TECHNOLOGY

We believe the best way to implement many of the Futures Committee's recommendations is to use technology to teach accounting. The following questions and issues represent some of the areas that could be investigated.

1. Use computer technology to teach beginning accounting. This may be done on a pilot basis or honors section basis. It may also be combined with other innovative approaches. For example, what are the implications of changing the format of beginning accounting courses to a 3-contact–hour lecture/discussion and a 3-hour lab setting for a total of 4 semester hours of credit? This approach is commonly used in the physical sciences and would provide the opportunity to address broad information and decision-making issues in class and to learn via computer-assisted instruction (CAI) tools in the lab. The latter pedagogy could probably accomplish much of the standard instruction surrounding the double-entry system common to traditional accounting.
2. A study of the experiences of using CAI in teaching accounting in the university environment may prove quite useful to provide a bench mark. For example, the University of Illinois used PLATO to teach elementary accounting on an experimental basis in the 1970s. The University of Virginia uses CAI to introduce the fundamentals of the accounting system to its entering MBA students. What have their experiences taught them? What have other universities learned that could be useful?
3. Use telecommunications media to aid in teach accounting classes. Michigan State University and Pennsylvania State University have used television to teach for a considerable period of time. What have they learned? How can it help? What have others done?
4. Combined approaches may also be useful but seem expensive currently. For example, one large, high technology company uses television transmission coupled with computer-driven slides and interactive remote audio. The instruction is live. What is the cost of such technology? Will they share it with educational institutions? What results have they obtained?
5. At least one large accounting firm has used CAI modules to teach selected topics. This firm has compared the results against live instruction of the same material and allegedly found CAI to be more effective. What have other firms done? What subject matter is best suited for CAI? Will these firms share these items with academics?
6. Some institutions have wired-in classrooms so each student can use a computer during the class. What can we learn from these experiences?
7. It is not uncommon for each member of an accounting faculty to have an electronic work bench. In some cases nearly identical equipment and software are available to the students. What impact has this had on computer integration? On faculty computer literacy? What barriers were overcome to integration?
8. Apparently some publishers are willing to sell parts of their textbooks in electronic media form. What implication does this have for bringing current material into the classroom? In the near future can instructors effectively pick and choose the best modules from various texts to design tailored "textbooks"?
9. Can audio/video tapes be made available for explaining especially difficult accounting topics? Can these be used in a lab-type setting or on an individual or small group setting for students wishing to clarify their understanding of the topic? Can they be broadcast at specified times over very low power television transmitters to students' rooms equipped with special decoders?
10. Where implementation of some technology has been successful, how has behavioral resistance to change been overcome? How has the reward structure dealt with such change? What level of assistance was needed? What capital support was required?
11. Can expert systems be used in a lab-type setting to help students gain insight into decision processes leading to professional judgments? This seems probable. Will developers share such systems at reasonable costs?
12. Can CD-ROM bases equipped with current accounting, auditing, or tax standards simplify the bibliographic reference process to the extent that students are able to refine simultaneously their basic accounting knowledge by reading the original accounting literature thereon and formulating answers (positions) on complex, unstructured cases? This seems likely at least in higher level courses. What are the implementation issues?

EXHIBIT 5
(CONTINUED)

13. Can a task force (possibly a conference) of accounting's and CAI's best people get together to discuss available practices and state-of-the-art technology as they relate to accounting educational applications? Can a subset of this group be commissioned to develop a "critical mass" of material to be used for introductory accounting labs? Is this the proper first step in broad application?
14. What role can interuniversity transmission systems (e.g., ARPA, BITNET) play in technology transfer?
15. How can existing computer-based information systems (e.g., NAARS, LEXIS, PHINET) be used in teaching?
16. Can the AAA establish and maintain a centralized optical scanning data base of available technological material and provide it reasonably to instructors?
17. Should an individual consulting expert be contracted to move among various accounting units to assist in technological implementation?

Matching Funding from Proposing Institution

Matching funding provides tangible evidence that the proposer is sincere about implementing the proposal and that the support may well have the wherewithal to continue restructuring beyond the grant stage.

Reward Teaching/Development Activity

At a minimum, an indication of support for teaching and development activity in the reward structure is needed during the grant stage. Other, longer-run commitments noted below are also meritorious.

New Teaching Evaluation Techniques

Many academics consider better measurements for true teaching effectiveness necessary. Agreement to explore these matters should be considered in evaluating a proposal. Exploratory ideas include working with students outside of the classroom, developing measures of perceived teaching effectiveness at various career points following graduation, and utilizing innovative technology.

Faculty Release Time

The proposing institution's willingness to grant release time for key faculty to work in development will assist in implementation.

Admissions Control

Having the ability to control admissions to the accounting courses or program reduces the time required to deal with marginal or unmotivated students, thus providing a better atmosphere in which to develop innovative teaching techniques.

Use of Graduate Assistants

Clearly, having full-time faculty to teach small sections of introductory accounting courses is desirable. However, the economic feasibility of this approach is elusive.

Thus, innovative use of graduate assistants, especially when coupled with laboratories using new teaching technologies, should be a particularly important element when viewed in conjunction with other components of the environment.

Existing Computer Capability

Existing capability in this area will obviously obviate the need for certain additional resource allocations and expedite implementation as well. Among other matters, existing hardware, software, and expertise (including existing classroom applications) contribute to this element.

Use of Practitioners

Willingness to use practitioner experts or those who can act as teachers while faculty developers are on release time should facilitate implementation.

Establishment of Learning Theory Seminars

These seminars can operate at several levels. First, faculty and graduate students will have a forum available for learning about experimental developments within their own unit. Second, experts can assist both groups in existing theory and application. Third, required courses may be established in the doctoral programs.

Evaluation and Feedback Mechanism

Does the proposal contain a plan to evaluate the success or failure of the implementation? For example, some accounting units that propose offering the traditional approach and the restructured approach in parallel for a period of time may be able to generate measures with relatively sound internal validity. Is feedback to the coordinating committee assured? Participation in conferences?

PROPOSAL 6—CURRICULUM INNOVATION AWARD

The AAA should devote considerable effort to promote the proper measurement and recognition of teaching/curriculum development to place it in a more prominent position. This recommendation is directed at individual and unit levels. Some of the ideas related to individual measurement are explored above. An added item within the reach of the AAA is to establish national awards for teaching/curriculum development, which would be highlighted at the annual convention. The AAA Executive Committee established an innovation in accounting education award at its August 1988 meeting.

More importantly, the AAA should strive to devise measurements of effectiveness at the unit level. Because academic reputation is believed to be extremely important to most academic administrators, we believe that a national ranking system, other than the pass rate on the CPA exam, will assist in focusing attention on teaching.

The AACSB is also interested in developing output measurements. This work may provide a basis from which to begin. Effecting this type of program to classify schools on some prior bases to include student input characteristics, size of student body, and so forth seems prudent. This will allow for awards in different categories.

PROPOSAL 7—DISSEMINATION

The coordinating committee or some of its member organizations should establish a mechanism to disseminate both new materials and new methods. For example, a clearing house could contribute to this function. Also, holding workshops and conferences on implementation should provide considerable assistance. Establishment of such vehicles should complement the efforts made locally by successful proposers, as noted earlier. Some existing fora (e.g, the Arthur Andersen New Accounting Faculty Seminar, the Price Waterhouse Professors' Seminar, the AAA/Touche Ross Trueblood Seminars) could assist in this regard. Some existing sectional activities could also assist. For example, the Auditing Section and the Managerial Accounting section routinely sponsor educational activities. The AAA annual convention could provide sessions as well.

CONCLUSION

Recent actions by the AAA, NASBA, AICPA Board of Examiners, and senior partners of the Big Eight firms all point to increased concern for and commitment to improvements in the capabilities needed for practice. The senior partners identify those for public accounting as communication skills, intellectual skills, and interpersonal skills. They recognize that academic education cannot alone be expected to accomplish all of these goals. Traditional areas continue to be a necessary component as they clearly indicate in the following passage:

> Post-secondary education should provide a strong fundamental understanding of accounting and auditing. This includes the history of the accounting profession and accounting thought, as well as the content, concepts, structure and meaning of reporting for organizational operations both for internal and external use [Arthur Andersen et al., 1989, p. 8].

This report sought to bring an operational tone to the effort to restructure accounting education, which began with the Futures Committee report. The recommendations made by the Futures Committee have generally received strong support among accounting academics and practitioners. We conclude that a significant opportunity for successful implementation exists at this time. We believe that failure to take immediate steps will substantially decrease the value that an accounting education can offer.

PROFESSORIAL ENVIRONMENT COMMITTEE
1986-87

Joseph J. Schultz, Jr.
Chairman
Arizona State University

David R. Campbell
Case Western Reserve University

Charles G. Carpenter
Miami University

Don Dupont
Arthur Andersen & Co.

Thomas W. Lin
University of Southern California

Jane T. Rubin
American Assembly of
Collegiate Schools of Business

Douglas Snowball
University of Florida

Shyam Sunder
Carnegie Mellon University

Miklos A. Vasarhelyi
AT & T Bell Labs and
Columbia University

REPORT OF THE PROFESSORIAL ENVIRONMENT COMMITTEE 1986–87

The charge to the Committee was as follows:

To document, in as much detail as possible, how the professorial environment of the accounting professor has changed during the past 25 years so that we might better anticipate the significance of these factors on the near-term implementation issues inherent in the 1986 (AAA) Report of the Committee on the Future Structure, Content, and Scope of Accounting Education.

The Committee interpreted the charge to include identifying those factors that shaped the professional practice of accounting (i.e., public, corporate, and not-for-profit/governmental) during the past 25 years and identifying how changes in these factors affected the professorial environment of accounting educators. Several areas relevant to the charge were identified: external environmental factors influencing professional accounting practice, professorial competence in relative and absolute terms, promotion and tenure process and criteria, terminal degree requirements, and specializations. The Committee formed two subcommittees: one examining the external factors that have driven the practice of accounting and the other measuring changes that have occurred in the environment of accounting faculty as perceived by a random sample of accounting faculty and business school deans. Implicit in this two-dimensional approach is the assumption of a correlation between changes in the accounting practice environment and the accounting professorial environment.

The report of the Committee includes a discussion of a conceptual overview of the professorial environment, an examination of the external environmental factors driving change in accounting education, a review of changes in higher education at the macro level, and an investigation of accounting educators' perceptions of changes that have affected the professorial environment.

CONCEPTUAL OVERVIEW OF THE PROFESSORIAL ENVIRONMENT

For purposes of this report the professorial environment is considered to consist of three elements: (1) a set of professorial activities (i.e., teaching, research, and service); (2) a system of selective rewards (e.g., tenure, promotion, and salary increases); and (3) a set of resources to stimulate the activities of accounting educators (e.g., individual education and practice work experience, institutional support such as released time, and external support such as access to practice for materials/resources). The framework depicted in Exhibit 1 (page 6) illustrates the professorial environment as being multidimensional in nature, influenced by changing *social, technological, economic, and political* conditions.

Although accounting education may have some influence on its external environment, for the most part the educational process reacts to changes in the external environment. As the external environment changes (e.g., competition, litigation, scope of services), the practice of accountancy changes and places new demands on the professional education of accountants. As the perception of educational needs change, the activities comprising the professorial environment are affected in varying degrees. This may call for the modification of resources and rewards of the professorial environment in order to meet the current and expected future needs of the practice environment.

EXTERNAL ENVIRONMENTAL FACTORS[1]

The process of identifying key factors that drove the explosive growth in the profession over the past 25 years involved informal discussions with colleagues in both the academic and practicing communities, as well as a review of the literature. The factors below, although not intended to be exhaustive, provide insight into external sources affecting the profession and the accounting educational process during the last quarter of a century.

GROWTH OF THE PROFESSION

The growth of the profession has far exceeded the growth of the population of the United States. Evidence of this growth can be illustrated by examining membership trends in several major accounting and financial organizations. For example, membership in the American Institute of Certified Public Accountants (AICPA) increased from 37,900 members in 1960 to over 230,000 in 1985. At the same time, membership in the Financial Executives Institute (FEI) increased from 5,200 to 12,800, while the National Association of Accountants (NAA) membership grew from 47,500 to 74,000 (Table 1). Additional evidence of the growing demand for the services of accountants is illustrated by the increase in the number of accountants, auditors, and bookkeepers from 476,000 in 1960 to 1.1 million in 1983. Looking at the projected increase in accountants and auditors alone, 882,000 were employed in 1984, with employment for 1995 expected to range between 1.1 to 1.3 million.[2]

TABLE 1
MEMBERSHIP IN PROFESSIONAL ACCOUNTING ORGANIZATIONS
1960 TO 1985

Year	AICPA	NAA	FEI
1960	37,897	47,476	5,238
1965	53,709	55,258	6,019
1970	74,413	69,820	6,987
1975	112,494	70,500	8,854
1980	161,319	79,883	11,272
1985	230,058	74,093	12,819

Source: American Institute of Certified Public Accountants, National Association of Accountants, and Financial Executives Institute.

This growing demand for skilled professionals has had a significant impact on the accounting educational system. One indication of this impact is the substantial increase in the number of students moving through the accounting education infrastructure. From 1961 to 1980 the number of students graduating with either a bachelor's or master's degree in accounting increased from 11,100 to 55,150. This trend, however, slowed during the period from 1980 to 1985, with the supply of accounting graduates increasing only modestly from 54,840 in 1981 to 57,890 in 1985 (Table 2).

TABLE 2
HISTORICAL TREND IN THE SUPPLY
OF ACCOUNTING GRADUATES
1961-85

Year	Bachelor's Degrees	Master's Degrees	Total Degrees
1961	10,632	469	11,101
1966	15,101	962	16,063
1972	23,800	2,200	26,000
1975	35,400	4,300	39,700
1980	49,870	5,280	55,150
1981	49,320	5,520	54,840
1982	50,300	5,570	55,870
1983	51,950	5,810	57,750
1984	53,020	6,330	59,350
1985	51,980	5,910	57,890

Sources: *Statistical Abstracts of the United States* (U.S. Bureau of the Census, 1961-1985) and *The Supply of Accounting Graduates and Demand for Public Accounting Recruits* (AICPA, 1961–85).

MACROECONOMIC FACTORS

Growth in the economic environment also has contributed to changes in the accounting profession and educational system. One measure of this increased economic activity is the growth in gross national product from $506.5 billion in 1960 to $3,662.8 billion in 1984. In addition, there have been over 8.6 million new business formations, 3.1 million business failures, and 20,000 mergers and acquisitions during this period. A review of the number of tax returns filed by corporations, partnerships, and proprietorships shows that over 11 million returns were filed in 1960, but that by 1983 this number had increased to over 17 million. During the same time frame the number of individual tax filings increased from 60 million to over 96 million (Table 3). If accounting services are correlated to economic activity, these data suggest that a portion of the growth in the profession can be attributed to an increasing level of economic activity during the past 25 years.

INTERNATIONALISM

Multinational business activity also has increased during the past 25 years. In 1960 U.S. imports and exports were $23.7 billion and $28.9 billion. By 1984 these figures had increased to $325.7 billion in imports and $217.9 billion in exports. In addition, the development of an international trading and financial community has led to an increased

TABLE 3
TAX RETURNS FILED BY CORPORATIONS, PARTNERSHIPS, PROPRIETORSHIPS, AND INDIVIDUALS
1960–83
(IN THOUSANDS)

Year	Corporations	Partnerships	Proprietorships	Individuals
1960	1,141	941	9,090	60,593
1965	1,424	914	9,078	67,199
1970	1,665	936	9,400	74,280
1975	2,024	1,073	10,882	82,229
1980	2,711	1,380	12,702	93,902
1983	2,999	1,542	13,074	96,321

Source: *Statistical Abstracts of the United States* (U.S. Bureau of the Census, 1960–83).

emphasis on international accounting and auditing standards, transfer pricing, and international taxation.

SOCIAL AWARENESS

Concern with the social responsibility of the accounting profession has played a major role in changes in the sociology of the profession. Two underlying and conflicting forces responsible for much of this change are (1) the ongoing professional desire for improved quality and extent of services provided and (2) the reduction of barriers to competition. This latter force was especially influential in the practice of public accounting. The mood of the 1960s resulted in an examination of values, particularly those traditionally set forth by those in authority. Accounting was no exception.

With regard to the academic environment, perhaps the major attempt during the 1960s to influence quality was the AICPA's advocacy of additional requirements for university-level education. In retrospect, the AICPA's sanctioning of the added university educational requirement in 1969 was probably quite appropriate. Only recently the AICPA membership voted overwhelmingly (82 percent) to require 150 semester hours of college work for persons seeking new membership in the AICPA beginning in the year 2000 (AICPA, 1988). Indeed, the pace of change (discussed throughout this section) seems to justify added competence. This advocacy, coupled with the perceived need for increased education, has resulted in significant changes in accounting education over the past 25 years. For example, while general graduate enrollment during this time period has increased only slightly (Table 6—see page 41), graduate education in accounting has soared (Table 2). Further evidence of this influence can be seen in one international public accounting firm's private data, which now reveal that nearly 40 percent of its partners hold advanced degrees (Arthur Andersen & Co., 1985). Similarly, a review of the educational credentials of the *new* partners of another international accounting firm reveals that in 1986 more than half possessed graduate degrees (Ernst & Whinney, 1986).

Driven by the concern for public accountability and sharp increases in litigation in the early 1970s, the mid-1970s resulted in consequential self-examination (e.g., The Commission on Auditors' Responsibilities) and Congressional scrutiny (e.g., Moss,

Metcalf, and, later, Dingell). These examinations led to the establishment of the Division of Firms within the AICPA and related peer review requirements and quality control standards. The Foreign Corrupt Practices Act, passed in late 1977, reaffirmed management's responsibility for the financial reporting process and the importance of the internal audit function. Membership in the Institute of Internal Auditors reflected this importance as it grew from 2,000 to 14,000 during the 1978–82 period. Business failures and concern over the public's understanding of the financial reporting process and the auditor's role in the process led to the "expectation gap" and the establishment of another commission (viz., the National Commission on Fraudulent Financial Reporting). Finally, the increased awareness of the social responsibility of accountants resulted in several amendments to the AICPA Code of Professional Ethics during the 1960–88 period. As these developments have occurred, the professorial environment has changed to meet the needs of entry-level professional accountants.

LITIGATION

One indicator of the increased legal awareness on the part of the general public is the number of lawsuits involving public accounting firms. For example, Palmrose (1987) found that the number of court cases involving the 15 largest public accounting firms increased dramatically during the past 25 years, with 93 cases from 1960 to 1969, 236 cases between 1970 to 1979, and 143 cases from 1980 to 1985.[3] This widely publicized increase in litigation has affected the professorial environment by placing a greater importance on providing entering professionals with an awareness of our litigious environment. In addition, the increase in litigation has contributed to an increase in technical pronouncements generated by the Securities and Exchange Commission and the Auditing Standards Board.

TECHNICAL STANDARDS

The explosive growth of technical standards concerning the practice of accounting is among the most significant external factors affecting the professorial environment during the past 25 years. In 1960 the technical financial reporting literature consisted of 43 Accounting Research Bulletins that totaled 412 cumulative paragraphs of pronouncements. By 1985 the financial reporting literature included over 5,000 effective paragraphs of Accounting Research Bulletins (51) and Accounting Principles Board Opinions (31), as well as over 90 Financial Accounting Standards Board (FASB) Standards (Table 4). In addition, there have been AICPA Statements of Accounting Positions and FASB interpretations, technical pronouncements, and statements of financial accounting concepts. In the public sector there were 86 SEC Accounting Series Releases (ASR) in 1960; by 1985 this number had increased to 473 combined Accounting and Auditing Enforcement Releases (AAER), Financial Reporting Releases (FRR), and Staff Accounting Bulletins. In addition, the recently formed Government Accounting Standards Board has begun to issue concept statements that will be followed by official pronouncements on accounting in the governmental area.

Official pronouncements of auditing standards have also proliferated during the past 25 years. In 1972 the AICPA Codification of Auditing Standards included 548 promulgated paragraphs. Since that time the Auditing Standards Board has issued 51 statements on Auditing Standards that have increased the paragraphs in effect to over 1,000. In addition, there have been Statements on Standards for Accounting and

TABLE 4
PRIVATE-SECTOR FINANCIAL REPORTING PARAGRAPHS
1960–85

Year	Paragraphs
1960	412
1965	500
1970	831
1975	1,742
1980	3,475
1985	5,003

Sources: Accounting Research Bulletins, Accounting Principles Board Pronouncements, and Financial Accounting Standards Board Statements.

Review Services, AICPA Industry Audit Guides, and various auditing interpretations issued.

Changing tax laws have also placed pressure on the practice and academic environments during the last quarter of a century. This is evidenced by the fact that through 1985 the Internal Revenue Code of 1954 had been amended 769 times. Similarly, although in 1965 the number of revenue rulings issued by the Internal Revenue Service totaled 5,775, this number had increased to over 15,100 rulings by 1985. Further evidence of the impact taxation has had on the professorial environment is illustrated by the implementation of master's of taxation programs at over fifty universities (Ernst & Whinney, 1987).

SCOPE OF SERVICES

An examination of the scope of services cannot be limited to the public accounting arena alone. But as the scope of services in public accounting changes, it tends to mirror developments in the corporate and governmental/not-for-profit areas that affect the responsibilities and knowledge of professionals in those areas as well. For example, an examination of the services performed by 847 public accounting firms in 1967 disclosed the following "frequently performed" services: audit (55 percent), write-up activities (74 percent), disclaimers on unaudited financial statements (45 percent), and special reports such as involvement in reports to credit-rating bureaus (46 percent). In the area of taxation, most of the activity concerned preparation of corporate (93 percent), partnership (90 percent), and individual (95 percent) tax returns. Areas of assistance to clients with tax problems included advice to closely held corporations (83 percent), payroll taxes (75 percent), and assisting the clients in IRS audits (77 percent). Management advisory services included insurance coverage analysis (33 percent), inventory control (27 percent), clerical work simplification (26 percent), selection of financing sources (24 percent), accounting machine and office equipment studies (19 percent), and business acquisition investigations (23 percent). Only 33 percent of the firms responding to the survey used punch card and EDP equipment in audit applications.[4]

Since 1967 the nature of public practice has changed dramatically. Auditing as a percentage of total practice revenues has declined for the major public accounting firms,[5] while compilation and review services have grown to be a significant portion of small and medium-sized firm revenues.[6] Tax services have continued to provide a substantial portion of the revenues generated by all public accounting firms, but the emphasis has shifted toward tax planning. Not surprisingly, management advisory services have grown as a percentage of revenues and appears to be the area of most growth for accounting firms in the future.[7] The scope of management advisory services, however, has changed markedly over the past 25 years, with computer system design and installation, financial planning, strategic planning, and psychological testing now included in the list of services performed by public accounting firms. The trends in the proportions of revenues contributed by auditing, tax, and consulting during the period from 1975 through 1986 for large public accounting firms are reported in Table 5.

A review of the expectations for the controllership function in 1964 included planning for control of operations (e.g., profit-planning, sales forecast, and budgets), reporting and interpreting the results of operations to management (e.g., formulation of accounting policy and coordination of systems and procedures), evaluating and consulting with management concerning any phase of the business, tax administration, government reporting, internal controls, and economic appraisal.[8] Although the functions of corporate accountants were quite extensive in the mid-1960s, today's corporate accounting executives are confronted with the new challenges that technology and technical pronouncements have imposed on their operating and financial reporting environment. Thus, in addition to their traditional roles, they are expected to participate in strategic planning and implementing information systems that provide more than the traditional financial/managerial reporting data.

The accountant's role in the governmental area also has expanded from one of budgeting and fund accounting to encompass the broader responsibilities of financial management. This increased responsibility may be attributable to the financial collapse, or near collapse, of major governmental units (e.g., New York City). As a result, greater emphasis is now placed on the disclosure of financial reporting data

TABLE 5

BIG EIGHT PERCENTAGE OF REVENUES GENERATED FROM AUDITING, TAX, AND CONSULTING DURING THE PERIOD 1975–86

Firm	Audit		Tax		Consulting	
	1975	1986	1975	1986	1975	1986
Arthur Andersen & Co.	66	47	18	21	16	32
Arthur Young	69	59	17	26	14	15
Coopers & Lybrand	69	61	19	21	12	18
Deloitte Haskins & Sells	74	66	15	22	11	12
Ernst & Whinney	73	58	17	22	10	20
Peat Marwick Main & Co.	68	56	21	26	11	18
Price Waterhouse	76	61	16	22	8	17
Touche Ross & Co.	62	55	24	23	14	22

Source: 1975 data gathered from *The Accounting Establishment: A Staff Study.* prepared by the Subcommittee on Reports, Accounting and Management of the Committee on Government Operations, United States Senate, December, 1976, U.S. Government Printing Office (Washington D.C., 1976), p. 30. 1986 data gathered from net fees reported to the SEC Practice Section of the AICPA.

related to the stewardship of governmental resources by elected officials and the planning, programming, and budgeting of resources.

These changes in the scope of services have contributed to increased specialization among both practicing and academic accountants. We revisit this issue in the internal study section of this report.

TECHNOLOGICAL INNOVATION

The development and integration of computer technology into the business environment has had a significant impact on the operating and information-generating environment of accounting professionals. Computerization has moved from a mainframe environment in the 1960s and early 1970s to a combination of mainframes, minis, and micros in the 1980s. The impact has not been limited, however, to the increased availability of computers alone; it is also related to the high speed in which technological change has occurred over the past 25 years and the rate of technology transfer. Thus this environmental factor has created significant pressure on accounting educators to modify traditional teaching approaches so as to train adequately entry-level professionals to meet the challenges caused by technological innovations.

One measure of the technological revolution is the increase in the number of computer programmers and operators from 332,000 in 1970 to over 1 million in 1983. The increase in the combined number of bachelor's and master's degrees awarded in computer science, from just over 300 in 1966 to over 25,000 in 1982, is additional evidence of the increased integration of computer technology into the information environment. Finally, the increase in sales of microcomputers from 750,000 in 1981 to over 4 million in 1985 illustrates the rapid rate at which the use of computer technology has spread to all areas of the business community.

Besides these numerical measures of the computerization of the information environment, other trends within this area have had a substantial influence on the knowledge levels and job responsibilities of accountants. Among those trends is the decentralization of computer power within organizations. This movement to distributive data-processing environments has had a direct effect on internal controls and the access to sensitive information within organizations. In addition, the lowered cost of computing power and the ability to store larger quantities of data for analysis within systems have expanded automation applications and spread the availability of computer usage to organizations of all sizes. The usage of satellite technology, telecommunications, and the change in processor speeds also have had an influence on the transmission of data and the speed of decision making within organizations.

The development of artificial intelligence (AI) and robotics is having dramatic affects on the accounting practice environment. Businesses and governments are developing applications using AI that will challenge public accountants to increase their knowledge base and methodologies for interfacing with this new wave of technological applications. In the area of robotics questions are being raised concerning, among other things, the traditional approaches to assigning cost within our manufacturing environment.

SUMMARY—EXTERNAL INFLUENCES

This portion of the study reviewed information related to changes in various social, technological, economic, and political aspects of accounting education's external environment. We identified factors that have influenced and will continue to influence the accounting professorial environment. Perhaps the greatest impact during this period came from the marked growth in the number of students majoring in accounting. As indicated by the number of graduates, the increase amounted to over 400 percent. This trend slowed over the last five years of our study period and is likely to slow or even decrease in the period from now until 1995.

Another factor of immense consequence was the sharp increase in the amount of codified knowledge related to accounting. As an example, the number of codified paragraphs of guidance concerning financial accounting grew from 412 in 1960 to over 5,000 by 1985. These figures include only the major guidance issued directly by the authoritative bodies (CAP, APB, and FASB) and exclude additional forms of codified literature, such as interpretations, which were numerous. The added guidance related to auditing, tax, and governmental accounting also registered major increases. Similarly, the consequential expansion of foreign trade and multinational ownership resulted in heightened concern for international standards. Moreover, the data indicate that this expansion will likely intensify in the future.

Increased concern for social welfare brought about conflicting forces in the forms of added critical scrutiny and free market competition. The number of lawsuits swelled, Congressional inquiries (and others) flourished, and competition led to new levels of efficiency. As a result, the expanding scope of services performed by public accounting firms was subjected to special examination. In addition, the relative mix of accounting services within firms took on different configurations and continue to expand in nontraditional accounting areas.

Contributing to efficiency and complexity was the distinct rise in the use of computers—first in main frames, followed by microcomputers near the end of the period. This influx resulted in far easier application and wider use of quantitative models. Near the end of the period, there was growing consensus that expert systems and artificial intelligence programs would gain increased use in accounting practice.

THE HIGHER EDUCATION ENVIRONMENT

Changes in the general state of higher education[9] play major roles in shaping the accounting professorial environment. The impact of particular changes on accounting faculty may not be felt directly and immediately, and some changes may affect accounting faculty less than their counterparts in other disciplines. Nevertheless, changes in the students, faculty, institutions, and funding of higher education help to explain the evolution of the accounting professorial environment over the past 25 years. Moreover, in the mid-1980s some dramatic shifts that will have substantial implications for the accounting professorial environment of the future occurred in higher education.

STUDENTS

Enrollment

Between 1963 and 1987, total student enrollment in U.S. universities grew from 4.8 million to an estimated 12.1 million, an increase of approximately 150 percent. Enrollment growth occurred in most years of this period, and at times the growth was dramatic (for example, a 30 percent growth took place between 1970 and 1975).

However, as Tables 6 and 7 indicate, the pattern has reversed in recent years, and the decline in student populations does not appear to be a temporary phenomenon.[10] Student enrollment peaked at around 12.5 million in 1983 and is expected to continue to decline through the early 1990s. Whereas enrollment increased 30 percent in the 10 years prior to 1983, it is expected to decrease by 6 percent in the 10 years following 1983. The predicted enrollment for 1993 (11.7 million) is less than the enrollment that occurred in 1980. These expectations reflect the aging of the U.S. population (see Figure 1). In 1983 the U.S. population included 30.1 million individuals aged between 18 and 24 years (the traditional college-age population); by 1993, the number of individuals in that age group is expected to drop to 24.6 million.

FIGURE 1

NATIONAL POPULATION TRENDS BY AGE GROUP

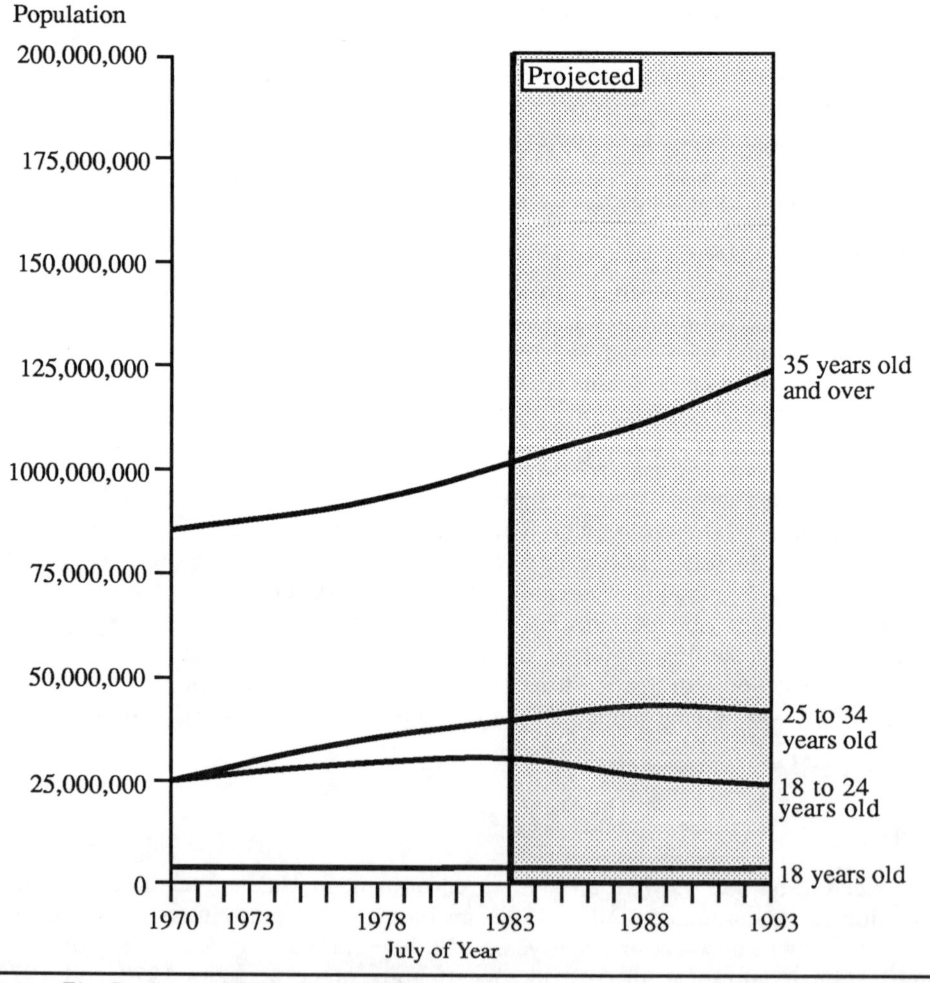

Source: *The Condition of Education 1985 Edition* (National Center for Education Statistics, Office of Educational Research and Improvement, U.S. Department of Education).

TABLE 6

PAST AND PROJECTED TRENDS IN TOTAL ENROLLMENT IN INSTITUTIONS OF HIGHER EDUCATION BY CONTROL AND TYPE OF INSTITUTION AND LEVEL OF STUDENT: UNITED STATES

FALL 1970–FALL 1993

(IN THOUSANDS)

		Control of Institution		Type of Institution		Level		
Fall of Year	Total Enrollment	Public	Private	4-Year	2-Year	Undergraduate and Classified	Graduate and Postbaccalaureate Unclassified	First-Professional
1970	8,581	6,428	2,153	6,358	2,486	7,376	1,031	175
1971	8.949	6,804	2.144	6,463	2,486	7,743	1,012	194
1972	9,215	7,071	2,144	6,459	2,756	7,941	1,066	207
1973	9,602	7,420	2,183	5,590	3,012	8,261	1,123	218
1974	10,224	7,989	2,235	6,820	3,404	8,798	1,190	236
1975	11,125	8,835	2,350	7,215	3,970	9,679	1,263	245
1976	11,012	8,653	2,359	7,129	3,883	9,429	1,333	251
1977	11,286	8,847	2,437	7,242	4,042	9,714	1,318	251
1978	11,259	8,784	2,533	7,353	4,217	9,684	1,319	257
1979	11,570	9,037	2,532	7,353	4,217	9,998	1,309	263
1980	12,097	9,457	2,640	7,571	4,526	10,475	1,343	276
1981	12,372	9,647	2,724	7,655	4,716	10,754	1,343	275
1982	12,426	9,696	2,730	7,654	4,772	10,825	1,323	278
1983	12,465	9,683	2,782	7,739	4,726	10,846	1,339	279
				Projected*				
1984	12,345	8,645	2,700	7,600	4,745	10,715	1,345	285
1985	12,247	8,591	2,656	7,437	4,810	10,551	1,398	298
1986	12,162	8,533	2,629	7,258	4,804	10,477	1,413	302
1987	12,136	9,518	2,618	7,317	4,819	10,410	1,424	302
1988	12,141	8,528	2,613	7,303	4,838	10,417	1,424	300
1989	12,161	8,548	2,613	7,306	4,855	10,439	1,425	297
1990	12,093	9,498	2,595	7,264	4,829	10,371	1,427	295
1991	11,989	5,419	2,570	7,195	4,794	10,266	1,430	293
1992	11,810	8,284	2,256	7,071	4,739	10,096	1,422	292
1993	11,676	8,125	2,491	8,969	4,708	9,958	1,418	290

Source: *Projections of Educational Statistics 1932–1993* (National Center for Education Statistics, U.S. Department of Education).
* For methodological details, see *Projections of Education Statistics to 1992–93*, 1985.

Table 7

TOTAL ENROLLMENT IN INSTITUTIONS OF HIGHER EDUCATION BY ATTENDANCE STATUS, SEX OF STUDENT, AND CONTROL OF INSTITUTION: UNITED STATES FALL 1963 TO FALL 1983

Year	Total Enrollment	Attendance Status		Sex of Student		Control of Institution	
		Full-time	Part-time	Men	Women	Public	Private
1963	4,765,867	*	*	2,955,217	1,810,850	3,065,848	1,700,019
1964	5,280,020	*	*	3,248,713	2,031,307	3,467,708	1,812,312
1965	5,820,864	*	*	3,630,020	2,290,844	3,969,596	1,951,268
1966	6,389,872	4,438,606	1,951,266†	3,856,216	2,533,656	4,348,917	2,040,955
1967	6,911,748	4,793,128	2,118,620†	4,132,800	2,778,948	4,816,028	2,095,720
1968	7,513,091	5,210,155	2,302,936	4,477,649	3,035,442	5,430,652	2,082,439
1969	8,004,660	5,498,883	4,505,777	4,746,201	3,258,459	5,896,868	2,107,792
1970	8,580,887	5,816,290	2,764,597	5,043,642	3,538,245	6,428,134	2,152,753
1971	8,948,644	6,007,232	2,871,412	5,207,004	3,741,640	6,804,309	2,144,335
1972	9,214,860	6,072,389	3,142,471	5,238,757	3,976,103	7,070,635	2,144,225
1973	9,602,123	6,189,493	3,412,630	5,371,052	4,231,071	7,419,516	2,182,607
1974	10,223,729	6,370,273	3,383,456	5,622,429	4,601,300	7,988,500	2,235,229
1975	11,184,859	6,841,334	4,343,526	6,148,997	5,035,862	8,834,508	2,350,351
1976	11,012,137	6,717,058	4,295,079	5,810,826	5,201,309	8,653,477	2,358,660
1977	11,285,787	6,792,925	4,492,862	5,789,016	5,496,771	8,846,993	2,438,794
1978	11,250,092	6,667,657	4,592,435	5,640,998	5,619,094	5,785,893	2,474,199
1979	11,589,889	6,794,039	4,775,860	5,682,877	6,887,022	9,036,882	2,533,077
1980	12,096,895	7,097,958	4,998,937	5,874,374	6,222,521	9,457,394	2,639,501
1981	12,371,672	7,181,250	5,190,422	5,975,056	6,396,616	9,647,032	2,724,640
1982	12,425,780	7,220,618	5,205,152	6,031,384	6,394,395	9,696,087	2,729,693
1983	12,464,651	7,261,050	5,203,611	6,023,725	6,440,936	9,682,734	2,781,927

*Data not available.

†Includes part-time resident students and all extension students.

Source: Office of Educational; Research and Improvement, U.S. Department of Education, *Digest of Education Statistics 1985–1986*.

Levels

Undergraduate enrollment (which accounted for 86 percent of the estimated 1987 enrollment) underlies both increased enrollment prior to 1983 and the subsequent decreases in enrollment (see Table 6). Undergraduate enrollment grew 32 percent between 1973 and 1983; it is expected to drop by 8 percent between 1983 and 1993. Enrollment in first-professional programs (e.g., law and medicine) has tended to trail the patterns displayed by undergraduate enrollment. Enrollment in these programs peaked in 1986 and should show a slight but steady decline into the 1990s. On the other hand, other graduate enrollment has shown modest but consistent growth over the 1962 to 1987 period, and this is expected to continue into the 1990s.

Gender

The proportion of female students has changed markedly over the past 25 years. In 1963 the total female enrollment in higher education was 1.8 million, and this represented 38 percent of total enrollment (see Table 7). This proportion has increased substantially (especially between 1970 and 1983, when an 82 percent increase in the number of female students occurred). In 1979 women composed the majority of college students for the first time, and the 1987 female enrollment represents 51 percent of the total student population. And although female student populations are expected to decline in the late 1980s and early 1990s, the decline will not be so dramatic as to cause females to lose their majority status.

Race

The 1987 student population is more racially diverse than that in the early 1960s. Indeed, the enrollment of minority students increased by 85 percent between 1973 and 1983 alone. The minority share of enrollment has not, however, changed significantly in recent years, and even in 1984 four of every five undergraduate students were white. Relative to the ethnic/racial composition of the general population, black, Hispanic, and Indian/Alaskan native students continue to be underrepresented in the student populations of the 1980s. A long-range trend has been a drop (to 16 percent in 1982) in the percentage of black students who attend traditionally black colleges.

Age

The aging of the U.S. population as a whole is reflected in statistics for students enrolled in institutions of higher education. In the very early 1960s, only three of every 10 students were older than 24. For the 1987 student population, it is estimated that 46 percent are above age 24. Continued increases in that percentage are expected, with an expected percentage for 1992 of 49 percent.

Attendance Status

In 1966, part-time students represented 30 percent of the total student enrollment (see Table 7). That percentage increased to 46 percent by 1987, and it is expected to continue to increase to 48 percent in 1992 as a large percentage of female students and students above age 24 continue to enroll on a part-time basis. In 1987, 50 percent of females and 75 percent of students above age 24 were part-time students. These percentages are expected to remain fairly constant through the early 1990s.

Admission Scores

Changes over time in the percentage of high school students who take college tests hamper the interpretation of admission test scores. Nevertheless, the steady decline in SAT scores between the early 1970s and early 1980s (see Figure 2) has been viewed with alarm. The average verbal score in 1972 was 453; by 1983 that average had dropped to 425. In 1972 mathematics scores averaged 484; that average dropped to 466 by 1981. The trend appears to have reversed in recent years. For example, the results of 1985 showed a 431 average for the verbal section and a 475 average for the mathematics section, with scores for prospective business students averaging 407 for the verbal section and 485 for the mathematics section. Higher scores by minority students appear, however, to underlie much of the recent improvement in average scores.

Graduate admission scores have tended to vary greatly by field and type of test; substantial declines in some social sciences and language disciplines (as well as a slight decline in GMAT scores) were experienced in the 1970s and early 1980s. Recently, GMAT scores have improved. For example, the average score in 1983–84 was 479; in 1986–87, 487. Average scores of those students intending to pursue an accounting or tax concentration have also increased. Relative to all GMAT taken, the scores of prospective accounting "majors" (1986–87 average, 475) have been consistently lower, although prospective tax "majors" (1986–87 average, 493) have been consistently higher. A somewhat different picture is presented by the GMAT scores of prospective doctoral students. Scores for this group have increased from 500 in 1983–84 to 514 in 1986–87. Those wishing to concentrate in accounting have stood out within this group and in 1986–87 had an average GMAT score of 519. The scores of doctoral students intending to concentrate on tax have changed dramatically in the middle 1980s. In 1983–84 the average GMAT score of these students was 486; but in 1986–87 that average had increased to 574.

Attitudes and Values

The attitudes and values of freshman students appear to have changed significantly between the late 1960s and mid-1980s.[11] Most conspicuously, 70.9 percent of 1985 freshmen endorsed the value of "being well-off financially," compared to 43.8 percent of freshmen in the mid-1960s (see Figure 3). Endorsements of the value "developing a meaningful philosophy of life" declined precipitously over the same period. It appears that money, power, and status have become more important to college students and that altruistic and social concerns and creative and artistic goals have declined in importance. Self-reported political attitudes of freshman students only partially support recent publicity about shifts toward greater political conservatism. The proportion of entering freshmen who consider themselves politically conservative remained in the 15–20 percent range between 1970 and 1985 while the proportion describing themselves as liberal dropped from 36.6 percent to 22.4 percent. At the same time, the students of 1985 indicated support for an array of fiscal and social positions that are traditionally viewed as liberal.

FIGURE 2
TRENDS IN PERCENTAGE OF STUDENTS WITH HIGH AND LOW SCHOLASTIC APTITUDE TEST (SAT) AND AMERICAN COLLEGE TESTING PROGRAM (ACT) SCORES

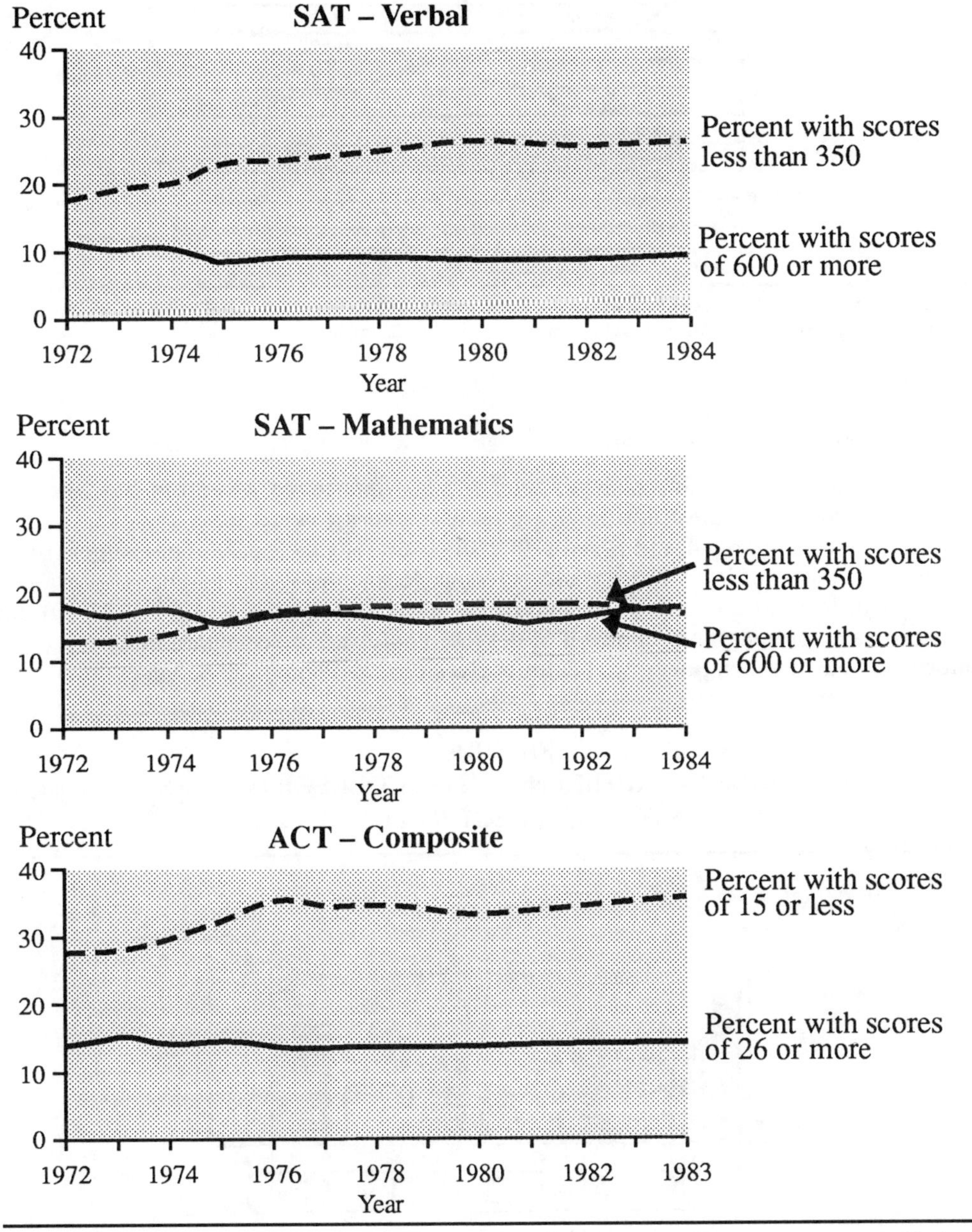

Source: *The Condition of Education 1985 Edition* (National Center for Education Statistics, Office of Educational Research and Improvement, U.S. Department of Education).

FIGURE 3
CHANGING LIFE GOALS, 1967–85
(IN PERCENTAGES)

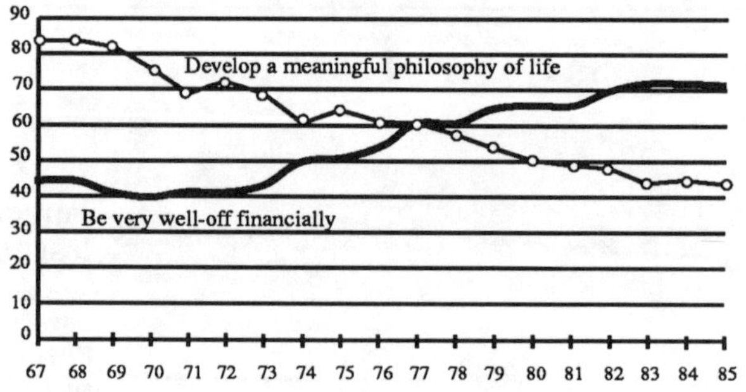

Source: *The American Freshman: Twenty Year Trends, 1966–1985* (Higher Education Research Institute, University of California at Los Angeles and American Council on Education).

Academic and Career Interests

One of the most striking changes over the last quarter of a century has been the movement away from the traditional arts and sciences toward more "occupationally oriented" fields. Figures 4 and 5 show this shift for selected years. The proportion of degrees granted conferred in arts and sciences (e.g., biological sciences, literature, history, and foreign languages) dropped by one-half between 1971 and 1981 alone. Over that same period, the proportion of degrees conferred in "occupationally oriented" fields (e.g., business, engineering, health professions, and computer sciences) increased

FIGURE 4
TRENDS IN PREFERENCES FOR COLLEGE MAJORS
PERCENTAGES, SELECTED YEARS, 1966–85

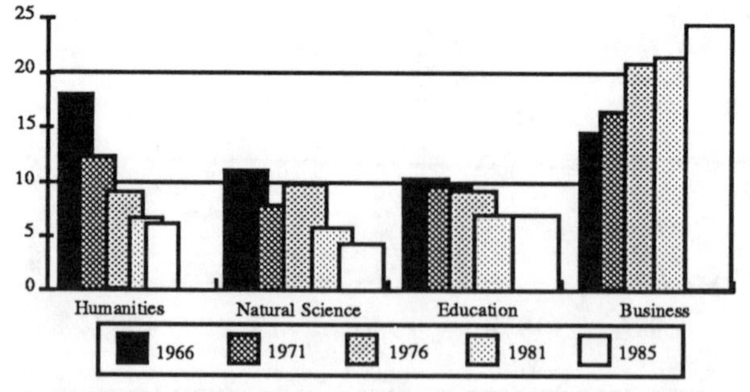

Source: *The Condition of Education 1985 Edition* (National Center for Education Statistics, Office of Educational Research and Improvement, U.S. Department of Education).

FIGURE 5

TRENDS IN CAREER PREFERENCES
(PERCENTAGES, SELECTED YEARS, 1966—88)

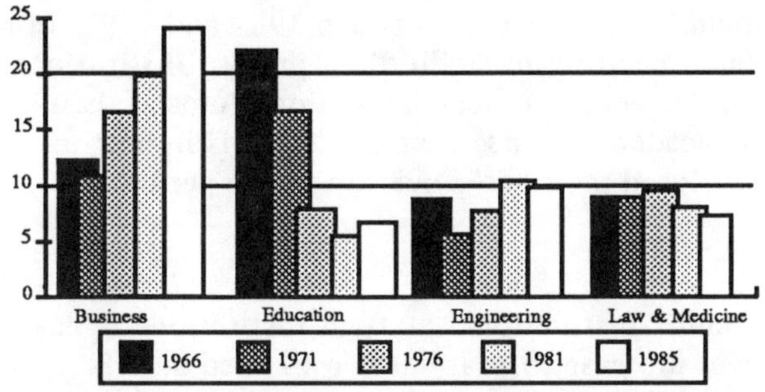

Source: *The Condition of Education 1985 Edition* (National Center for Education Statistics, Office of Educational Research and Improvement, U.S. Department of Education).

from 25 percent to 43 percent. The career plans of freshman students mirror these trends. In Fall 1966, 11.6 percent of freshmen planned to pursue business careers; in Fall 1986 the percentage was 25.5 percent.

INSTITUTIONS

In the 1962–63 academic year there were 2,093 institutions of higher education (see Table 8). By the 1984–85 academic year this number had increased 50 percent to 3,146 (excluding branch campuses). The number of public institutions grew 80 percent over this period, with most of this growth attributable to two-year institutions. The number of two-year institutions more than doubled over the period, and four-year institutions increased by 23 percent. Private institutions grew 34 percent and showed

TABLE 8

NUMBER OF INSTITUTIONS OF HIGHER EDUCATION, BY CONTROL AND TYPE OF INSTITUTION: UNITED STATES, 1962–63 AND 1984–85

	1962–63			1984–85		
	Public	Private	Total	Public	Private	Total
Two-Year Institutions	376	1092	1468	461	1450	1911
Four-Year Institutions	346	261	625	868	367	1235
Totals	740	1353	2093	1329	1817	3146

Source: Digest of Education Statistics 1985–1986, Office of Educational Research and Improvement, U.S. Department of Education.

comparable growth rates for four-year institutions (33 percent) and two-year institutions (41 percent). The proportion of students enrolled in private institutions, however, dropped from 36 percent in 1963 to 22 percent in 1987. Despite this downward trend, the data reported in Figure 6 and Table 6 indicate that the proportionate enrollments in private and public institutions (and in two-year and four-year institutions) should be fairly stable between 1987 and 1993. In terms of survival, public institutions have been more stable than private institutions. Only 36 public institutions (of which 35 were two-year institutions) closed their doors between the 1960–61 and 1982–83 academic years, although 218 private institutions (including 122 four-year institutions) closed their doors over that same period.

FACULTY

The number of senior instructional staff in institutions of higher education has more than doubled over the past 25 years; it is estimated at 678,000 in 1987. Of these, 65 percent are full-time, 73 percent are employed in public institutions, and 71 percent work in four-year institutions. Data for 1985 reveal that faculty are predominantly male (65 percent) and white (92 percent). Trends in faculty numbers correspond with trends in student enrollment (See Figure 7). Thus, total faculty numbers increased 33 percent in the 10 years prior to 1983 but are expected to drop 10 percent (to 635,000) in the 10 years subsequent to 1983. Over the 1973–83 period, more extreme increases occurred in part-time faculty (78 percent, versus 17 percent for full-time faculty), for faculty employed by public institutions (39 percent, versus 20 percent for private institutions), and for faculty in two-year institutions (60 percent, versus 25 percent for four-year institutions). The decline in faculty numbers between 1983 and 1993 is expected to be more severe at private institutions (a 12 percent decrease, versus 9 percent for public institutions) and four-year institutions (an 11 percent decrease, versus 7 percent for two-year institutions). Full- and part-time faculty numbers are expected to decline at about the same percentage rate. In considering these trends, it should also be noted that between the early 1960s and 1985 there was an 85 percent decline in the proportion of freshmen students interested in faculty careers. Furthermore, Figure 8 data indicate that a drastic decline in the purchasing power of faculty salaries occurred in the period 1972–73 to 1980–81. Although some of these losses were recouped in the early and mid-1980s, real salaries for the 1983–84 academic year were still below those for the 1972–73 time horizon.

FINANCING

In the 1985-86 academic year total expenditures by colleges and universities ($100.9 billion) represented more than a 10-fold increase over expenditures in the 1961–62 period (see Table 9). Inflation, however, underlies much of the increase. For example, in the 10-year period from 1971–72 to 1981–82, current-fund expenditures increased 175 percent; measured in constant (1981–82) dollars, the real increase (29 percent) actually corresponds closely to the increase in student population over that period.

Sources of funding largely depend on the control of the institution (i.e., public versus private). In the case of public institutions, states contribute the largest share of funding. In the 1981–82 period states provided 44 percent of current-fund revenue for four-year institutions and 50 percent for two-year institutions. Conversely, for private

FIGURE 6
ENROLLMENT TRENDS IN INSTITUTIONS OF HIGHER EDUCATION BY INSTITUTIONAL CHARACTERISTICS

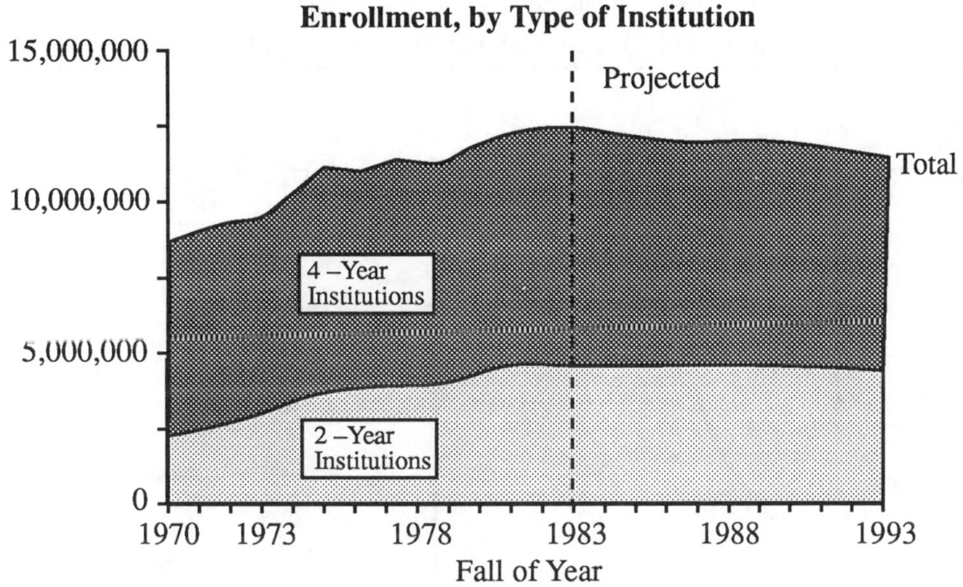

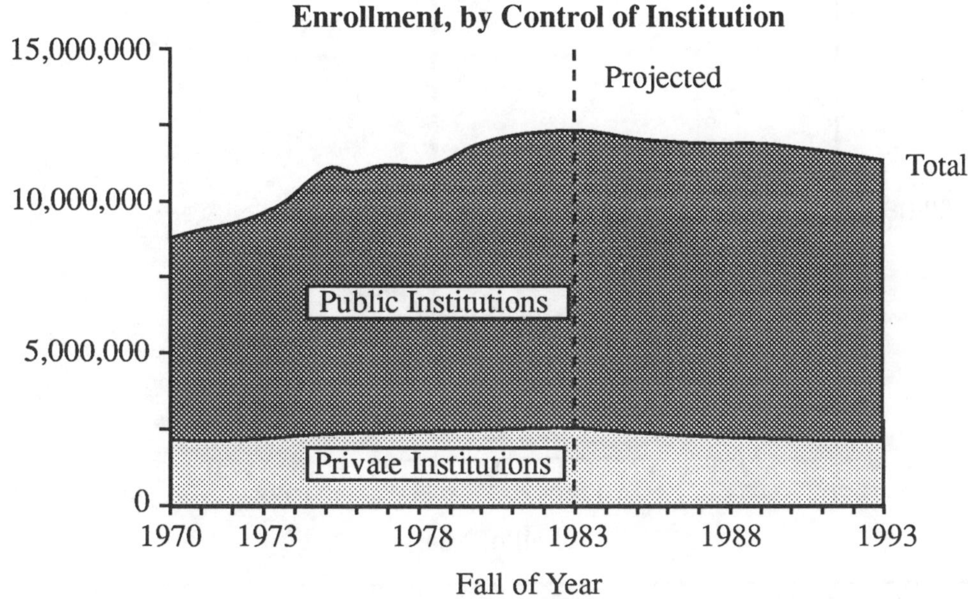

Source: *The Condition of Education 1985 Edition* (National Center for Education Statistics, Office of Educational Research and Improvement, U.S. Department of Education).

institutions, student sources provide the largest share of funding, with 37 percent of the funding for four-year institutions and 67 percent of the funding for two-year institutions coming from students in the 1981–82 period.

FIGURE 7

SENIOR INSTRUCTIONAL STAFF
IN INSTITUTIONS OF HIGHER EDUCATION

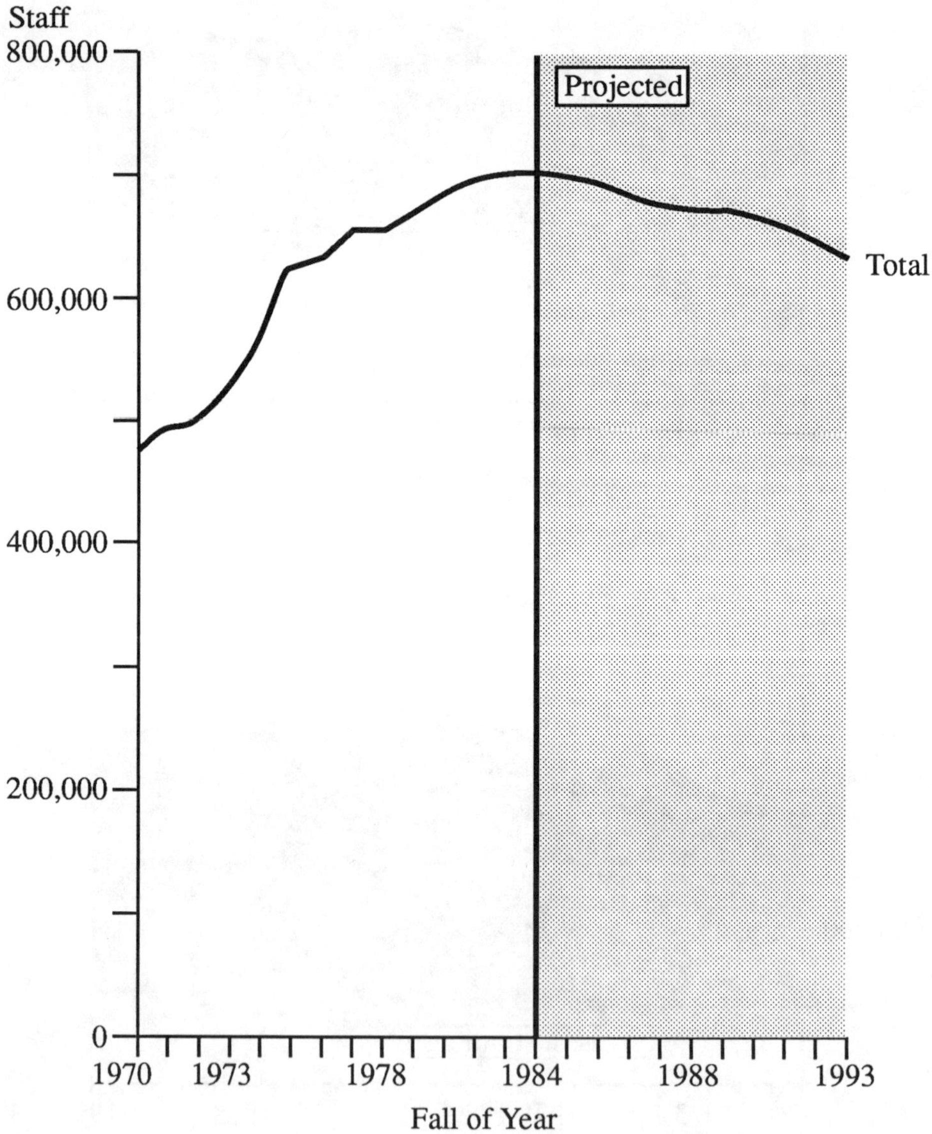

Source: *The Condition of Education 1985 Edition* (National Center for Education Statistics, Office of Educational Research and Improvement, U.S. Department of Education).

Changes in sources of funding have occurred over time. Important funding trends that became apparent in the early 1980s are (a) increases in the proportion of funding by states, (b) decreases in the proportion of funding from federal sources (from 19 percent in the 1970–71 period to 13 percent in the 1981–82 period), and (c) stability in

FIGURE 8

AVERAGE SALARY OF FULL-TIME INSTRUCTIONAL STAFF, ALL ACADEMIC RANKS COMBINED

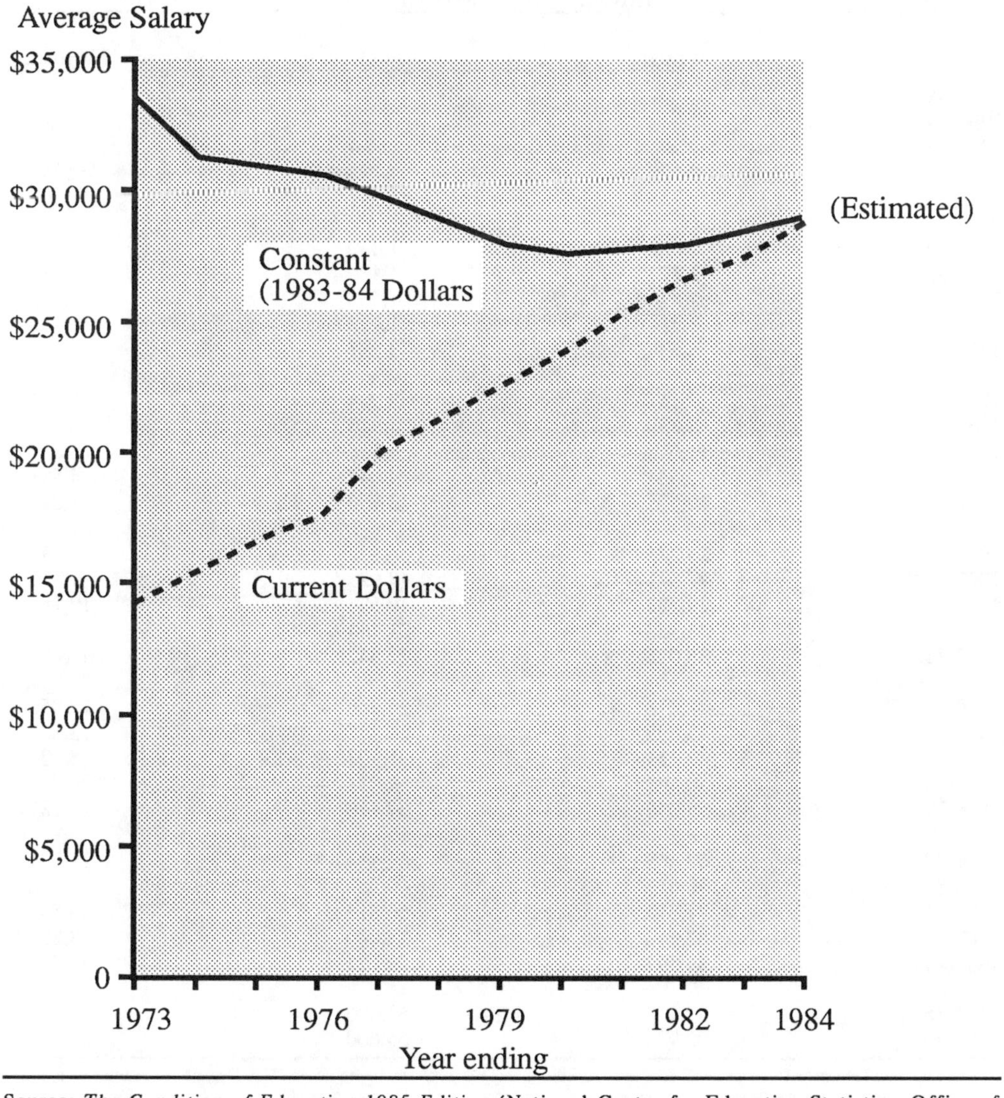

Source: *The Condition of Education 1985 Edition* (National Center for Education Statistics, Office of Educational Research and Improvement, U.S. Department of Education).

the proportion of funding provided by students (around one-third), despite substantial increases in tuition charges. Figure 9 shows that the increases in tuition costs over the last 20 years are far less dramatic than publicized when measured in constant dollars. Moreover, voluntary support has increased markedly, particularly in recent years. Total

TABLE 9
EXPENDITURES OF HIGHER EDUCATIONAL INSTITUTIONS BY CONTROL OF INSTITUTIONS: UNITED STATES, 1899–1900 TO 1985–86 (AMOUNTS IN MILLIONS)

	Total	Public	Private
1899–1900	—	—	—
1909-10	—	—	—
1919-20	—	—	—
1929-30	$632	$292	$341
1939-40	758	392	367
1949-50	2,662	1,430	1,233
1951-52	2,874	1,430	1,233
1953-54	2,874	1,565	1,309
1955-56	3,414	1,912	1,832
1957-58	5,530	3,237	2,293
1959-60	7,147	3,904	3,244
1961-62	8,830	4,919	3,911
1963-64	11,615	6,558	5,057
1965-66	15,634	9,047	6,588
1967-68	20,575	12,750	7,824
1969-70	25,276	16,234	9,041
1970-71	27,541	18,028	9,513
1971-72	29,722	19,538	10,184
1972-73	31,923	21,144	10,799
1973-74	35,026	23,542	11,484
1974-75	39,818	26,966	12,852
1975-76	43,605	29,736	13,869
1976-77	47,223	31,997	15,226
1977-78	50,498	34,031	16,467
1978-79	55,296	37,110	18,187
1979-80	62,465	41,434	21,031
1980-81	70,524	46,559	23,956
1981-82	77,313	50,813	26,500
1982-83	82,642	53,840	28,803
1983-84*	89,597	58,124	31,473
1984-85†	95,500	62,000	33,500
1985-86†	100,900	65,600	35,300

Source: *Digest of Education Statistics 1985–86* (Office of Educational Research and Improvement, U.S. Department of Education).
Note: Because of rounding, details may not add to totals.
* Preliminary
† Estimated

FIGURE 9
ESTIMATED AVERAGE CHARGES FOR TUITION AND REQUIRED FEES PER FULL-TIME EQUIVALENT STUDENT IN ALL INSTITUTIONS OF HIGHER EDUCATION WITH ALTERNATE PROJECTIONS,* BY CONTROL OF INSTITUTION: UNITED STATES, 1966–67 TO 1986–87

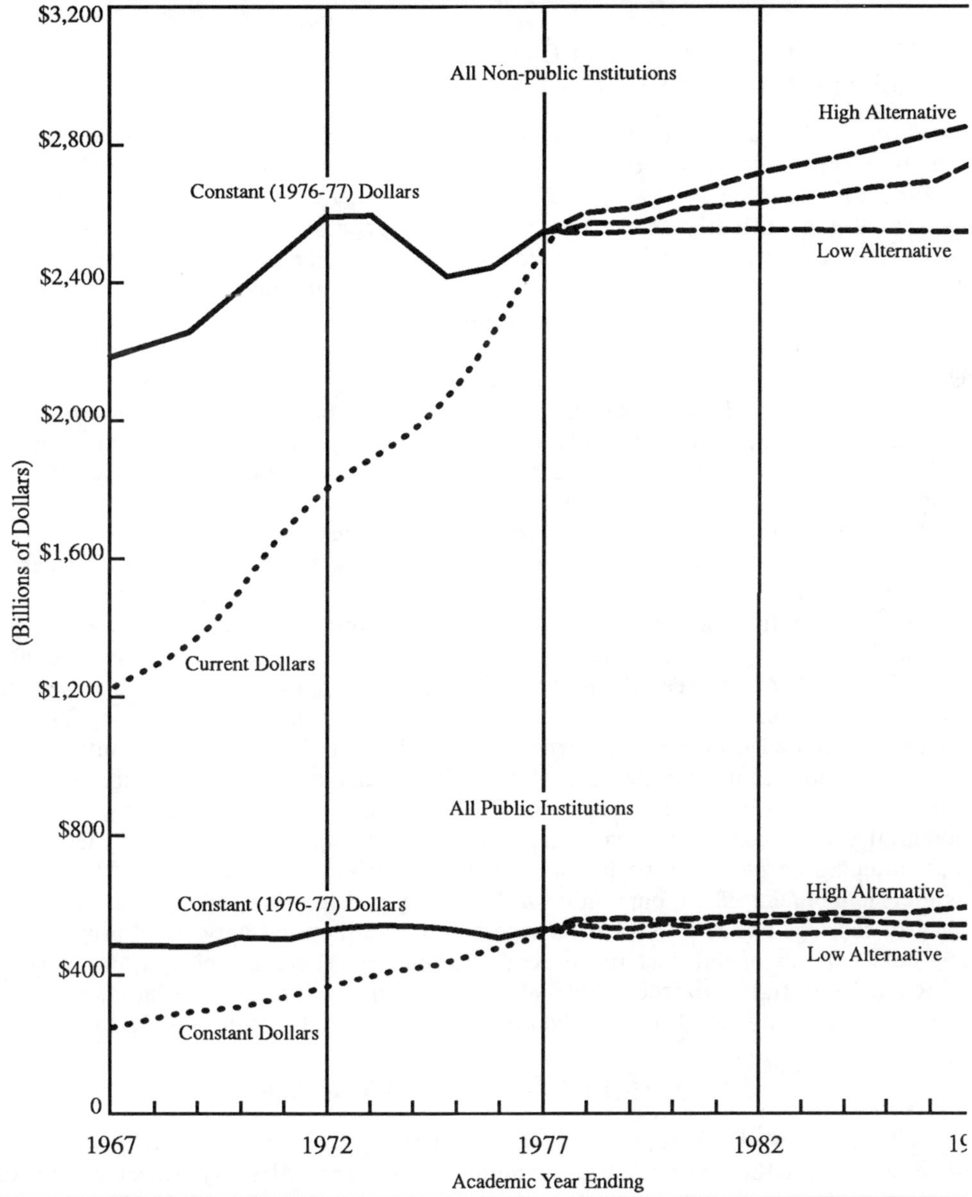

Source: *The Condition of Education 1985 Edition* (National Center for Education Statistics, Office of Educational Research and Improvement, U.S. Department of Education).
*Projections are in constant (1976–77) dollars.

voluntary support in the 1983–84 academic year was $5.6 billion, which represented a 73.4 percent increase (15.6 percent after adjustment for inflation) over the preceding five years. This voluntary support came from alumni (23.3 percent), private nonalumni (23.5 percent), foundations (19.3 percent), business (22.7 percent), religious organizations (3.4 percent), and other (7.8 percent). The proportion provided by business represents a 17.2 percent increase over the 1978–79 period, whereas the proportion provided by foundations registered a 21.7 percent decline.

SUMMARY OF TRENDS AFFECTING THE UNIVERSITY ENVIRONMENT

Over the last quarter of a century, the student population has increased markedly (nearly 150 percent from 1963 to 1983) as have the percentage of women (38 percent in 1963 to 52 percent in 1983) and the typical student age. Students' attitudes also have changed radically as evidenced by a far greater desire to be very well off financially. In part, this desire is reflected by statistics that show 26 percent of recent entering freshmen selecting a business-related major as compared to 12 percent 20 years ago. In addition, a far larger proportion of students presently attend public universities (about four of five) as compared to 20 years ago (about five of eight). University expenditures also have risen dramatically but proportionally to student enrollment when adjusted for inflation. Likewise, contributed support has risen markedly over the period, especially since 1980. During the same time, minorities have made slight proportional gains but continue to be underrepresented based on their proportion of the total populations. In addition, admission scores have moved down slightly, and graduate enrollment in business has increased marginally.

By the close of the decade ending in the mid-1990s, the 18-to 24-year-old population will decline by nearly 20 percent. However, total enrollments are expected to decrease by only 6 percent. The typical student is therefore likely to be older (nearly half will be over age 24) and attending on a part-time basis. In spite of some concern (e.g., Palmer, 1986) expressed about the decline in the quality of top students selecting accounting, the underlying data noted in this section point to a stable population of relatively talented students with directed goals. Several factors that may influence the matter favorably or unfavorably include the widespread adoption of a postbaccalaureate requirement for either licensing or membership in the AICPA (AICPA, 1988), the potential shift to urban/suburban universities as the population ages and increasingly must attend on a part-time basis, and the success of attracting more minority students as their component of the population at large is growing more rapidly than the whole. Faculty shortages in certain areas may persist due to the relatively small proportion of students expressing interest in an academic career. The remaining major variable, which is essentially unpredictable at this writing, is the public's attitude toward education generally (cf., Carnegie Commission Report and *A Nation at Risk*).

THE INTERNAL ENVIRONMENT

This portion of the report focuses on changes over the last two and one-half decades within the university environment that more directly affect accounting professors. Recall that the charge to the Committee was to document changes in the accounting professorial environment during the past 25 years so that it might better anticipate the significance of these factors on the near-term implementation of the report of the American Accounting Association Committee on the Future Structure, Content, and Scope of Accounting Education (1986). Within the context of the internal environment, the Committee was encouraged to document changes in professorial competence in relative and absolute terms, changes in the promotion and tenure process and criteria, changes in the requirements for terminal degrees, and changes in the extent of specialization. Other factors reviewed included salary compression and other matters adjudged appropriate.

Investigating such factors as competence, specialization, and the like presents a substantial challenge, and, although some archival data are available, they are severely limited. Thus, the principal bases for conclusions consist of mail surveys of accounting professors, chairpersons of academic accounting units, and deans of business colleges. After an explanation of the overall methodology, the discussion will follow the general framework developed in Exhibit 1.

Some of the data may prove controversial. The intent is to provide descriptive data, *not* normative data. The reader should bear this in mind.

METHODOLOGY

The structure of the survey consisted of two fundamental divisions within the accounting professorial environment. First, the Committee believed that accounting professors beginning their academic careers at different times during the 25–year period could be expected to have entered different environments with different personal characteristics and educational backgrounds. Second, it was believed that professors employed by institutions of higher learning that either grant doctoral degrees with a concentration in accounting, or do *not* do so, would exhibit different expectations, educational backgrounds, and environments. In addition to these major experimental grouping variables, other information was gathered on survey respondents in order to fit the model better. These are discussed in conjunction with later analyses. The chairpersons and deans selected to receive questionnaires were strictly determined by the faculty members responding to the survey.

Start Times

The Committee chose to survey professors listed in *The Accounting Faculty Directory* (Hasselback, 1986) from three time periods within the 25-year time frame covered by the charge. Table 10 presents a frequency distribution of accounting faculty by the dates of their highest degree along with other information. The date of the highest degree acted as a surrogate for the faculty members' start date. Comparison of the data collected by questionnaires indicated some imprecision in this surrogation, but not enough to be significant. Furthermore, it is the only reasonable ex ante referent to the population as it appears in Hasselback (1986). In addition, the date of highest degree may well represent other respondent characteristics regarding their perception of the environment (e.g., experiences while in their degree programs). Limitations related to the use of Hasselback (1986) as a sample referent are discussed later.

The first time period, *1961 to 1966*, characterizes the "early" group. It comprises the beginning point of the 25–year period and spans six years to provide for sufficient population in the cells of interest.

The second time period, *1971 to 1974*, represents the "middle" group. It is believed to reflect the influence of the AACSB's terminal degree requirement that became effective in 1969 but was phased in for many universities during the early

TABLE 10
OVERALL POPULATION FREQUENCIES OF ACCOUNTING FACULTY BY VARIOUS TIME PERIODS AND CHARACTERISTICS

	Dates of Highest Degrees of Accounting Faculty							
Row Description	Pre-1961	1961-66	1967-70	1971-74	1975 -79	1980-81	1982-86	Totals
Group Designation		Early		Middle		New		
Type of Institution								
1. Doctoral Granting	243	120	120	179	249	131	358	1,401
(Percent)	(19)	(26)	(24)	(23)	(23)	(27)	(32)	(25)
2. Nondoctoral Granting	1,004	342	380	583	855	357	767	4,278
(Percent)	(81)	(74)	(76)	(77)	(77)	(73)	(68)	(75)
3. Total	1,247	463	500	762	1,104	478	1,125	5,679
4. Time Cumulative Totals (Summation of line 3)		1,710	2,210	2,972	4,076	4,554	5,679	
5. Average Number per Year	N/A	93	125	191	184	239	225	N/A
Doctoral Degrees in Accounting Granted								
6. Total/Time Period	348*	348*	444	606	601	506	610†	3,463†
7. Per Year/ Time Period	N/A	58	111	152	120	153	122†	N/A
8. Cumulative Totals of line 6		696	1,140	1,746	2,347	2,853	3,463	
9. Maximum Percent of Total Faculty with Accounting Doctoral Degree by Time Period (line 8 / line 4)		41	52	59	58	63	61	

Source: Hasselback, *The Accounting Faculty Directory* (1982 and 1987).

Note: Throughout this study, the three groups of faculty receiving their highest degrees in 1961-66, 1971-74 and 1980-81 are referred to as early, middle and new.

* Data available for total prior to 1966 only. Half of the 696 degrees awarded prior to 1966 allocated to 1961-66 time period.

† Data available only through 1985. Total for period estimated.

1970s. In addition, the 1971–74 time period provides for detection of the effects of some changes related to the growing emphasis on empirical research (i.e., the late 1960s and 1970s are commonly cited as the beginning of empirical research in accounting—Ball and Brown, 1968; Beaver, 1968, etc.).

The third time period, *1980 to 1981*, is the "new" group. This period includes professors who are almost ready for promotion and tenure and who have had an adequate length of time to develop stable perceptions of the professorial environment. The time period covers only two years because of the larger number of subjects available.

Even though the preponderance of the population of professors attained their highest degree following the middle group (see Table 10), the median time falls within that group. Also, there are approximately as many faculty with highest degree dates attained prior to the early group (1,247) as there are after the new group (1,125). Thus, even though the purpose in establishing groups was to detect what we considered to be major changes during the period, the findings may, to an extent, apply to the population at large. Throughout the tabular presentations in this section, the marginal means are weighted by the relative population frequency within the groups and the statistical analyses are similarly weighted (Burdick, 1983). A more detailed discussion of data analysis techniques and relevant limitations is presented later.

Type of Institution

The Committee decided to partition the population on the basis of those professors at universities that offer a doctorate with a concentration in accounting and those that do not. The justification for this was based on studies (e.g., Cargile and Bublitz, 1986; Campbell and Morgan, 1987) that suggested significant differences in these two environments. Some of the characteristics anticipated to be greater at doctoral-granting (D-G) schools were (1) faculty size (this is supported by data from Hasselback (1986), which shows that the actual mean size of the faculty of the 81 schools granting doctoral degrees was 17.3 as compared to that of the faculties of nondoctoral-granting (ND–G) of 9.6); (2) numbers of teaching and research assistants with greater expertise; (3) availability of resources; and (4) expectations for research/publication. In addition, a somewhat "newer" faculty at doctoral schools was expected (this is borne out by the percentages of new faculty in Table 10, lines 1 and 2). It is noteworthy that three of four accounting faculty are at ND–G schools. Other beliefs are developed later as specific hypotheses are discussed and evidence presented.

The Questionnaires

The questionnaires presented in Appendices B, C, and D were used to elicit responses from the accounting faculty, business college deans, and accounting chairpersons. After an initial Committee meeting during which numerous ideas were exchanged to develop surrogates for attacking the relevant issues, a draft questionnaire was formulated and circulated to each Committee member. At a later meeting, several major concerns arose regarding the use of questionnaires.

First, there was concern whether dimensions such as competence could really be determined through a survey instrument. Yet this approach seemed to be the only feasible way in which to supplement existing archival data such as the proportion holding a doctoral degree, professional certification, and so forth. Another major issue involved the notion of distant recall. To measure change over time, the questionnaires asked members of the sample in the early and middle groups to recall the environment during the early part of their careers as full-time academicians. No doubt a considerable amount of error might be present in any such recollections. In addition, the philosophical issue of maturation was an acknowledged reality (e.g., switching from a ND–G school to a D-G school during this period). In spite of these concerns, it was resolved that there was little option for accomplishing the task other than to elicit such recall. And, because the study primarily is concerned with changes over time, specific responses are perhaps not so significant as directionality.

The Committee also realized that application of sophisticated statistical techniques would prove quite a target for pure statisticians. Some members of the Committee believed that raw data and, perhaps, marginal means should be presented, leaving the

Committee (and eventually the reader) to determine the "significance" of the pattern of data. Certainly, the large amount of information requested, the recall problems inherent in the questionnaires, and the data of varying quality from different archival sources presented consequential problems in obtaining statistical significance. Furthermore, there was the realization that conducting numerous statistical tests would almost certainly result in some being significant. In spite of these limitations, the Committee decided to report statistical significances for data that readily lent themselves to such analyses.

Mailing Procedures

Prior to the mailing of the accounting faculty questionnaire, Professor Ray Sommerfeld, then President of the American Accounting Association, sent a letter encouraging each randomly selected faculty member to complete and return the questionnaire. Due to the length of the questionnaire, this letter was necessary to secure a reasonable response rate. In contrast, only a letter from the Committee chairperson was sent to the deans and accounting chairpersons because their questionnaires were quite short.

Two hundred forty-five questionnaires were mailed to accounting faculty members. Professor James Edwards provided the Committee with randomly selected individuals from a computerized data base of Hasselback (1986). The sample was evenly divided among the six subpopulations created by the three start dates and the two types of institutions. Five additional questionnaires were sent to the nondoctoral-early group because this group exhibited a lower response rate than the other five groups (see Table 11). Efforts at follow-up with this group proved ineffective. The number of responses across groups was relatively stable, ranging from 22 to 31.

In addition to questionnaire response rate, several other limitations existed due to the use of Hasselback (1986). One limitation is that the population of the faculty appearing in the 1986 edition of Hasselback represents the faculty *currently* employed.

TABLE 11

SAMPLE DATA AND AVERAGE AGE

	Faculty Start Date			
	Early	Middle	New	Totals
Questionnaires Returned/Mailed:				
Doctoral Granting	28/40	25/40	31/40	84/120
Nondoctoral Granting	22/45	25/40	25/40	72/125
Response Rates:				
Doctoral Granting	70%	63%	78%	70%
Nondoctoral Granting	49%	63%	63%	58%
Average Age:				
Doctoral Granting	56	45	37	
Nondoctoral Granting	53	47	39	

Undoubtedly, many of the persons employed initially in the early group's period (1961–66), as well as some in each of the other periods are not represented in this source. As the results are discussed, this limitation, and its likely impact, will be considered.

Another limitation attributable in part to the use of Hasselback (1986) for the sample frame of reference is that part-time faculty are likely to be omitted at a higher rate than full-time faculty. For example, the respondents' set contains only full-time academics even though there was no intention to eliminate part-time faculty members. Archival data from Williams (1979), when combined with more recent survey data from Williams et al. (1985), reflect substantial changes in the ratio of part-time faculty to full-time faculty over time. Table 12 reflects a sharp downward trend from 86 part-time per 100 full-time faculty in the 1967–68 period to about 40 part-time per 100 full-time faculty in the 1985–86 period. This downward trend, which is nearly obscured in the Committee's data collection due to the sample referent, very likely contributes to differences in the typical professorial profile and environment over time. This is so because it seems likely that part-time faculty would (1) hold doctorates less frequently, (2) pursue research and publication less often and with different methods, and (3) be less conceptually oriented than full-time faculty. The impact of this trend will be discussed when reaching conclusions from analyses.

TABLE 12

NUMBER OF PART-TIME (FTE) FACULTY
PER 100 (FTE) FACULTY IN ACCOUNTING
AT FOUR-YEAR AND GRADUATE INSTITUTIONS

	Time Period			
	1967-68	1972-73	1977-78	1985-86
Ratio	86	68	37	40

Sources: All data prior to 1985-86 from Williams, "Ten Years of Changes in Accounting Education" (1979). Data for 1985-86 is estimated from information appearing in Table 6, p. 17 of Williams et al., "Accounting Data Base: 1985-86" (1985).

Note: The part-time faculty reflected in the 1985-86 column are primarily involved in teaching principles (86 percent of all principles are taught by part-time faculty). By contrast, only 32 percent of other undergraduate and graduate classes are taught by part-time faculty. Most of the part-time faculty in the 1985-86 column are graduate teaching assistants (52 percent) followed by instructors/lecturers (40 percent).

Business college deans and accounting chairpersons were mailed questionnaires only if an accounting faculty member from their school returned the questionnaire. This procedure was followed for contrasting perceptions of deans and accounting faculty who worked at the same institutions. Also, perceptions of certain issues (e.g., the importance of various activities for promotion) would not vary significantly along start date times, allowing for pooling of different "start time" faculty responses into the doctoral/nondoctoral dichotomy. Of the 138 questionnaires mailed to current deans and chairpersons listed in Hasselback (1986), 70 went to D-G schools and 68 to ND–G schools. Of the deans' questionnaires mailed, 36 (51 percent response rate) and 26 (38 percent response rate) were returned from the two groups, respectively. Of the chairpersons' questionnaires, 30 were returned from D-G institutions (43 percent response rate), and 41 were returned from ND–G institutions (60 percent response rate). In addition, surveys were mailed to former deans, but an insufficient number were returned for analysis.

Data and Statistical Procedures

The data collected in this study resemble those appearing in Cargile and Bublitz (1986). As with that study, MANOVA was the primary method of analysis. *SAS* (1985) was used as the basic statistical package and was supplemented with manual computations where needed, especially for simple, nonparametric analyses. Where MANOVA indicated significance in a variable with more than two levels, the Bonferroni test was used to determine the source. This is explained in *SAS* (1985). In general, the tests employed are not referred to, but they consist of MANOVA and, where appropriate, Bonferroni tests. For a further discussion of the data characteristics needed to meet the assumptions of MANOVA, see Appendix A.

As noted earlier, some members of the Committee believed that no analyses were needed for straightforward, nonparametric data. Thus formal analyses (e.g., Chi square) have been used only when it was believed that the data might be difficult for the reader to analyze personally. In these cases, the type of test and significance levels are noted.

INDIVIDUAL RESOURCES

As depicted in Exhibit 1, the initial focal point in describing the accounting professorial environment consists of examining available resources. This section presents information on the individuals composing that environment. In this section available data relating to the absolute and relative competence of the individual and the extent of specialization will be reviewed. Following the study of the individuals composing the accounting professorial population, attention will be given to the resources afforded by the institution and the environment external to the institution. Lastly, the reward structure within the accounting professorial environment will be focused.

Competence

The typical accounting faculty member, as reflected by the sample medians, began his career in the 1971–74 time period, is 46 years old, holds a doctoral degree with a concentration in accounting, possesses professional certification, and has work experience of just over six years prior to beginning employment as a full-time academician. Thus, as represented by traditional indicators of competence, it is clear from the outset that the population consists of well-qualified individuals. In the analyses that follow, however, readers are encouraged to reach their own conclusions.

Archival data. Formal credentials consist of highest degree attained as well as professional certification achieved. Table 13 presents information gathered principally from archival sources that avoids the problems associated with the sample referent as noted above. The proportion of doctorates among full-time faculty has risen dramatically over the 20-year period reflected in the table. Indeed, even allowing for the proportion of doctorates drawn from the sample referent (which contains some

TABLE 13
PROPORTION OF FULL-TIME FACULTY WITH DOCTORATES AND PROFESSIONAL CERTIFICATION BY TIME

	Time Period			
	1967-68	1972-73	1977-78	1986-87
Doctorate	31%	41%	50%	60%* (54%)
Professional Certification	60%	58%	72%	(60%)

Sources: All data prior to 1986-87 from Williams, "Ten Years of Changes in Accounting Education" (1979). Doctorate in 1986-87 from Williams et al., "Accounting Data Base: 1986-87" (1986). Numbers in parentheses are based on samples of 100 faculty each from doctoral- and nondoctoral-granting schools, according to Hasselback, *The Accounting Faculty Directory* (1987), approximately weighted to arrive at overall percentages. The faculty member was deemed to possess professional certification if he or she was listed as having a CPA, CMA, or CIA.
* Contains persons holding Master of Law

part-time faculty), the trend is clear. The information in Table 10, line 9, moreover, confirms that faculty holding doctorates in accounting have increased generally, in both absolute and relative terms. For example, the maximum percentage of accounting faculty in the 1966–67 academic year that could have had doctorates in accounting was 41 percent as compared to 61 percent in the 1986–87 period.

The trend associated with the proportion of faculty holding professional certification is less clear because the only data for the 1986–87 period is extrapolated from random samples drawn from Hasselback (1987). This referent would contain primarily, but not exclusively, full–time faculty. Thus there is an unknown error component in the 1986–87 information. It seems quite likely that many of the part-time faculty who were present in greater abundance in earlier periods possessed professional certification. This issue will be addressed later.

Doctoral degrees held. The percentage of doctoral degrees held by respondents in the sample as compared to the percentage that exists in the population reported in Hasselback (1987) is presented in Table 14. The percentages are also separated as to type of institution. It is important to remember that the members of the sample were not intended to represent a random sample of the population at large, but rather random samples of the populations from three "start date" time periods and from two types of

TABLE 14
PROPORTION OF DOCTORAL DEGREE HOLDERS IN SAMPLE VERSUS POPULATIONS BY TYPE OF INSTITUTION

	Type of Institution		
	Doctoral Granting	Nondoctoral Granting	Overall
Sample Respondents	92%	63%	70%
Population	74%	47%	54%

Source: Population data are estimated from two random samples of 100 each from doctoral- and nondoctoral-granting schools from Hasselback, *The Accounting Directory* (1987).

institutions within each of the time periods. This method was employed to study trends. Nevertheless, it seems sound to note differences between the sample respondents and members of the population generally because they will bear on the validity of some interpretations. As indicated in Table 14, the respondents in the sample are more likely to possess a doctorate than those in the professorial environment population. Also, the faculty at D-G institutions are more likely to possess a doctorate than those at ND–G schools.

Table 15 reflects the same general trend in the proportion of accounting faculty holding doctoral degrees as was reported earlier in Table 13. But there is an increasing tendency among both D-G and ND–G institutions to employ persons holding doctorates with a concentration in accounting as opposed to those holding doctorates in other fields (Table 16). This trend may reflect, in part, the increased emphasis of the AACSB on doctorally qualified accounting faculty, as well as an overall increase in the number of accounting doctorates available for employment.

Another clue into differences that exist between the entrants to faculty posts over time is provided in Table 17. That is, a significant trend exists in terms of the proportion of faculty who gained experience as research assistants during their graduate programs. Faculty members in the new group are far more likely to have had experience as a researcher prior to their becoming full-time academics. Also, a greater likelihood exists that faculty at D-G institutions had research experience during their graduate programs than did those at ND–G schools.

TABLE 15

SAMPLE NUMBER AND PROPORTION
OF DOCTORAL DEGREE HOLDERS
BY START DATE AND TYPE OF INSTITUTION

	Type of Institution		
Start Date	Doctoral Granting	Nondoctoral Granting	Overall
Early	25/28 (89%)	11/22 (50%)	60%
Middle	25/25 (100%)	18/25 (72%)	79%
New	27/31 (87%)	16/25 (64%)	70%

TABLE 16

SAMPLE NUMBER AND PROPORTION OF DOCTORAL DEGREES IN
ACCOUNTING TO ALL DOCTORATES
BY TYPE OF INSTITUTION AND START DATE

	Type of Institution		
Start Date	Doctoral Granting	Nondoctoral Granting	Overall
Early	23/25 (92%)	6/11 (55%)	64%
Middle	21/25 (84%)	12/18 (67%)	71%
New	25/27 (93%)	16/16 (100%)	98%

Chi square is significant at $p < .05$ for accounting versus not accounting across start date for doctoral granting- and nondoctoral- granting institutions. It is not significant overall.

TABLE 17

SAMPLE NUMBER AND PROPORTION OF FACULTY WHO SPENT TIME AS A DOCTORAL STUDENT RESEARCH ASSISTANT TO ALL FACULTY

	Type of Institution		
Start Date	Doctoral Granting	Nondoctoral Granting	Overall
Early			
6/28 (21%)	3/22 (14%)	16%	
Middle	6/25 (24%)	3/25 (12%)	15%
New	15/31 (48%)	8/25 (32%)	36%
Totals	31%	18%	

Overall, the data in this section support the notion that the more recent the faculty member's entrance to academia, the greater the research expertise. Also, those faculty at D-G schools are more likely to possess greater research skills than their counterparts at ND–G schools.

Professional certification. As noted above, no clear-cut trend appears as to the proportion of faculty holding professional certification. The information in Table 18 indicates that the sample respondents were more likely to be certified than their counterparts in the population. Table 19 includes more substantive trend data as the groups are separated by start date.

This information tends to confirm the suspected decline in the proportion of accounting faculty who are certified. In particular, the declining proportion of those entering the faculty ranks over time is rather clear. Based on the data in Tables 13 and 19, the proportion of certified faculty appears to have peaked sometime in the middle to late 1970s and is now declining. As reported in Table 20, this may be due in part to the fact that more faculty are entering the accounting professorial ranks with less practice experience. Accreditation emphasis on the doctoral degree and not on the master's-CPA combination that existed until 1969 may also contribute to the decreased importance of professional certification.

Practice work experience. In addition to formal credentials, the Committee believed that the amount of practice work experience accumulated by faculty prior to

TABLE 18

PROPORTION HOLDING PROFESSIONAL CERTIFICATION IN SAMPLE VERSUS POPULATION BY TYPE OF INSTITUTION

	Type of Institution		
Start Date	Doctoral Granting	Nondoctoral Granting	Overall
Sample Respondents	67%	72%	71%
Population	56%	62%	60%

Source: Population data are estimated from two random samples of 100 each from doctoral and nondoctoral granting schools according to Hasselback, *The Accounting Faculty Directory* (1987). Determination of certification status is determined in all cases from Hasselback, *The Accounting Faculty Directory* (1987). Certification means CPA, CMA, or CIA.

TABLE 19
PROFESSIONAL CERTIFICATION
BY START DATE AND TYPE OF INSTITUTION

	Type of Institution		
Start Date	Doctoral Granting	Nondoctoral Granting	Overall
Early	19/28 (68%)	16/22 (73%)	72%
Middle	19/25 (76%)	20/25 (80%)	79%
New	16/31 (52%)	15/25 (60%)	58%
Proportion Certified	67%	72%	71%

Source: Certification data for our sample respondents are from *The Accounting Faculty Directory* (Hasselback, 1987). Chi square is significant at $p < .05$ for certified versus not certified across start date for the overall columns. It is not significant for either the doctoral-granting or nondoctoral-granting institutions.

their appointment as full-time academics may bear on their competence. To measure this experience, the respondents were asked to identify the number of months they spent in various types of organizations (e.g., Big 8 firms, non–Big 8 firms, large corporations) and the nature of their work (e.g., auditing, tax). MANOVAs using type of institution and start date as the two independent variables were run. No significant pattern of activity was noted. However, the information presented in Table 20 is believed to be noteworthy.

The data in Table 20 reflect a decreasing trend over time in months of experience. This trend is probably understated because part-time faculty constituted a far larger proportion of the faculty in earlier periods and, as discussed, they are generally not included in the sample referent, especially for the early and middle groups. Thus the Committee believes that it is highly likely that the trend toward decreasing experience is significant.

The difference in the typical amount of experience between faculty at D-G schools and those at ND-G schools did register significance at the .10 level. Again, it is believed that the relatively heavy omission of many part-time faculty from the early and middle groups resulted in a bias that suppressed statistical significance. The fact that part-time faculty were more prevalent in earlier periods and more experience rich than existing faculties is a conclusion also reached by the American Accounting Association Committee on Changes in Accounting Education (1987).

TABLE 20
PRACTICE EXPERIENCE PRIOR TO FULL–TIME
ACADEMIC POSITION
BY START DATE AND TYPE OF INSTITUTION
(IN MONTHS)

	Type of Institution		
Start Date	Doctoral Granting	Nondoctoral Granting	Overall
Early	67	90	84
Middle	64	77	74
New	47	70	64
Overall	60	--------------- 79	74

Significant at p<.10. ----

Perhaps the importance of this trend is overstated because even the lowest typical amount of experience was 47 months, a considerable amount. In terms of total experience, just over one year on average was listed in the "other" category, which may well have been nonaccounting experience.

Relevant practice experience. From their inception, accounting accreditation standards (AACSB, 1980) have called for recent relevant experience in the area of one's teaching. In theory, the extent to which one is involved in the practice of an area, the better he or she should be at teaching the area. Thus we were primarily interested in whether the practice experience as measured above was related differently either for faculty at different types of institutions or for faculty with different start dates.

The information in Table 21 presents the structure for the study of this matter. The first three columns of data relate to the percentage of time on average reported for each of the areas we used to partition the teaching of accounting. As would be expected, faculty at D-G schools taught more heavily in the accounting research area than did their counterparts at ND–G institutions. Conversely, faculty at ND–G schools taught much more heavily in the managerial/cost accounting area. No obvious explanation exists for this disparity.

The overall column reflects that nearly half of all teaching is done in the financial accounting area and that only a small proportion (1 percent) is done in the governmental area. The large proportion devoted to financial accounting, however, may be inflated because much of the structure and general theoretical constructs of accounting is dealt with in these courses. No ready explanation for the small percentage of time devoted to governmental accounting is apparent.

The far right column in Table 21 reflects the overall average in terms of months of practice experience by accounting area. If the experience reported in this far right column were positively related to the area in which the respondents' taught, it would seem that their experience was indeed relevant. One way to relate this would be to run an intercorrelation matrix for the overall sample to determine the extent to which

TABLE 21

TEACHING AREA AND PRACTICE EXPERIENCE
BY AREA AND TYPE OF INSTITUTION
(IN PERCENT OF TIME AND MONTHS)

	Type of Institution			
Teaching and Practice Area	Doctoral Granting	Nondoctoral Granting	Overall	Practice Experience (in months)
Audit	13%*	10%*	11%*	16
Finance	48	43	44	11
Managerial/Cost	9 ———	25	21	8
MAS/Systems	7	5	5	5
Tax	11	9	10	9
Government	0	1	1	8
Accounting Research	8 ———	1	3	N/A

* Numbers in these columns represent the proportion of teaching time (expressed in percentage) devoted to each area in the first column.
Significant at p .05. ____

teaching activity within each area related to the amount of practice experience by area. This interrelation resulted in a six-by-six matrix of correlation coefficients (some redundant). Each coefficient measured the strength of association between the six areas of teaching and practice experience.

To determine whether these correlation coefficients showed a positive relationship between similar areas of teaching and practice, the number of significant coefficients of the six diagonal cells (e.g., audit with audit, financial accounting with financial accounting) were counted. The number of significant coefficients for the 15 nonredundant off-diagonal cells (e.g., audit with financial accounting, audit with managerial/cost) were then counted. To the extent that the frequency of significant coefficients was relatively greater for the diagonal than the off-diagonal coefficients, it was concluded that a strong relationship existed between practice experience and teaching areas.

An explication of this analysis is facilitated by referring to the bottom row of Table 22. An interpretation of the bottom row of this table is four significant ($p < .05$) correlation coefficients that related the amount of teaching and experience in auditing (A), managerial/cost accounting (M), systems/management advisory services (S), and tax (T). Continuing across the row, 44 percent of all teaching was done in these areas, the total amount of experience per respondent directly relevant to these four areas was 35 months, and the total amount of experience per respondent in this overall group was 74 months. The off-diagonal correlation coefficients revealed that only 2 of 15 were significant (not reported in the table). Because four of six represented a greater frequency than 2 of the 15, it was concluded that this evidenced a positive relationship between practice experience and teaching areas overall.

Although this overall measure provided evidence that a positive relationship existed between the respondents' experience and their area of teaching, it did not provide any insight as to differences between faculty by types of institution or by their career start date. To overcame this problem, the sample was separated into the six grouping divisions (early, middle, and new start dates at both D-G and ND–schools). In addition, two more groups composed of doctoral and nondoctoral respondents were formed. Eight intercorrelation matrices were then computed. The results appear in the first eight rows of Table 22. In reviewing column one, the reader should know that significant off-diagonal correlations were found to equal three in only one case. The rest of the analyses resulted in two or fewer off-diagonal coefficients. Because the frequencies of significant coefficients are much greater for the diagonals than the off-diagonals, it was again concluded that practical experience is positively related to teaching.

This conclusion is especially supported when one considers that no significant relationships existed in the financial accounting area between practice and experience (probably due to its breadth) and that the relative amount of teaching in financial accounting amounts to 44 percent of all instructional activities. Furthermore, accounting research constitutes 3 percent of all teaching, resulting in only 53 percent left to be explained. Together, these factors imply that the actual percentage of teaching that can be explained is about twice the amount reported in Table 22. For example, the 44 percent on the bottom row translates to about 88 percent.

The information in Table 22 supports the notion that accounting faculty tend to teach in their areas of expertise. In addition, it supports the proposition that newer

TABLE 22

INDICATORS OF WORK RELATED EXPERTISE TO TEACHING AREAS BY TYPE OF INSTITUTION AND START DATE

Type of Institution	Start Date	1	2	3	4
Doctoral Granting	Early	2 (A,S)	19	22	67
	Middle	3 (A,M,S)	32	38	64
	New	3 (A,M,T)	42	27	47
	All	4 (A,M,S,T)	41	31	60
Nondoctoral Granting	Early	2 (A,M)	34	18	90
	Middle	1 (S)	4	6	77
	New	3 (A,M,T)	34	45	70
	All	4 (A,M,S,T)	48	40	79
Both	Early	2 (A,M)	27	20	84
	Middle	2 (A,S)	21	26	74
	New	3 (A,M,T)	38	35	64
Overall		4 (A,M,S,T)	44	35	74

Column Legend:
1—The number of work-related areas showing a significantly positive relationship with the same teaching area as indicated by the Pearson product moment correlation coefficient. Significance is at less than 5 percent. *Maximum is 6*. The areas of significant positive relationship are in parentheses, where A is auditing, F is financial accounting (not shown in table, but in questionnaire), M is managerial cost, S is management advisory/systems, T is taxation and G is governmental (not shown in table, but in questionnaire).
2—The total percent of teaching done in that group by areas shown in column 1. For example, members of the early group at doctoral-granting schools do 19 percent of their teaching in the areas of auditing and management advisory/systems courses.
3—The number of months of experience in the areas shown in column 1.
4—The total number of months of experience.

faculty tend to teach more intensively in their practice experience areas than do the members of the other two start-date groups.

Summary—Competence. Over the past 20 to 25 years, accounting faculty have become far more competent in terms of formal education and research experience. The proportion of full-time faculty has increased approximately 50 percent. Another measure of competence, practice experience, has decreased somewhat, although the proportion of faculty with professional certification rose and then declined to its 1960 level. Presently, a substantial proportion of faculty possess relevant experience in the subject area they teach.

The proportion of all faculty with doctorates has increased from 31 percent in the 1967–68 period to about 57 percent in 1986–87 period. Of faculty in the new group, 87 percent possess doctorates. However, the sample contains about 40 percent more doctorates than would be expected in a random sample (77 percent versus 54 percent). Only 16 percent of the members of the early start-date group (1961–66) had experience as a research assistant during their graduate work as compared to 36 percent in the new group (1980–81).

The proportion of faculty holding professional certification changed from 60 percent in the 1967–68 period to 72 percent in the 1977–78 period and to 60 percent in the 1986–87 period. The start-date groups reflect this same pattern (early—72 months; middle—79; new—58). Practice experience evidenced a decrease among the start-date groups (early—84 months; middle—74; new—64), with members of the new group at D-G schools showing the least at 47 months.

Allocation of Time

The Committee believes that the total number of hours allocated to one's professional area and the allocation of those hours among various professorial activities are likely to influence the competence of the individual. Furthermore, this information may provide some indication of changes in emphasis over time. In order to investigate these issues, the respondents were asked to estimate the number of hours they devoted to six different activities in a nine-month academic year and a three-month summer period during the most recent three-year period. In addition, the middle and early groups were asked to give their best assessments of how they allocated their time during the first three years of their career as a full-time academicians for similar time frames.

As discussed earlier, recall is a limiting factor on all of this information, especially because it relates to the first three-year period of the early and middle groups' careers. Furthermore, overall accuracy is subject to question. In spite of these limitations, the Committee believes that concern with *differences* mitigates these problems because in many instances differences over time relate to within-subject changes, thereby reducing the variance inherent between individuals. However, the probable exclusion of part-time faculty or faculty in the early and middle groups who are no longer employed as faculty remains a limitation.

Current allocations of time. Information on the typical work week during the nine-month academic year by type of institution is presented in Table 23.[12] No overall difference exists in the total number of hours worked between D-G and ND–G faculties, nor does any difference exist among the various groups on the basis of start date. Thus the average work week of 51.1 hours seems representative of accounting faculty overall.

The differences in the activities between different types of institutions are reflected primarily in research and secondarily in teaching and outside remunerative activities. Faculty at D-G schools spend more time on research and less time on teaching and outside remunerative activities than their colleagues at ND–G schools.

The only significant interaction term involving type of institution and start date relates to research. The data in Table 24 indicate that members of the newer group tend

TABLE 23

ALLOCATION OF TIME DURING THE NINE-MONTH ACADEMIC YEAR BY ACTIVITY AND TYPE OF INSTITUTION

(IN HOURS PER WEEK)

	Type of Institution		
Activity	Doctoral Granting		Nondoctoral Granting
Teaching	20.9	-----	23.5
Research	12.9	——	7.5
Service/Administration	7.5		8.0
Remuneration	3.9	-----	6.6
Continuing Education	2.8		3.2
Other	2.8		2.4
Totals	50.8		51.2

Significant at p <.05. ——
Significant at p <.10. -----

TABLE 24

TIME ALLOCATED TO RESEARCH DURING THE NINE-MONTH ACADEMIC YEAR BY START DATE AND TYPE OF INSTITUTION (IN HOURS PER WEEK)

	Type of Institution		
Start Date	Doctoral Granting	Nondoctoral Granting	Overall
Early	8.7	4.3	5.4
Middle	11.9	7.8	8.8
New	18.1	10.0	12.0
Overall	12.9	7.5	8.8

Significant at p <.05. ——
Significant at p <.10. - - - -

to work more on research than members of the early group. Indeed, a slight trend over time exists in this direction, which, due to limitations in the sample referent (already discussed), is probably understated in the analysis.

The information in Table 25 reflects the allocation of time during the three-month summer period. As would be expected, those at D-G schools spend more time on research and less on outside remunerative activities than their counterparts at ND–G schools. Information in Table 26 indicates that research also varies across faculty start dates in the expected direction, with newer faculty more heavily engaged in research.

To estimate the effect of differences for the whole year, the reported times for the nine-month academic year and the three-month summer period were combined on a pro rata basis. Table 27 data indicate that both research and remunerative activity reflect differences in the same direction as the nine-month data. Table 28, which represents the only significant interaction, reflects the same pattern as the summer data.

Early career allocations of time. The above data may reflect the effects of change either as (1) a function of the length of time a faculty member has been full-time or (2) the differences that existed from the outset of the faculty member's career. To provide

TABLE 25

ALLOCATION OF TIME DURING THE THREE-MONTH SUMMER PERIOD BY ACTIVITY AND TYPE OF INSTITUTION (IN HOURS PER WEEK)

	Type of Institution		
Activity	Doctoral Granting	Nondoctoral Granting	Overall
Teaching	9.1	9.8	9.7
Research	18.5	9.0	11.4
Service/Administration	4.4	5.5	5.2
Remuneration	5.0	9.6	8.4
Continuing Education	2.7	3.1	3.0
Other	4.3	3.3	3.5
Totals	43.9	40.3	41.2

Significant at <p .05. ——

TABLE 26

TIME ALLOCATED TO RESEARCH DURING THE THREE-MONTH SUMMER PERIOD
BY START DATE AND TYPE OF INSTITUTION
(IN HOURS PER WEEK)

	Type of Institution		
Start Date	Doctoral Granting	Nondoctoral Granting	Overall
Early	12.0	5.1	6.8
Middle	18.1	8.5	10.9
New	24.9	13.5	16.4
Overall	18.5	9.0	11.4

Significant at <p .05.——

some insight into these alternative explanations, members of the early and middle groups were asked to recall how they allocated their time during the first three years of their careers as full-time faculty. These responses together with the new group's responses then were analyzed.

Data in Table 29 indicates that for the nine-month academic year, type of institution was a significant factor in the allocation of time for teaching, research, and outside remunerative activities. Moreover, these significant findings held in the same directions as above. Teaching and service activities also varied significantly among start dates. The newer the faculty member's start date, the less time was spent in teaching. The newer members also indicated that they spent more time on service activities than their colleagues in either of the other groups. Possibly this latter finding may reflect an increase in the aggregate amount of service performed now as compared to 10 and 20 years ago.

As reported in Table 30, the time expended in the summer of the early part of the respondents' careers suggests that faculty at D-G institutions taught less and researched more. One interpretation of this significant difference in research activity may be that faculty

TABLE 27

ALLOCATION OF TIME DURING THE WHOLE YEAR
BY ACTIVITY AND TYPE OF INSTITUTION
(IN HOURS PER WEEK)

	Type of Institution		
Activity	Doctoral Granting	Nondoctoral Granting	Overall
Teaching	17.9	20.1	19.6
Research	14.2	7.9	9.5
Service/Administration	6.8	7.4	7.2
Remuneration	4.2	7.4	6.6
Continuing Education	2.8	3.2	3.1
Other	3.2	2.7	2.8
Totals	49.1	48.6	48.7

Significant at <p .05. ——

TABLE 28

TIME ALLOCATED TO RESEARCH DURING THE WHOLE YEAR BY START DATE AND TYPE OF INSTITUTION (IN HOURS PER WEEK)

	Type of Institution		
Start Date	Doctoral Granting	Nondoctoral Granting	Overall
Early	9.5	4.5	5.8
Middle	13.4	8.0	9.4
New	19.8	10.9	13.2
Overall	14.2	7.9	9.5

Significant at $p < .05$.——
Interaction is significant at $p < .05$.

at D-G institutions face substantially greater research expectations than faculty at ND–G institutions. It also may be that the greater availability of research grants at D-G schools has allowed faculty at these institutions to devote more time to research than their counterparts at nondoctoral schools. Additionally, because the sample is drawn from faculty currently at doctoral institutions, these "survivors" may be the ones who applied themselves more successfully to research/publication than those no longer employed at D-G institutions.

TABLE 29

ALLOCATION OF TIME DURING THE NINE-MONTH ACADEMIC PERIOD BY ACTIVITY, START DATE, AND TYPE OF INSTITUTION FOR FIRST THREE YEARS IN CAREER (IN HOURS PER WEEK)

		Type of Institution		
Activity	Start Date	Doctoral Granting	Nondoctoral Granting	Overall
Teaching	Early	26.3	30.6	29.5
	Middle	24.4	27.0	26.3
	New	18.9	24.2	22.9
	Means	23.3	27.2	26.2
Research	Early	14.8	6.2	8.4
	Middle	20.0	9.2	11.9
	New	18.1	10.0	12.0
	Means	18.0	7.8	10.4
Service/Administration	Early	3.3	4.2	4.0
	Middle	3.2	4.5	4.2
	New	5.2	6.8	6.4
	Means	3.8	5.0	4.7
Remuneration	Early	2.4	4.7	4.1
	Middle	1.1	4.1	3.3
	New	3.1	7.2	6.2
	Means	2.1	5.1	4.3

Significant at $p < .05$.——
Significant at $p < .10$.----

TABLE 30

ALLOCATION OF TIME DURING THE THREE-MONTH SUMMER PERIOD BY ACTIVITY, START DATE, AND TYPE OF INSTITUTION FOR FIRST THREE YEARS IN CAREER (IN HOURS PER WEEK)

		Type of Institution		
Activity	Start Date	Doctoral Granting	Nondoctoral Granting	Overall
Teaching	Early	15.7	13.1	13.8
	Middle	9.3	17.2	15.2
	New	5.7	11.5	10.0
	Means	10.0	14.5	13.4
Research	Early	17.4	8.4	10.7
	Middle	26.0	7.9	12.5
	New	24.9	13.5	16.4
	Means	23.2	9.6	13.0
Service/Administration	Early	2.1	1.2	1.4
	Middle	1.5	2.3	2.1
	New	2.8	4.1	3.8
	Means	2.1	2.5	2.4
Totals	Early	44.4	33.5	36.3
	Middle	45.4	35.7	38.2
	New	41.2	42.9	42.5
	Means	43.8	37.1	38.8

Significant at $p < .05$. ——

Table 30 data also reveal that newer faculty engage in teaching less than their counterparts of 10 years ago and service more than their colleagues of the two earlier periods. The teaching trend is especially noticeable at the D-G institutions where less than six hours a week is devoted to such activity. As noted above, the greater availability of research grants and the higher expectations of productivity in the research/publication area may contribute to this trend. However, probably because of the absence of many part-time faculty from the earlier groups, the research trend is not statistically significant. In addition, the research trend at nondoctoral schools seems to be lagging that at doctoral schools, with the faculty at D-G schools reportedly working significantly more hours per week in the summer than their counterparts at ND–G schools.

Table 31 reflects estimates of the 12-month behavior pattern and produces no surprises as to significant differences in activities. Again, the early careers of those at D-G schools focus more heavily on research and less on outside remunerative activities than those at ND–G schools. The big change in time allotted to research appears to have begun sometime between the early careers of the early group (1961-66) and that of the middle (1971-74). The time of this change is consistent with the selection of the time periods for these two groups, which reflected a change in the requirement for terminal status (CPA with a master's degree) by the AACSB and increasing emphasis on empirical research methodologies.

Change between middle and early start dates. How does the allocation of time change over the course of a faculty member's career? The prior two analyses presented static comparisons of the time allocations of faculty at different types of institutions for the current time period and at similar stages of their careers. Of additional interest is the

TABLE 31
TIME ALLOCATED DURING THE WHOLE YEAR
BY START DATE AND TYPE OF INSTITUTION
FOR FIRST THREE YEARS IN CAREER*
(IN HOURS PER WEEK)

		Type of Institution		
Activity	Start Date	Doctoral Granting	Nondoctoral Granting	Overall
Research	Early	15.5	6.8	9.0
	Middle	21.5	8.9	12.0
	New	19.8	10.9	13.1
	Means	19.3	8.2	11.0
Remuneration				
	Early	2.7	5.2	4.6
	Middle	1.8	4.6	3.9
	New	3.4	7.5	6.5
	Means	2.6	5.9	4.8

* Significant relationships only. No significant differences in teaching, service/administration continuing education or other categories.
Significant at $p < .05$. ——

issue of change within an individual's career over time. Tables 32 through 34 present some indication of how the respondents in the study have changed their time allocations during their careers. These tables do not include the new group because its members have not been involved in academia on a full-time basis long enough to track change.

The data in Table 32 relate to activity measures over the nine-month academic year. These measures indicate a significant decrease in the amount of time devoted to research between the early career years and today, as well as a significant increase in time allotted to service. In addition, the time spent in teaching reflects a decline that is significant at the .10 level. The decrease in research differs significantly between those at D-G schools and their counterparts at ND–G schools. No other patterns related to changes over time are evident in this table, nor are there any changes peculiar to those in the early or middle start groups. As with prior analyses, those at doctoral institutions spend more time on research and less time on remunerative activities.

The information in Table 33 indicates similar patterns of time allocations for the summer months. Time devoted to service, outside remunerative activities, and continuing education activities have increased significantly over time, but the amount of time spent on teaching has decreased considerably. However, this decrease is not statistically significant due to the high variance in the responses. But the relative decrease in time devoted to teaching at ND–G schools is significantly greater than the small decrease at D-G schools. Conversely, the relative decrease in time spent in research is significantly larger at D-G schools than at ND–G schools. Faculty at ND–G schools indicate a significantly greater increase in time devoted to continuing education. But, as before, the amount of time devoted to research overall is still greater at D-G schools, and the time spent on outside remunerative activities is less.

The final table in this area, Table 34, reports the pattern of activity for the 12-month period. The table data indicate a significant decrease in the time devoted to teaching and research and a significant increase in the time allocated to service. The

TABLE 32

ALLOCATION OF TIME DURING THE THREE-MONTH SUMMER PERIOD BY ACTIVITY, PHASE OF CAREER AND TYPE OF INSTITUTION (IN HOURS PER WEEK)

	Type of Institution								
	Doctoral Granting			Nondoctoral Granting			Overall		
Activity	Early Career	Current	Difference	Early Career	Current	Difference	Early Career	Current	Difference
Teaching	25.2	21.7	–3.5	28.3	23.2	–5.1	27.5	22.9	–4.6
Research	17.9	10.6	–7.3	8.1	6.5	–1.6	10.6	8.5	–3.1
Service/Admin.	3.2	8.5	5.3	4.4	8.4	4.0	4.1	8.5	4.4
Remuneration	1.6	4.1	2.5	4.3	6.4	2.1	3.6	5.8	2.2
Continuing Education	2.9	3.0	0.1	2.2	3.4	1.2	2.3	2.8	0.5
Other	1.0	3.6	2.6	0.8	2.8	2.0	3.0	1.9	–1.1

Note: Not reflected in the above table is the significant difference between types of institutions for research and remunerative activities across both career phases (early in career and current).
Significant at $p < .05$. ______
Significant at $p < .10$. - - - -

TABLE 33

ALLOCATION OF TIME DURING THE THREE-MONTH SUMMER PERIOD BY ACTIVITY, PHASE OF CAREER, AND TYPE OF INSTITUTION (IN HOURS PER WEEK)

	Type of Institution								
	Doctoral Granting			Nondoctoral Granting			Overall		
Activity	Early Career	Current	Difference	Early Career	Current	Difference	Early Career	Current	Difference
Teaching	11.9	10.6	–1.3	15.7	9.2	–6.5	14.7	9.6	–5.1
Research	22.5	15.0	–7.5	8.1	7.2	–0.9	11.7	9.4	–2.6
Service/Admin.	1.7	5.2	3.5	1.8	6.0	4.2	1.8 ——	5.8	4.0
Remuneration	3.8	5.2	1.4	7.0	11.2	4.2	6.4 ——	11.0	4.6
Continuing Education	4.0	4.4	4.2	3.4	6.3	2.9	3.5 ——	5.8	2.3

Note: Not reflected in the above table is the significant difference between types of institutions for research and remunerative activities across both career phases (early in career and current).

Significant at $p < .05$.——

faculties at D-G and ND–G schools differ significantly on the extent of change in research and continuing education, with research decreasing more heavily for those at D-G schools and continuing education increasing more extensively for those at ND–G schools. Moreover, the overall differences between research and remunerative activities continue to reflect significance.

Summary—Allocation of Time. The survey findings indicate that the newer the faculty member, the more time spent on research. Faculty at D-G institutions spend more time on research and less time on teaching and outside remunerative activities than faculty at ND–G schools. During the summer months, these differences are more pronounced due in part to faculty at doctoral schools reporting a longer work week.

During the early parts of their careers, faculty in the middle and new groups spent more time on research than faculty in the early group. The new faculty devoted less time to teaching than those in the other groups. Interestingly, the new faculty also spent more time on service.

As faculty matured in their careers, they spent more time on service and outside remunerative activities and less time on research and teaching. Faculty at D-G schools exhibited a greater decrease in time allocated to research than faculty at nondoctoral schools, even though they continued to allocate more time in total to research than faculty at ND–G schools. Faculty at ND–G schools increased the time allotted to continuing professional education more than faculty at D-G schools.

Job Satisfaction

As with the allocation of time, the Committee believes that job satisfaction is positively related to the quality of performance in the various professorial activities. As part of the job satisfaction assessment, the respondents were asked to assign 100 points to the same six activities used for the allocation of time. Again, the respondents were asked to make this allocation for the past three-year period, with those in the middle and early groups also asked to make the assessments for their first three years as full-time faculty members. Because the total amount of any one respondent's job satisfaction is set at 100, the analyses pertain to the *relative* job satisfaction among various activities.

Significant results for the most recent three-year period are presented in Table 35. Faculty at D-G schools derive less satisfaction from teaching and more satisfaction from research than their counterparts at ND–G schools. Start date also plays an important role in differentiating the respondents in terms of the enjoyment they reportedly derive from teaching and research. Members of the early group enjoy teaching significantly more than members of the other two groups. Conversely, members of the early group derive significantly less satisfaction from research than the others in the sample. Members of the middle and new groups do not differ noticeably on either of these dimensions. One possible explanation for this finding may be that the sample referent allowed for selection of only "survivors" in the early and middle groups.

In an attempt to reduce the problem of maturation that may have occurred over the professional life of the respondents, the data in Table 36 compare job satisfaction for all respondents during the first three-year period of their careers. As in the above analysis, faculty at D-G institutions indicate less satisfaction from teaching and more from research than those at ND–G institutions. The gap in these areas, however, is far wider than that measured in Table 35 and therefore may indicate changes over time. As

TABLE 34
ALLOCATION OF TIME DURING THE WHOLE YEAR BY ACTIVITY, PHASE OF CAREER, AND TYPE OF INSTITUTION (IN HOURS PER WEEK)

	Type of Institution								
	Doctoral Granting			Nondoctoral Granting			Overall		
Activity	Early Career	Current	Difference	Early Career	Current	Difference	Early Career	Current	Difference
Teaching	21.9	18.9	–3.0	25.2	19.8	–5.4	24.3	19.6	4.7
Research	19.1	11.8	-7.3	8.1	6.7	–1.4	10.9	8.0	2.9
Service/Admin.	2.8	7.7	4.9	3.7	7.9	4.2	3.5	7.8	4.3
Remuneration	2.2	4.5	2.3	4.8	7.3	2.5	4.1	6.6	2.5
Continuing Education	2.9	2.9	0.0	2.1	3.2	1.1	2.3	3.1	0.8

Note: Not reflected in the above table is the significant difference between types of institutions for research and remunerative activities across both career phases (early in career and current).
Significant at $p < .05$.——

TABLE 35

JOB SATISFACTION BY ACTIVITY, TYPE OF INSTITUTION, AND START DATE FOR THREE MOST RECENT YEARS*

(ON A 100-POINT SCALE)

		Type of Institution		
Activity	Start Date	Doctoral Granting	Nondoctoral Granting	Overall
Teaching	Early	47.1	65.4	60.8
	Middle	41.2	52.5	49.6
	New	46.0	48.1	47.6
	Means	44.3	54.8	52.1
Research	Early	19.6	6.1	9.5
	Middle	29.0	14.8	18.4
	New	38.6	21.7	26.0
	Means	29.3	14.3	18.1

* Significant relationship only. No significant differences in service/administration, remunerative activities, continuing education or other categories.
Significant at $p < .05$. ——
Significant at $p < .10$. ----

to service and outside remunerative activities, faculty at ND–G schools indicate more enjoyment than their colleagues at D-G schools.

Start date also influences the enjoyment derived during these early career years in the areas of teaching, research, and outside remunerative activities. In general, the more recent the start date, the more likely it is that the typical faculty member enjoys research and outside remunerative activities more and teaching less. The significant differences, however, occur only between members of the new group and members of the other two groups. But again, because of the large number of part-time faculty not included in the early and middle groups of the sample, these differences may be understated.

Table 37 reveals differences in job satisfaction arising over time, as reported by members of the early and middle groups. Overall, the measures of teaching and research satisfaction continue to differentiate the faculties of D-G and ND–G schools. The only significant change over time in job satisfaction is, however, a decrease in the amount of enjoyment in teaching. A significant change in the amount of enjoyment derived from research also is shown for the faculties at D-G and ND–G schools, with doctoral faculty indicating substantially less enjoyment. The doctoral faculties, nevertheless, continue to report greater satisfaction from research. The only difference in the changes between the members of the early and middle groups arises in the area of continuing education, where members of the latter group reported an increase in their satisfaction, but the other members did not.

Specialization

In reviewing competence measures, the data indicated that the respondents spent less time on teaching and research and more time on service activities as their careers progressed. They also revealed a sharp difference in the allocation of time among

TABLE 36

JOB SATISFACTION BY ACTIVITY, TYPE OF INSTITUTION, AND START DATE FOR THREE YEARS EARLY IN CAREER*
(ON A 100-POINT SCALE)

		Type of Institution		
Activity	Start Date	Doctoral Granting	Nondoctoral Granting	Overall
Teaching	Early	50.7	74.6	68.6
	Middle	52.0	68.3	64.2
	New	46.0	48.1	47.6
	Means	49.8	64.5	60.8
Research	Early	29.1	9.6	14.5
	Middle	40.0	10.0	17.6
	New	38.6	21.7	26.0
	Means	36.5	13.1	9.0
Service/ Administration				
	Early	6.5	4.4	4.9
	Middle	1.8	6.8	5.5
	New	3.4	8.4	7.1
	Means	3.6	6.6	5.8
Remuneration	Early	4.6	5.0	4.9
	Middle	1.8	8.1	6.5
	New	6.0	13.5	11.6
	Means	3.9	11.8	7.5

* Significant relationship only. No significant differences in continuing education or other categories.
Significant at $p <.05$. ——
Significant at $p <.10$. - - - -

different start-date groups—especially on research. The reduction in time allocated to teaching seems incongruous when the increasing measures of codified knowledge documented in the first part of the study is considered. For example, the past decades have seen marked increases in financial accounting standards, auditing standards, and tax laws/rulings. Indeed, the American Accounting Association Committee on Changes in Accounting Education (1987) found that current intermediate textbooks had nearly 50 percent more words than similar books of 15 years before. One explanation for this apparent incongruity lies in increased specialization. To investigate this proposition, the Committee reports on measures and changes in faculty size, practice work experience, teaching in concentrated subject areas and various other related dimensions.

Faculty size. The size of accounting faculties has increased significantly over the 13 years that *The Accounting Faculty Directory* (Hasselback, 1974 to 1987) has been published. Although there may have been a tendency not to include part-time faculty in the directory—and part-time faculty did constitute a larger proportion during the early part of the directory's existence—the trend is still quite clear. Table 38 indicates that, on average, the size of faculties at D-G schools increased by six members from the 1974-75 period to the 1986-87 period and that nondoctoral faculties increased by four. One possible consequence of these increases of nearly 50 percent may be that faculty

TABLE 37
JOB SATISFACTION BY ACTIVITY, TYPE OF INSTITUTION, START DATE, AND PHASE OF CAREER*
(ON A 100-POINT SCALE)

		Type of Institution								
		Doctoral Granting			Nondoctoral Granting			Overall		
Activity	Start Date	Early Career	Current	Difference	Early Career	Current	Difference	Early Career	Current	Difference
Teaching	N/A*	51.5	43.5	−8.0	70.8	57.7	−13.1	66.0----	54.2	−11.8
Research	N/A*	35.6	25.2	−10.4	9.8	11.2	1.4	16.2	14.6	−1.6
Service/Administration	N/A*	3.7	9.4	5.7	5.8	14.2	5.4	5.3	10.8	5.5
Continuing Education										
	Early	5.4	5.8	0.4	4.5	4.1	−0.4	4.7	4.7	0.0
	Middle	3.0	3.5	0.5	2.7	7.6	4.9	2.5	6.7	3.8
	New	3.9	4.4	0.5	3.4	6.2	2.8	3.6	5.8	2.2

* Significant and other selected relationships only. No significant differences occurred in remunerative and other activities or between the early and mid start date groups other than in continuing education.
Significant at $p < .05$ ——
Significant at $p < .10$ ----

TABLE 38

FACULTY SIZE BY TYPE OF INSTITUTION
(1974–75 AND 1986–87)

Type of Institution	Date 1974-75	1986-87
Doctoral Granting	11.6 ——	17.6
Nondoctoral Granting	7.2 ——	11.3

Significant at p < .05. ———
Source:Hasselback, *Accounting Faculty Directory* (1974 and 1986).
Note: The *Accounting Faculty Directory* was first published in 1974. The means in the cells were computed from a random selection of 60 institutions—30 each from the different type of institution. In 1974-75, there were 64 schools listed as granting doctorates with concentrations in accounting; in 1986-87, there were 81 schools. The comparable numbers for nondoctoral granting schools were 77 and 473, respectively.

members were provided with the opportunity to concentrate their teaching within a particular subject area. Indeed, this growth in faculty size, coupled with the sharp increase in codified knowledge and perceived research and service needs, would seem to encourage such specialization.

Concentration in practice work experience. Another factor that would likely encourage specialization within teaching areas would be practice work experience that focused more strictly on particular accounting areas. To determine the extent, if any, of this tendency among the surveyed faculty members, the Committee constructed a Herfindahl measure of concentration for each of the respondents (cf., Stigler, 1968; Eichenseher and Danos, 1981). This measure essentially represents the variance present in a fixed pool of activity, and although it is typically used to measure concentrations within industries, it is applicable as a measure of any dispersion.

Referring to Table 39, the results of an ANOVA with type of institution and start date as the independent variables indicate that respondents in the new group reported a significantly greater propensity to specialize in their practice experience than did members of either the middle or early groups. Moreover, the results of a MANOVA, which analyzed the different practice areas by type of institution and start date, indicate that respondents in the new group reported a marked increase in the amount of experience in the tax area as compared to those in the other groups. This finding, reported in Table 40, is consistent with the growing importance of tax services within public accounting firms. Table 40 also shows that the members of the middle group

TABLE 39

CONCENTRATION OF PRACTICE EXPERIENCE
BY START DATE AND TYPE OF INSTITUTION

Start Date	Type of Institution: Doctoral Granting	Nondoctoral Granting	Overall
Early	1.8	1.8	1.8 - - ┐
Middle	1.9	1.8	┌— 1.8 ¦
New	1.4	1.5	└— 1.5 - - ┘

Concentration data are based on respondents' Herfindahl measures (Stigler, 1968). Lower measures indicate greater concentration.
Significant at p <.05.____
Significant at p <.10._ _ _ _

TABLE 40
PRACTICE EXPERIENCE BY ACTIVITY AND START DATE
(IN MONTHS)

Activity	Start Date Early	Middle	New
Auditing	13.8	15.1	19.5
Financial	8.9	11.9	7.4
Managerial/Cost	4.9	12.2	4.1
MAS/Systems	3.6	7.9	2.5
Taxation	6.5	6.0	16.8
Government	12.1	8.6	1.8

Significant at p <.05.——
Significant at p <.10.- - - -

tend to have more experience in the managerial/cost area than those in the other two groups. No other main effects registered significance, but the experience level in governmental accounting is apparently decreasing while that in auditing is increasing.

More detailed analysis of the reported auditing experience proved to uncover a significant interaction between start date and the type of institution. Table 41 data indicate a decreasing level of auditing experience for the respondents at D-G granting schools and an increasing level for those at nondoctoral schools. Although there is no ready explanation for this trend, the Committee speculates that having degrees in majors other than accounting plays a role in this pattern of experience.

Evidence of the trend toward nonaccounting bachelor's degrees is presented in Figure 10. Note that 30 percent of the respondents in the early group hold bachelor's degrees in areas other than accounting, but this figure rises to 36 percent for the middle group. The new group registers a 50-50 split between those with bachelor's degrees in accounting and those in other areas. For the respondents at D-G schools, the resulting numbers are even more pronounced over time because the proportion without bachelor's degrees in accounting moves from 25 to 32 to 55 percent. These trends parallel the overall reductions in practice experience reported in an earlier section.

Concentration in teaching area. Table 42 reports the Herfindahl measures on teaching concentration grouped by type of institution and start date. ANOVA indicated a significant interaction for this pattern of responses from the groups, but no significant main effect between either the type of institution or the start date. The sharpest indication of specialization appears in the new group at D-G schools.

TABLE 41
PRACTICE EXPERIENCE IN AUDITING
BY TYPE OF INSTITUTION AND START DATE
(IN MONTHS)

Type of Institution	Start Date Early	Middle	New
Doctoral Granting	19.2	18.2	9.0
Nondoctoral Granting	12.0	14.0	23.0

The interaction is significant at p <.05.

FIGURE 10

PROPORTION OF RESPONDENTS WITH BACHELOR DEGREES NOT IN ACCOUNTING OVERALL AND BY TYPE OF INSTITUTION AND BY START DATE

(IN PERCENTAGES)

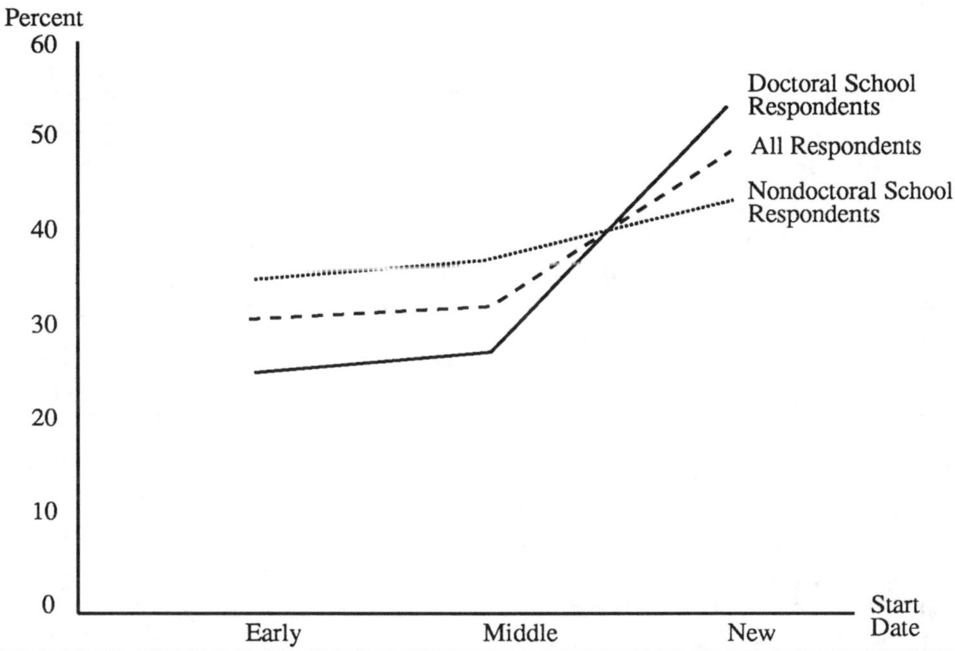

However, the pattern is different for ND-G schools, with the middle group registering the largest concentration. Only a weak pattern of increased specialization over time is evident in these data.

Table 43 presents similar concentration measures for the first three years of the respondents' careers as full-time faculty. Here the pattern of greater specialization, which exists over time and between D-G and ND-G schools, fits many of the assumed

TABLE 42

CONCENTRATION OF TEACHING AREAS

BY START DATE AND TYPE OF INSTITUTION

Start Date	Type of Institution	
	Doctoral Granting	Nondoctoral Granting
Early	1.6	1.8
Middle	1.6	1.4
New	1.3	1.7

Concentration data are based on respondents' Herfindahl measure (Stigler,1968). Lower measures indicate greater concentration.

The interaction is significant at p .<05.

TABLE 43
CONCENTRATION OF TEACHING AREAS BY START DATE AND TYPE OF INSTITUTION

	Type of Institution		
Start Date	Doctoral Granting	Nondoctoral Granting	Overall
Early	1.8	2.1	2.0
Middle	1.7	2.1	2.0
New	1.3	1.7	1.6
Overall	1.6	2.0	

Concentration data are based on respondents' Herfindahl measures (Stigler, 1968). Lower measures indicate greater concentration.
Significant at p <.05. ——
Significant at p <.10. ----

relationships. For example, doctoral faculties tend to be larger and to stress research more heavily than nondoctoral faculties. Thus, as speculated, these faculties register significantly more concentration. Similarly, more emphasis is on research for new faculties now than in the past. Again, the data show significantly greater specialization in teaching among newer faculty as compared to those who started 10 and 20 years earlier.

The data in Table 44 reinforce the shift toward greater specialization in teaching over the past 25-year period. As shown in this table, the concentration measures for members of the early and middle groups decreased significantly from 2.0 to 1.6. In addition, two other relationships that registered significance at the 10 percent level deserve mention. Referring to the overall column, the interaction between start date and time of career indicates that the respondents in the middle group, which still focus more heavily on research than those in the early group, have become more specialized than those in the early group. One possible consequence of increased teaching specialization, therefore, is a greater availability of time to pursue research and related activities. The other interesting pattern among the data is that the middle group at nondoctoral granting schools has become more specialized over time as compared to those in the other groups. Nevertheless, all groups report a greater tendency toward teaching specialization.

TABLE 44
CHANGES IN CONCENTRATION OF TEACHING AREAS BETWEEN CURRENT ASSIGNMENTS AND ASSIGNMENTS BY START DATE AND TYPE OF INSTITUTION FOR FIRST THREE YEARS IN CAREER

	Type of Institution					
	Doctoral Granting		Nondoctoral Granting		Overall	
Start Date	Early	Current	Early	Current	Early	Current
Early	1.8	1.6	2.1	1.8	2.0	1.8
Middle	1.7	1.6	2.1	1.4	2.0	1.4
Overall	1.8	1.6	2.1	1.6	2.0	1.6

Concentration data are based on respondents' Herfindahl measures (Stigler, 1968). Lower measures indicate greater concentration.
Significant at p <.05. ——

TABLE 45

PROPORTION OF TEACHING AREA BY START DATE

(IN PERCENTAGE)

Teaching Area	Start Date Early	 Middle	 New
Managerial/Cost	22	24	15
Taxation	12	5	12

No relationships are statistically significant.

Subject areas taught. Because of the shift over time toward greater teaching specialization, the Committee decided to examine whether a pattern existed for the subject areas taught by faculty at different types of institutions with different start dates. Recall that an early MANOVA, which analyzed current teaching areas by start date as well as by type of institution (Table 21), uncovered no significant differences among the faculties beginning their careers at different times. However, the information presented in Table 45 indicates a slight decrease in the amount of teaching in the managerial/cost area and a slight increase in the amount of teaching in the taxation area by members of the new group. But because these trends are not significant, there is little to explain a higher degree of specialization in the data.

The Committee also investigated the teaching patterns that existed during the first three years of the respondents' careers as full-time faculty. Table 46 indicates that in the managerial/cost area, the emphasis during this early career phase was greater for the respondents in the middle group than for those in the other two groups. Conversely, for the respondents in the new group the emphasis on taxation was greater than for those in the other groups. One explanation for this trend may be that many of the tax courses taught in earlier times were staffed by part-time persons. In addition, a greater number of tax classes may be taught currently than previously.

To explore changes over time in teaching emphasis by members of the early and middle groups, the Committee conducted a MANOVA using type of institution, start time, and phase of career (early and current) as the independent variables. According to the data in Table 47, no significantly different patterns were detected. However, the proportion of teaching in the taxation area doubled from 4 percent during the first three

TABLE 46

PROPORTION OF TEACHING AREA

BY START DATE FOR FIRST THREE YEARS IN CAREER

(IN PERCENTAGE OF TIME)*

Teaching Area	Start Date Early	 Middle	 New
Managerial/Cost	18 ----	27 ----	15
Taxation	5	3 ——	12

Significant at p <.05. ——

Significant at p <.10. - - - -

*Significant relationships only.

TABLE 47

PROPORTION OF TEACHING TIME IN SUBJECT AREA
BY PHASE OF CAREER
(IN PERCENTAGES)

	Phase of Career		
Subject Area	Early Career	Current Career	All Current Teaching*
Auditing	10	12	11
Financial	45	42	44
Managerial/Cost	24	24	21
MAS/Systems	5	4	5
Taxation	4	8	10
Government	1	1	1
Accounting Research	4	4	3

No relationships are statistically significant.

* These figures include teaching done by members of the new group as well as members of the other two groups.

years of the respondents' careers to 8 percent currently. The right column, which reflects the proportion of teaching currently for all of the early, middle, and new respondent groups, reflects the patterns discussed above.

Teaching loads—Number of sections per semester/quarter. In addition to concentrating one's teaching in specific subject areas, factors such as the number of sections taught per semester/quarter, the number of different preparations undertaken per time period, and the level of the courses taught may affect the degree of teaching specialization. In this section, the investigation focuses on the number of sections taught during a semester/quarter currently as well as over time. Other measures that may allow for greater concentration or reduction of time allocated to teaching are examined shortly.

Table 48 contains information related to the number of sections taught currently per semester/quarter. The only significant relationship occurred between doctoral- and nondoctoral-granting schools, with the data reflecting a heavier emphasis on teaching at the latter. The table also indicates that the respondents in the three groups reported no difference in the number of sections taught currently per semester/quarter. However, between the two types of institutions, nearly a full section difference exists in the teaching loads.

Differences in the number of sections taught during the first three years in the respondents' careers are reported in Table 49. As shown in this table, those in the early

TABLE 48

NUMBER OF SECTIONS TAUGHT PER SEMESTER/QUARTER
BY START DATE AND TYPE OF INSTITUTION

	Type of Institution		
Start Date	Doctoral Granting	Nondoctoral Granting	Overall
Early	1.9	2.8	2.6
Middle	1.5	2.7	2.4
New	2.1	2.7	2.5
Means	1.8 ————	2.7	2.5

Significant at p< .05. ——

TABLE 49

NUMBER OF SECTIONS TAUGHT PER SEMESTER/QUARTER
BY START DATE AND TYPE OF INSTITUTION
FOR FIRST THREE YEARS IN CAREER

	Type of Institution		
Start Date	Doctoral Granting	Nondoctoral Granting	Overall
Early	2.5	3.4	3.2
Middle	1.8	2.7	3.0
New	2.1	2.7	2.5
Means	2.1	3.2	2.9

Significant at $p < .05$. ——
The interaction between type of institution and start date is also significant at $p < .05$.

group taught significantly more sections than those in the new group. A trend over time also appears toward teaching fewer sections. In addition, the interaction between type of institution and start date is significant, with the doctoral faculty teaching fewer sections than the nondoctoral faculty.

Table 50 reports the results of a MANOVA used to examine the relationships between the number of sections taught per semester/quarter, the phase of a faculty member's career, type of institution, and start date for the early and middle groups. On average, the respondents in the study began their careers teaching just over three sections per semester/quarter and now teach two and one-half. The greater emphasis on classroom contact at the nondoctoral-granting schools remains in evidence. This difference is emphasized by averaging current teaching loads with beginning loads to estimate the approximate teaching loads over the course of the respondents' careers (Table 51). Note that a significant pattern emerges between the type of institution and the two start-date groups. Clearly, the teaching loads are quite different for faculties depending on the nature of their institutions and when they began their full-time academic careers.

Teaching loads—Number of course preparation and levels. Another indicator of teaching specialization is a reduction in the number and level of different preparations required of a faculty member. Table 52 represents the primary relationships from a MANOVA that used type of institution and start date as independent variables to study

TABLE 50

NUMBER OF SECTIONS TAUGHT PER SEMESTER/QUARTER
BY PHASE OF CAREER AND TYPE OF INSTITUTION
(EARLY AND CURRENT)

	Type of Institution		
Phase of Career	Doctoral Granting	Nondoctoral Granting	Overall
Early Career	2.1	3.4	3.1
Current	1.7	2.7	2.5
Overall	1.9	3.1	2.8

Significant at $p < .05$.___
The interaction between type of institution and start date is also significant at $p < .05$.

TABLE 51

NUMBER OF SECTIONS TAUGHT PER SEMESTER/QUARTER BY START DATE AND TYPE OF INSTITUTION

	Type of Institution	
Start Date	Doctoral Granting	Nondoctoral Granting
Early	2.2	3.1
Middle	1.7	3.1

The interaction is significant at $p < .05$.

TABLE 52

NUMBER OF DIFFERENT COURSE PREPARATIONS BY LEVEL OF COURSE AND TYPE OF INSTITUTION FOR MOST RECENT THREE YEARS

	Type of Institution	
Level of Course	Doctoral Granting	Nondoctoral Granting
Undergraduate	2.5	4.1
Master's	2.1	1.2
Doctoral	0.8	0.0
Overall	5.4	5.5

The interaction is significant at $p <.05$.

the level of courses taught and the number of different preparations for the most recent three-year period of the respondents' careers. The results indicate a clear difference in the level of courses taught by faculties at doctoral- and nondoctoral-granting schools. Reference to the last row indicates no significant difference in the number of courses that faculty have prepared at the different types of institutions. In addition, start date was not significant in any of these relationships, indicating that faculty in the new group who are generally in the last phase of their probationary period for tenure consideration have a similar number of preparations as their more experienced counterparts. Furthermore, the large number of different course preparations reported overall makes it difficult to support a strong conclusion of specialization.

Perhaps the most striking finding in Table 52 is the fact that more than half of the different course preparations by faculty at D-G schools are at the graduate level. Indeed, faculty at the ND-G schools averaged more than one graduate preparation during the most recent three-year period. Because the report of the American Accounting Association Committee on the Future Structure, Content, and Scope of Accounting Education (1986) called for additional education, this finding suggests that the preparation effort required to meet this recommendation may not be difficult to accomplish.

Table 53 presents information about course preparations for the first three years in the careers of the respondents. As with the previous table, type of institution and start date were used as the independent variables, with level of course included as a repeated measure. Reference to the last row indicates that on average faculty at D-G schools prepared about one course less than their counterparts at nondoctoral schools. Moreover, those at ND-G schools tended to heavily at the undergraduate level and less at the graduate level.

TABLE 53

NUMBER OF DIFFERENT COURSE PREPARATIONS
BY LEVEL OF COURSE, START DATE,* AND TYPE OF INSTITUTION
FOR FIRST THREE YEARS IN CAREER

Level of Course	Start Date	Type of Institution: Doctoral Granting	Type of Institution: Nondoctoral Granting	Overall
Undergraduate	Early	3.9	6.3	5.7
	Middle	3.4	6.2	5.5
	New	2.2	3.8	3.4
	Means	3.2	5.6	5.0
Master's				
	Means	2.2	1.3	1.5
Doctoral				
	Means	0.5	0.1	0.2
Totals	Early	6.9	7.6	7.4
	Middle	5.8	7.6	7.1
	New	5.0	5.2	5.1
	Means	5.9	6.9	6.7

* Start date included only when significant.
Significant at p< .05. ——

As shown in the bottom row and the right-most column, new faculty tend to teach fewer preparations than their more experienced colleagues. Coupling this pattern with the concentration data presented earlier suggests a trend toward greater specialization. It should be noted, however, that almost all of the difference in course preparations arises at the undergraduate level. The teaching loads of the new group, therefore, are likely to be quite challenging because they may require thinking about accounting issues from considerably different perspectives.

Table 54 presents the results of a MANOVA that analyzed changes in the number of course preparations during the first three-year period and the most recent three-year period of the early and middle groups' careers. The type of institution and level of course also were included in the model. As with Table 53, similar patterns of course

TABLE 54

NUMBER OF DIFFERENT COURSE PREPARATIONS
BY PHASE OF CAREER, TYPE OF INSTITUTION,
AND LEVEL OF COURSE*

Phase of Career	Type of Institution: Doctoral Granting	Type of Institution: Nondoctoral Granting	Overall
Early Career	6.2	7.6	7.2
Current	5.6	5.6	5.6
Overall	5.9	6.6	6.4

* The courses and type of institution interaction and the courses and time of career interaction are each significant at p <.05.
Significant at p .<05. ——

preparations exist for the type of institution. In addition, the expected reduction in the number of courses prepared over time is supported clearly. Although this reduction again lends support to the trend toward greater specialization over time, the large number of different preparations does not suggest a sharp concentration in teaching areas.

Teaching loads—Number of preparations per semester/quarter. In this final section on teaching loads, examination focuses on the number of different preparations per semester/quarter during the current and first three-year periods in the respondents' careers. The purpose of this investigation lies in the belief that the number of different courses taught in a semester/quarter influences the amount of time needed for the teaching function. Initially, all respondents were asked to estimate the average number of different course preparations they had engaged in per semester/quarter over the most recent three-year period. The respondents in the early and middle groups were also asked this same question for the first three-year period in their careers. As with prior analyses, the independent variables of the ANOVA were type of institution and start date.

The only significant relationship detected for the most recent three-year period was type of institution. Those at D-G schools averaged 1.5 different courses per semester/quarter while their counterparts at nondoctoral granting schools averaged 1.9. Similarly, for the first three-year period significant differences were noted in the expected direction between the types of institutions. And, as shown in Table 55, fewer different course preparations during the early part of faculties' careers have occurred over time.

Examination of changes between the early and current phases of the respondent's careers revealed the type of institution and the change over time (reduction from 2.0 to 1.8 different course preparations) to be significant. In addition, the start date and phase of career interaction indicated that the early group began their careers preparing 2.2 different courses per semester/quarter, but the middle group started at 1.9. Currently, however, both report 1.8 different course preparations per semester/quarter.

American Accounting Association—Sections. Another indicator of emerging specialization is represented by the formation and growth of sections within the American Accounting Association (AAA).[13] Sections were formed to provide a critical

TABLE 55

DIFFERENT COURSE PREPARATIONS PER SEMESTER/QUARTER BY START DATE AND TYPE OF INSTITUTION FOR FIRST THREE YEARS IN CAREER

	Type of Institution		
Start Date	Doctoral Granting	Nondoctoral Granting	Overall
Early	1.8	2.4	2.2
Middle	1.5	2.1	1.9
New	1.5	1.9	1.8
Means	1.6	2.1	2.0

Significant at p <.05. ——
Significant at p <10. - - -

mass of AAA members (100 or more, originally) with a forum for interaction in their particular areas of interest. As currently structured within the AAA, sections came into existence in 1976, when six sections were formed. In 1977 another was added, and one each in 1980, 1981, and 1982 to arrive at the existing total of 10. (This does not include the Academy of Accounting Historians, which is not an AAA section.)

An overall gauge of interest in the sections can be constructed by comparing the change in membership in the sections to the change in membership in the parent organization. In making such a comparison, it is important to realize that many AAA members hold memberships in two or more sections, resulting in some multiple counting for section totals. From 1982, the earliest year of the data, to the present, membership in the AAA fell from 11,258 to 9,367 (a decrease of 17 percent). During the same time period, aggregate section membership rose from 5,368 to 7,778 (a 45 percent increase). A somewhat surprising factor, and perhaps significant beyond the original purpose in reviewing this information, is that essentially the decrease in the AAA membership during this period is due to a reduction in practitioner membership (4,988 to 3,146, or a decrease of 37 percent).

Another measure of specialization lies in the level of activity in the sections. Because the major purpose of sections is to provide a forum for the exchange of ideas, concepts, teaching notes, and so forth within the specialized area, it is not surprising that newsletters and meetings at the AAA annual convention are commonplace. However, it is noteworthy that three have started and sustained journals in their short existence. These three and the start-up dates for their journals are Taxation, Summer, 1979; Auditing, Summer, 1979; and Information Systems/Management Advisory Services, Fall, 1986.

Summary—Specialization. An extreme amount of specialization may hinder the implementation of the Bedford Committee Report (AAA, 1986) recommendations that focus on accounting as a total information system. Among the factors militating for specialization are increases in faculty size and codified knowledge. Faculty size has increased nearly 50 percent over the 12 years ending in 1986–87 and probably more during the past 25 years.

The data show significantly more concentration in practice experience over time—especially between the new group and the other groups. This seems related generally to less experience in the new group and to increasing emphasis in taxation. Less experience over time may be related to the increasing number of faculty who do not hold bachelor's degrees in accounting. Also, there is a trend for those joining ND-G faculties to have more auditing experience. The reverse is true for doctoral schools.

Teaching has generally become more concentrated over time, especially at D-G schools. Increasing concentration is due in part to (1) decreased teaching loads, (2) increased teaching in tax—particularly among new faculty, and (3) increased concentration over the course of one's career. The proportion of teaching among the six areas studied has remained remarkably stable.

The data reflect a greater load of one section per term for faculty at nondoctoral schools, although the gap is narrowing gradually. The number of sections per term has decreased over time.

Faculty have prepared about five different courses over the past three-year period. Compared to faculty at ND-G schools, those at D-G schools have taught more at the graduate level. In fact, more than half their different course preparations have been at the graduate level. Respondents from ND-G schools taught 1.2 different course preparations at the graduate level. Trends point to increasing emphasis on graduate education and a decreasing number of different preparations.

The number of different preparations per term was 1.5 for faculty at D-G schools and 1.9 for faculty at ND-G schools. Those in the early group taught more in the early phase of their careers than those in the other two groups. As to changes as the career matured, a slight decrease in courses taught was found.

Since their inception in 1976, AAA sections have exhibited tremendous growth while the AAA has shrunk, indicating a tendency toward specialization. Surprisingly, all shrinkage in AAA membership since 1982 is attributable to the net defection of practitioner members.

The models used in this section to analyze the data ignored faculty size, which could contribute to the findings. For example, more specialization was found at D-G schools, which are larger than ND-G schools. The evidence does not support strong concentration at present, but the trend is in that direction.

INSTITUTIONAL RESOURCES

In the preceding portion of the examination of the internal environment, the resources the individual brings to the professorial environment were investigated. In this section, attention turns to the effects of the university, private sector, and AACSB on accounting faculty.

Intrauniversity Effects

Within the institutional environment of the university, substantial changes have occurred over the past 25 years. Among the changes examined in this section are student/faculty relationships, class sizes, and computer resources. In addition to archival data, much discussion relies on the responses of surveyed accounting faculty and business college deans. Using a 7-point scale with 1 equal to favorable to 7 equal to unfavorable, the respondents were asked to rate the effects of numerous factors on the quality of accounting education for the most recent three-year period.

Increased enrollment. Table 2 data, which were reviewed earlier, showed that the total number of bachelor's and master's degrees in accounting had increased nearly 400 percent for the period beginning in 1961 and ending in 1985. Moreover, information in Table 10 indicated that the rate of accounting faculty growth did not equal the ratio of increase in total accounting graduates. Comparative data showed that university enrollment in total increased only 150 percent from 1963 to 1987. This disparity therefore indicates that accounting faculty were subject to much higher demand for their services over the last of a quarter century than other faculty generally.

In spite of this imbalance in the demand for and supply of accounting faculty, the respondents indicated that this condition did not represent a significantly favorable or unfavorable influence on the quality of the accounting educational environment because the mean response on a 7-point scale was 4.2. Indeed, Figure 11 shows that the ratio of students to faculty may be decreasing. This is consistent with the earlier analysis of university student enrollments and stabilization in the number. of accounting graduates since 1980.

Quality of accounting students. According to the respondents, one favorable result that occurred during the past 25 years was an overall increase in the quality of

FIGURE 11
RATIO OF TOTAL STUDENT CREDIT HOURS TO TOTAL FULL-TIME FACULTY EQUIVALENTS OVER TIME

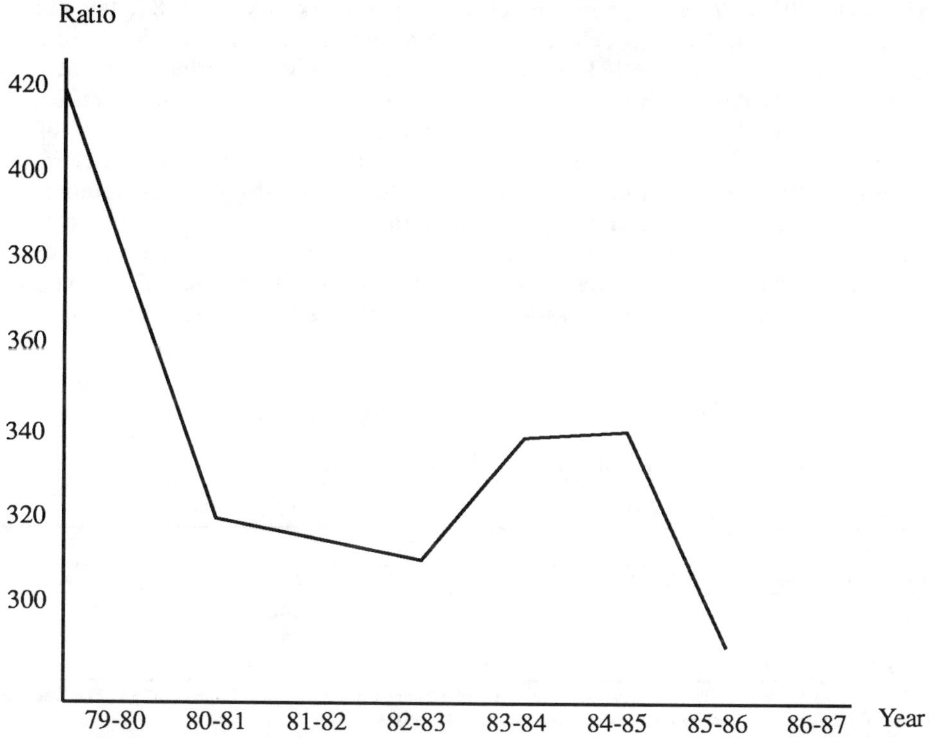

Source: *Administrators of Accounting Programs Data Base Survey* (Williams et al., 1979–85). Data for 1981–82 and 1986–87 were not available.

accounting students. The respondents ranked this as the second most favorable change of the last two and one-half decades by assigning it a mean rating of 2.3. However, feeling was mixed among the respondents depending on their start dates. The early group assigned 2.4, the middle group 2.7, and the new group 1.9. Although no ready explanation for these differences is apparent, it is noteworthy that all are quite favorable.

Reduced student/faculty contact outside the classroom. The most unfavorable change over the past 25 years according to the respondents is the reduced student/faculty interaction outside the classroom, which seems related to the substantial increase in accounting enrollments. The mean response on this item was 5.5 and did not differ between faculty at doctoral- or nondoctoral-granting schools or among faculty in the three start-date groups. This result is interesting because the Committee originally suspected selective recall of the "good old days" by members of the early group. The consistency across all start-date categories in the study was unexpected.

Decreased teaching loads. In spite of the increase in the demand-supply ratio, the amount of time devoted to teaching has decreased over the past 25 years. One reason for this trend is the decreased amount of classroom contact hours taught per week. As noted in Table 56, just over half of the faculty responding to a survey in 1967-68 taught 10 to 12 classroom contact hours per week. By 1986-87, two-thirds taught less than 10. The Committee's own survey reflected a significant decline in the time devoted to teaching as well. For example, Table 23 indicates that those at D-G institutions currently devote about 21 hours per week in total to teaching and those at ND–G schools about 24 hours. The comparable number for the first three years of all faculty reporting in the 1961-66 group was 30 hours per week and for all faculty in the 1971-74 group, 26 hours (Table 29). Review of the other tables constructed from survey responses leads to the conclusion that generally more time is now allocated to research, service, and outside remunerative activities than in the past. The respondents ranked the reduction in teaching loads as having the fourth most favorable impact on the quality of accounting education, assigning it a mean of 2.7.

TABLE 56

DISTRIBUTION OF TEACHING L0AD
FOR FULL-TIME FACULTY OVER TIME
(IN CONTACT HOURS PER WEEK)

	Time Period			
Contact Hours Per Week	1967–68	1972–73	1977–78	1986–87
Less than 10	37	42	48	67
10-12	51	48	45	21
More than 12	12	10	35	12

Source: All data except 1986-87 from Williams, "Ten years of Changes in Accounting Education" (1979). Data for 1986-87 from Williams et al., "Accounting Data Base: 1986-87" (1986).

Megasections. The decrease in teaching loads, together with the increasing demand for accounting instruction, has resulted in several approaches to make such instruction more efficient. One of these is a movement to teach some classes, especially financial accounting principles, in large sections often referred to as *megasections*. Megasections typically involve delivering lectures to several hundred or more students either live or by television. The use of megasections may or may not employ much smaller "breakout" sections that provide for more intimate discussion of problems, concepts, and so on. Efficiency results from one full-time faculty member instructing several hundred to a thousand students per semester. This reduces the teaching load of other faculty so that they may pursue other activities. Figure 12 indicates the increase in the use of megasections over the past several years (data were not available for earlier years). Accredited schools have led the way in implementing megasections, with nearly 30 percent having at least one megasection of principles of financial accounting. However, relatively few schools employ megasections outside of the principles courses.

Class sizes. Figure 13 presents information regarding the reported trend in class sizes from 1979 to 1986. The trend is essentially stable, probably reflecting the fact that the data began in 1979 and overall university enrollments peaked in 1983 (Table

FIGURE 12

USE OF MEGASECTIONS BY COURSE TYPE AND ACCREDITATION STATUS

1984–86

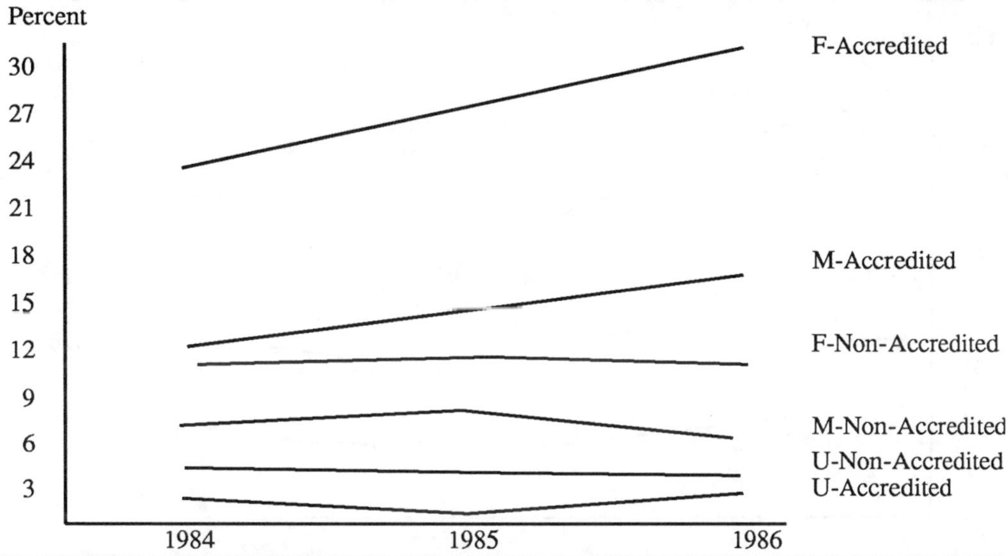

Note: Reflects proportion of schools using at least one megasection to teach Principles of Financial Accounting (F); Principles of Managerial Accounting (M); or other upper-level accounting courses (U).
Source: Williams et al., *Accounting Data Bases*.

7). Also, the period of most rapid growth (30 percent from 1970 to 1975) occurred before the start of the data on class sizes. Consistent with this assessment is the fact that growth in accounting graduates has dissipated since 1980 (Table 2). Figure 11 further reinforces the significant drop in the demand-supply imbalance at the outset of the 1980s and the relatively stable trend since that time. These trends were cited because the respondents ranked increased class size as the second most unfavorable factor affecting accounting education during the past 25 years, assigning it a mean of 5.3.

Multiple-choice items. Another factor that recently has drawn special concern in the accounting academic community is the increased use of multiple-choice items for testing. The concern has been fueled by discussions of the AICPA toward moving to an all-objective format for the CPA exam. Arguments favoring such a move include the belief that more knowledge can be tested and that grading can be accomplished more efficiently and reliably than under the current format. The current format involves a mixture of objective questions and open-end response items that are graded solely for content. Academics are concerned that an all-objective CPA exam will not test certain knowledge domains adequately and will decrease concern for writing skills (AICPA, 1987). Overall, the respondents ranked the increased use of multiple-choice questions as the third most unfavorable factor contributing to change in the quality of accounting education over the past 25 years. However, the severity of the ranking

FIGURE 13
AVERAGE CLASS SIZE BY LEVEL
(EXCLUDING MEGASECTIONS)
1979–86

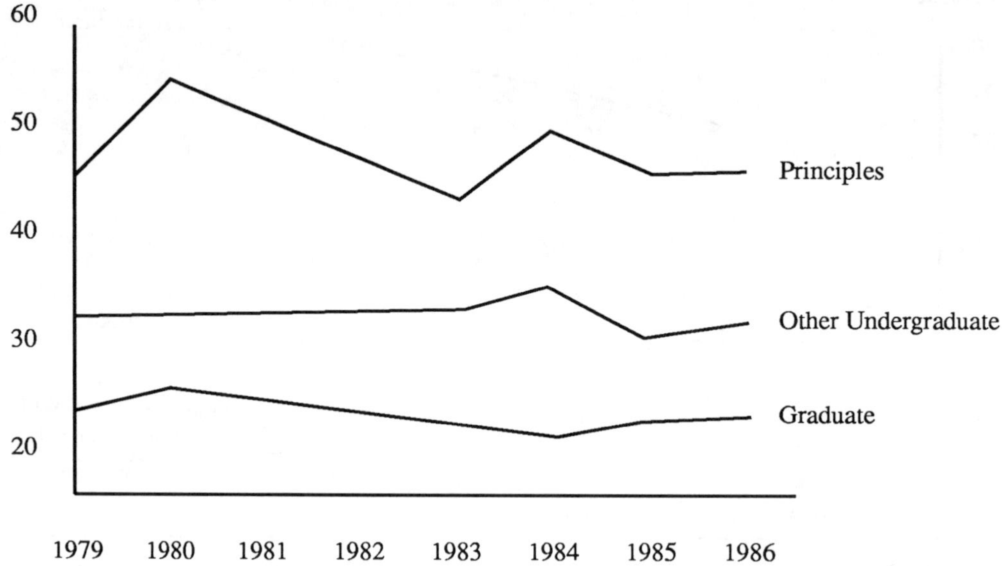

Note: The data from 1986 have been aggregated on a weighted basis to be comparable to data from other times.
Source: Williams et al., *Administrators of Accounting Programs Data Base Survey* (1979–85). Data for 1981–82 and 1986–87 were not available.

differed significantly between faculty at D-G schools (mean of 5.5) and those at nondoctoral schools (mean of 4.7).

Computers. A final matter of concern in the university area is the availability and impact of the computer on accounting education. The respondents ranked the increased availability of the computer as having the most favorable impact of all on accounting education over the past 25 years (mean of 2.2). In addition to the rather obvious applications in the classroom, the increased availability of computers has facilitated implementation of more sophisticated research methodologies into accounting. Cargile and Bublitz (1986) report that their survey of different facilitators of accounting research placed the computer as most important.

Summary—Intrauniversity effects. Increased enrollment and efforts to cope with it over the past 25 years have resulted in mixed costs and benefits. The increased quality of students, the reduction in the teaching loads, and the increased availability of computers have contributed favorably. On the other side of the ledger, reduced contact between students and faculty outside of class, the increased class sizes (including the use of megasections), and the use of multiple-choice items are perceived as harming the accounting educational environment. The mixture of activities (e.g., teaching, research) have also changed substantially, which contributes both favorably and unfavorably.

Other Effects

Private support.[14] The primary sources of external support come through contributions of time, instructional materials, research participation, conference sponsorship, and monetary donations from alumni and large public accounting firms. During the time period addressed by the study, the support from Big Eight accounting firms has escalated tremendously in all of these areas. To document this support, data were secured from three world headquarters offices of Big Eight firms that reported the amounts that had come from their foundations. However, because local office contributions are not included in the data, the figures reported in Table 57 are understated.

TABLE 57
THREE FOUNDATIONS' CONTRIBUTIONS
BY RELATIVE INCREASE AND TIME

Year	Amount	Percentage of Increase Over Prior Period
1966	$ 100,000	—
1971	616,000	616
1976	3,041,000	494
1981	5,871,000	193
1986	10,243,000	174

Source: Donald P. Dupont, Managing Director—Personnel for Arthur Andersen & Co., secured private information from the foundations of three Big Eight accounting firms. Amounts do not include local office contributions.

The rise in participation is marked and impressive. The concern for improved quality in the accounting educational environment evidenced by this pattern results from a close interaction between accounting academia and practice unparalleled in other disciplines. Furthermore, based on projections from experts, the trend should not abate because the practitioner arm of the profession is quite concerned about potential decreases in the number and quality of students produced by the academic sector. Indeed, the trend may even increase.

Another indicator of this private support is the number of externally funded fellowships or professorships. These posts carry stipends that increase the probability of the recipient university retaining the holder and reduce the potential of financial pressure for the holder. By reducing this pressure, the holder is freed to place more emphasis on other areas directly related to the academic environment. Table 58 indicates the substantial increase in the number of these designations since the 1974–75 period. As with the prior data, the commitment of external resources is impressive.

Other examples of financial support also exist. To name a few, they are the Arthur Andersen Foundation's Doctoral Dissertation Program, the Arthur Young

TABLE 58
NUMBER OF SPECIAL FACULTY DESIGNATIONS OVER TIME

1974–75	1978–79	1982–83	1986–87
0	57	83	168

Source: Hasselback, *Accounting Faculty Directory* (1974, 1978, 1982 and 1987).

Foundation's Tax Research Program, the Coopers & Lybrand Computer Integration Program, the Deloitte Haskins & Sells Foundation's Doctoral Grant Program, the Ernst & Whinney Foundation's Doctoral Dissertation Program, the Peat Marwick Foundation's Research Opportunities in Auditing, the Price Waterhouse Foundation's Professorship Program, and the Touche Ross Foundation's Trueblood Seminar Program. These programs, together with the trends discussed above, convey the essence of the relationship between the private sector and the professorial environment. Accordingly, the faculty respondents ranked the increase in research support as the sixth most favorable factor affecting change in the accounting educational environment over the past 25 years, assigning a mean of 2.9.

Research opportunities in auditing. Perhaps the most visible program in terms of affecting the direction and output of academic accounting is the Peat Marwick Foundation's Research Opportunities in Auditing (ROA) Program. In 1975, the firm of Peat, Marwick, Mitchell & Co. issued a series of auditing research ideas listed by priority. In the latter part of 1976, $1 million was committed to expedite the progress in this area. During the 1976-77 academic year, the first grants were issued. According to the 1986 report on the program (Peat Marwick Foundation, 1986), 72 projects had been completed and 30 more were in process. Perhaps of equal importance, during that year's submission period 83 proposals were received. Thus by the 1986-87 period, $2,148,400 in grants had been awarded to 142 researchers at 58 schools.

The impact of this program on auditing research is substantial. According to Vasarhelyi et al. (1987), the total number of articles published in six academic journals increased significantly during the 20-year period ending in 1986 (discussed later). Even so, during the 10-year period ending in 1986, their data base reveals that on average 23.6 percent of all articles published during that time were auditing related. During the 10-year period preceding 1976, the comparable percentage was 9.2. Although it must be acknowledged that the Commission on Auditor's Responsibility (1976) and several Congressional inquiries were in progress during the mid-1970s (discussed in an earlier section), the fact that the proportion of academic auditing articles nearly tripled seems strongly related to the availability of, and organized forum for, funding such research.

Accreditation standards.[15] Through the accreditation of accounting programs and business schools, the American Assembly of Collegiate Schools of Business (AACSB) exerts considerable influence on the professorial environment of accounting faculty. Part of this influence results from the fact that more than 260 business schools and more than 70 accounting schools/ departments are accredited by the AACSB. More far reaching, however, is the influence of the AACSB, which results from the large number of (1) individuals who serve on AACSB committees or attend AACSB–sponsored workshops, (2) faculty members who move between accredited institutions and nonaccredited institutions, and (3) articles written about or referring to AACSB standards, and schools that spend many years aspiring to accreditation.

Approximately 25 years ago, the reports of Gordon and Howell (1959) and Pierson (1959) were published. These reports were extremely critical of business school education for numerous reasons, such as the poor quality of student admissions, the overemphasis on vocationalism, the narrowness of curricula, the low level and quality of faculty research, the heavy reliance on part-time faculty, the sparsity of doctorally qualified faculty, and the minimal coverage of liberal arts subject matter. Largely as a consequence of these criticisms, the AACSB accreditation standards for business schools and faculty were substantially revised in the early 1960s. The adoption of a formal requirement for doctorally qualified accounting faculty, however, was postponed until 1969. Prior to that date, a master's degree with a CPA certificate had been considered sufficient.

Several changes in the professorial environment of accounting faculty appear to have resulted from the terminal degree requirement of the AACSB. First, the terminal degree requirement probably caused an imbalance in the supply of and demand for doctorally qualified accounting faculty. On the supply side, data reported by Campbell and Hermanson (1987) indicate that prior to 1966, only 554 accounting doctoral degrees had been awarded, but in the 1966–70 period, 504 doctoral degrees were awarded. Beginning in 1971, however, the number of new accounting doctorates increased markedly, up to 761 in the 1971–75 period, 738 in the 1976–80 period, and 883 in the 1981–85 period. Similar data gathered from Hasselback (1987) appear in Table 10. Together, these two data sources indicate that in slightly more than the last decade the overall production of accounting doctorates has more than doubled from all previous years, with approximately two of three doctorally qualified accounting faculty having received their degrees since 1971.

On the demand side the trend is more difficult to quantify, but AAA reports (Williams et al., 1979–87) have consistently indicated a shortage of doctorally qualified accounting professors (Table 59). For example, according to these data 5.0 vacancies existed in the 1979–80 academic year for every new accounting doctorate; in the 1985–87 period 3.9 vacancies existed per accounting doctoral candidate. A similar trend appears in AACSB data, which indicate that the ratio of openings per doctoral graduate declined from 7.1 in the 1981–82 period to 3.9 in the 1982–83 period, 4.3 in the 1983–84 period, and 3.2 in the 1984–85 period. Thus, despite a narrowing of the demand/supply gap, the data still indicate a substantial imbalance in the supply of and demand for accounting doctorates.

Second, the combined effect of the terminal degree requirement, the imbalance in the supply of and demand for accounting doctorates, and the dramatic growth in accounting student enrollment (discussed earlier) caused substantial faculty shortages, which resulted in upward pressure on starting salaries for new accounting doctorates.

TABLE 59

RELATIONSHIP BETWEEN NUMBER OF DOCTORAL DEGREES GRANTED AND NUMBER OF NEW FACULTY MEMBERS SOUGHT

1979–87

	79-80	80-81	81–82	82–83	83–84	84–85	85–86	86–87	Totals
Total Positions Authorized	571	624	N/A	564	533	486	486	414	3,678
Number of Degrees Awarded	115	119	N/A	113	116	123	86	142	814
Relationship	5.0	5.2	N/A	5.0	4.6	4.0	5.7	2.9	4.5

Note: Because the 1985–86 and 1986–87 years exhibit high variance, an average ratio of 3.9 is believed to be more representative. Computation of a similar ratio for the 1987–88 year from the Report on Supply and Demand for Accounting Professors (AAA, 1987) was 4.05.

Source: Williams et al., "Accounting Data Base: 1979–87" (1979–87).

For instance, according to AACSB data, the starting salary for new accounting doctorates was $15,000 in 1972. By the 1986–87 academic year, however, this salary had increased to $42,000 ($16,300 after adjustment for inflation). The real salary of new accounting doctorates therefore rose 8.7 percent over this time period. In comparison, data reported by Robert Half (1987) indicate the salary of managers in public accounting changed from $21,000 in 1972 to $46,000 in 1986 ($17,600 after adjustment for inflation). Thus managers employed by public accounting firms experienced a real salary decrease of 16.2 percent over this same time horizon.

A similar trend emerges when the salaries of new accounting doctorates are contrasted with those of new doctorates in other business school disciplines. Here the AACSB data indicate that the starting salary for accounting doctorates in 1972 was approximately equal to that for other business school disciplines. However, for the 1986–87 academic year, the salary of new accounting doctorates was approximately $5,000 (14 percent) higher. Further evidence of this relative increase in the salary of new accounting doctorates is shown in data gathered by Oklahoma State University (Figure 14). According to these data, the ratio of assistant accounting professors' salaries to all assistant professors' salaries increased from 1.16 in the 1974–75 period to 1.34 in the 1985–86 period.

A third change in the professorial environment is the emphasis placed on rigorous research. This change results in part from the AACSB adoption of a terminal degree requirement and in part from increasing demand for accounting services as well

FIGURE 14

RATIO OF ACCOUNTING FACULTY SALARIES TO OVERALL AVERAGE ACADEMIC SALARIES 1974–1986

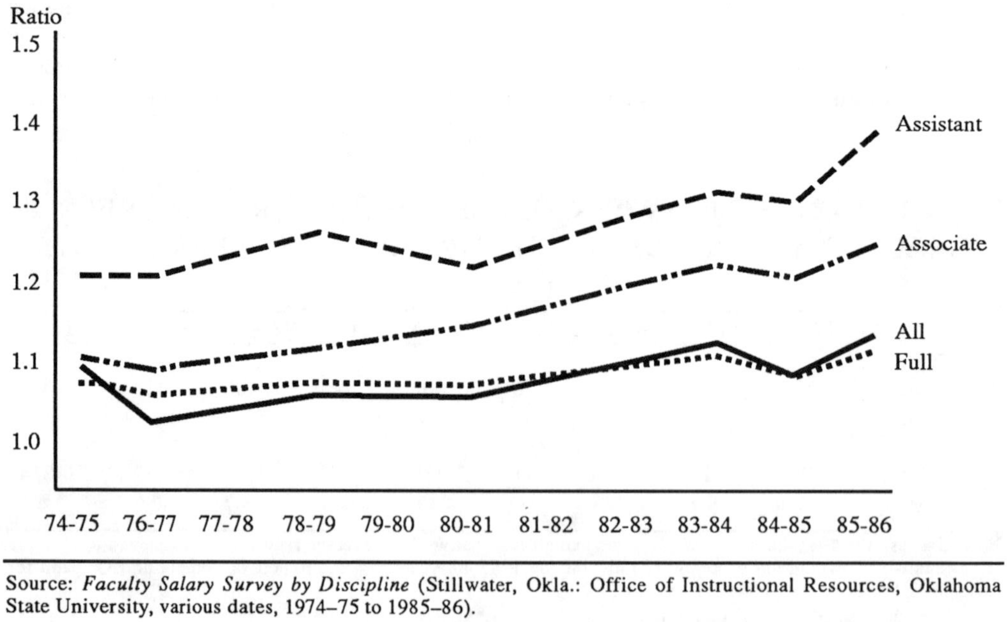

Source: *Faculty Salary Survey by Discipline* (Stillwater, Okla.: Office of Instructional Resources, Oklahoma State University, various dates, 1974–75 to 1985–86).

as the introduction of richer research methodologies (e.g., Ball and Brown, 1968; Beaver, 1968) . As an illustration of this changing emphasis, consider that in 1963 only 11.7 percent of the 94 articles published in *The Accounting Review* and the *Journal of Accounting Research* employed rigorous or empirical methods.[16] However, by 1975 this figure had increased to 86.2 percent. The introduction of several new journals during the following decade, such as *Accounting Organizations and Society* in 1976, the *Journal of Accounting Auditing and Finance* in 1977, the *Journal of Accounting and Economics* in 1979, and *Auditing: A Journal of Practice and Theory* in 1981, provided even greater opportunities for the publication of rigorous accounting research. As a result, of the 149 articles published in these six journals in 1986, 98 percent employed rigorous analytical or empirical methods. A graphic display of this shift toward rigorous research is presented in Figure 15.

In terms of the content of accounting research, a similar change in emphasis also has occurred over the past 25 years. To elaborate, 73.9 percent of all articles published in *The Accounting Review* and the *Journal of Accounting Research* in 1963 dealt with

FIGURE 15
ARTICLES AND RIGOROUS ARTICLES OVER TIME

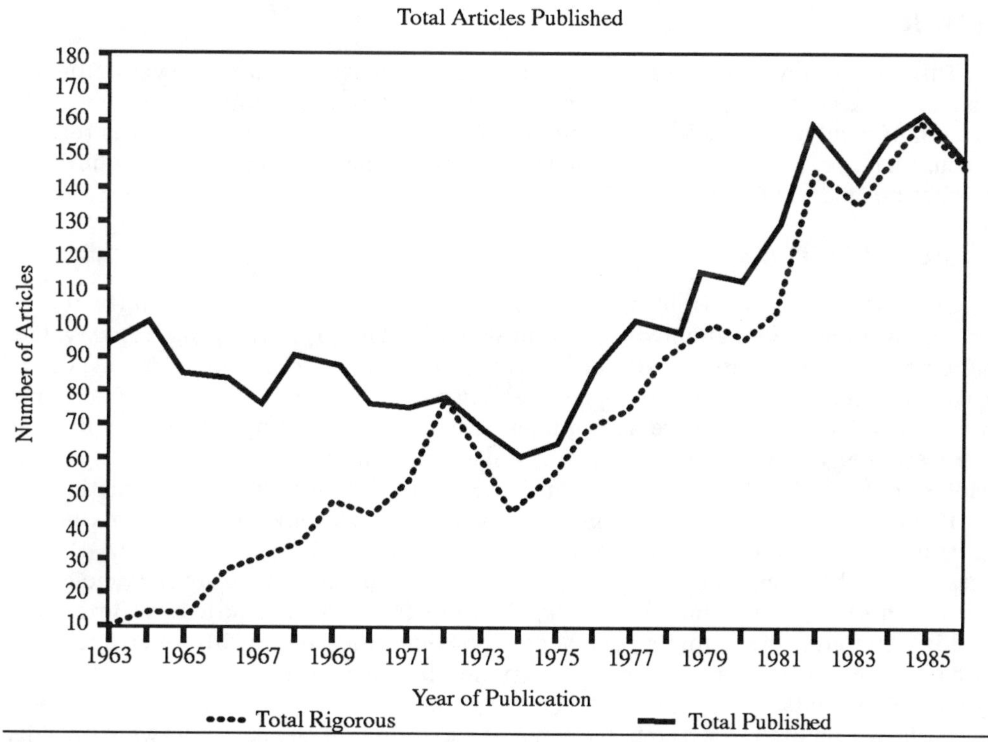

Source: M.A. Vasarheyli, D. H. Bao, and J. Berk, "Date Base of Six Accounting Journals" (1987).

accounting theory or history. By 1986, this figure had declined to 25.7 percent for the six journals mentioned above. Replacing these two topic areas were behavioral studies, up from less than 1 percent in 1963 to 19.6 percent in 1986, and statistical modeling, jumping from 8.5 percent in 1963 to 43.2 percent in 1986.

In addition to the terminal degree requirement, the AACSB accreditation standards also have influenced accounting curriculum. One example of this influence is the 1983 requirement for students to receive instruction in the "design, use, control and audit of computerized information systems." Although this requirement is frequently claimed to have caused a substantial revision in the content of accounting courses, it is important to recognize that neither this nor other changes in the AACSB accreditation standards have occurred separately and apart from other developments in the environment.

Instead, business and academic leaders have stimulated changes in educational requirements that the AACSB has then spread throughout academia more broadly. Thus, in the case of the requirement for computerized management information systems, the AACSB responded to the changing environment of accounting professionals by gradually requiring additional computerized accounting course work (i.e., the study of "management information and computer systems" was part of the original accounting standards for the 1980–81 academic year, and the study of "information systems" has been part of the business curriculum standards since at least 1969).

REWARDS

This section reviews a broad range of factors contributing to the reward structure available to accounting professors. Perhaps the most striking observation herein is the plethora of combinations open to accounting faculty. The inquiry covers issues relating to tenure and promotion, salary, sabbaticals, mobility, business opportunities, intrinsic satisfaction, and academic status.

Tenure and Promotion

Success within any field closely relates to formal recognition manifested by promotion. In addition, employment by an organization that mirrors one's own values and emphases contributes positively to job satisfaction. To examine one aspect of academic success, the discussion focuses on temporal changes in the types of activities that are involved in the tenure and promotion decision, including related factors such as differential treatments of publications and determinants of market value. Again, readers are reminded that the findings are intended to be descriptive, not normative.

Hours of work. Respondents in the survey indicated they worked approximately 51 hours each week during the regular nine-month academic year and about 41 each week during the three-month summer period. The weighted average for the whole year resulted in 48.7 hours, which is remarkably close to the 49.3 reported by Boze et al. (1986). Although these totals represent a considerable amount of "overtime" in a normal sense, the preferred work week reported by Boze et al. (1986) only decreased by five to six hours.

Perhaps of more relevance is the issue of flexibility, or the extent to which faculty can select how to allocate their time. Earlier results in this paper indicated a tremendous opportunity for such flexibility. For example, Table 22 indicated that faculty often teach most heavily in their areas of practice experience—presumably their primary areas of interest. Moreover, Tables 23 and 25 reflected significant differences—both statistically and practically—between faculty at D-G and ND–G institutions as to the time spent on various activities. This leads to the speculation that faculty can, to a considerable extent, choose the areas they wish to emphasize by selecting their schools. Both this data and that of Boze et al. (1986) point to more satisfaction among those at D-G schools for research. Comparing the time allocated to this activity during the regular academic year and the summer period for this group (Tables 23 and 25) represents a substantial change—from 12.9 hours per week to 18.5, respectively. Other comparisons between time allocated to such pursuits as teaching and outside remunerative activities during the academic year and the summer period also reflect the ability of many faculty to shift their areas of emphasis. Therefore, this observed flexibility among the respondents supports the assertion of Campbell and Hermanson (1986, p. 14) that faculty can select from among "multiple types of doctoral programs" to prepare themselves for the areas of emphasis (e.g., teaching, research) that they most prefer.

The ability to effect changes in time allocation is further evidenced by the shift across one's career toward greater emphasis on those activities more closely related with job satisfaction. For example, Table 34 shows that the respondents in the early and middle groups currently devote less time to teaching and research activities and more to service than during the early phase of their careers. In conjunction with this shift, Table 37 reflects movements in these same directions for reported job satisfaction, thereby implying an ability of accounting faculty to alter their areas of emphasis in the desired direction. Thus, it appears that the ability to determine areas of emphasis, coupled with typical faculty teaching loads of six to nine hours per week, various choices for publication outlets (discussed below), and relatively generous breaks between semesters and for holidays, allows for considerable flexibility as compared to many professions that are subject to potentially erratic client demands.

Teaching, research, and service. The key criteria for tenure/promotion decisions revolve around faculty performance in teaching, research, and service. Campbell et al. (1983) found substantial differences in the emphasis placed on these criteria depending on whether the institution granted doctorates and whether it was accredited by the AACSB. As expected, D-G institutions exhibited a "research profile"; ND–G but accredited schools exhibited a "teaching/research profile"; and nonaccredited schools exhibited a combination of the three. In other work, Campbell and Morgan (1986) reported that faculty promoted to full and associate professors at D-G schools publish at a significantly higher rate than those promoted at ND–G schools. Likewise, Cargile and Bublitz (1986) reported a similar pattern of disparity among different types of institutions and also noted that political action plays a role in promotion decisions.

This report revisits and supports some of these findings while also tracing changes over time. One shift over time presented in Table 60 is the increasing proportion of full-time faculty in the higher and presumably tenured ranks.[17] Because tenure effectively guarantees a position until retirement or death and because the growth in faculty sizes has slowed dramatically, it is reasonable to expect some changes attributable to an increasing proportion of faculty at higher or tenured ranks.

Current perceptions. Tables 61 and 62 note distinct differences between types of institution in the importance attached to different criteria both for the tenure decision of associate professors and the promotion decision of full professors. As shown in these tables, a much stronger emphasis is on research at D-G schools and a much heavier emphasis on teaching at ND–G schools.

TABLE 60
PROPORTION OF FULL-TIME ACCOUNTING FACULTY
BY RANK AND TENURE STATUS
1967–87

	Time Period		
Rank/Tenure Status	1967–68	1977–78	1986–87
Professor	21.9	24.4	27.0
Associate	26.0	25.6	27.2
Tenured	47.9	50.0	54.2
Assistant	34.2	30.9	29.4
Instructor/Lecturer	16.0	16.8	16.4
Untenured	50.2	47.7	45.8

Source: All data except 1986-87 from Williams, *Ten Years of Changes in Accounting Education* (1979). Data for 1986-87 from Table 6, Williams et al., "Accounting Data Base: 1986-87" (1986).

TABLE 61
IMPORTANCE OF TEACHING, RESEARCH, AND SERVICE IN
ASSISTANT TO ASSOCIATE PROFESSOR
TENURE DECISION BY TYPE OF INSTITUTION
(ON A 100-POINT SCALE)

	Type of Institution	
Activity	Doctoral Granting	Nondoctoral Granting
Teaching	27	47
Research	66	42
Service	7	10

The interaction is significant at $p < .05$.

TABLE 62
IMPORTANCE OF TEACHING, RESEARCH, AND SERVICE IN
ASSOCIATE TO FULL PROFESSOR
PROMOTION DECISION BY TYPE OF INSTITUTION
(ON A 100-POINT SCALE)

	Type of Institution	
Activity	Doctoral Granting	Nondoctoral Granting
Teaching	27	42
Research	59	44
Service	12	12

The interaction is significant at $p < .05$.

Early career perceptions. To gain insight into changes over time in the relative importance of the tenure/promotion criteria, respondents in the early and middle groups were asked to assess the importance of teaching, research, and service with respect to tenure and promotion decisions for the first three years of their careers. Tables 63 and 64 indicate the same pattern of differences between D-G and ND–G schools as existed in the respondents' answers for the current time. However, during these early periods, research was not perceived to be as important as it is currently at either type of school, and teaching was perceived to be more important. Yet it appears that the difference between teaching and research for the two types of institution was approximately the same as in the current time.

An examination of Table 63 reveals that the shift at D-G schools toward greater emphasis on research and less on teaching seems to have begun between the early and middle groups' start dates (early 1960s to early 1970s). To elaborate, assessments of the respondents in the early and middle groups at D-G schools reflect a 14-point difference in teaching (49 to 35) and a 13-point difference (39 to 56) in research. This harbinger of change is manifested in the current time weights as approximately two-thirds of all accounting doctorally qualified faculty have begun their academic careers after 1971 (Campbell and Hermanson, 1986). Table 64 data indicate no differences within teaching and research for the promotion decision between associate and full professor for the start-date groups. The difference between the research and teaching criteria between the two types of institutions shows little change for this higher promotion decision.

Evidence of the increased emphasis on research and the decreased emphasis on teaching during the past 25 years is shown in Tables 65 and 66. For both D-G and ND–G schools, the overall emphasis has moved from research being weighted about one-third to the present weighting of approximately one-half. Separately, however, the emphasis on research at D-G schools has increased to an assigned weight of two-thirds

TABLE 63

IMPORTANCE OF TEACHING, RESEARCH AND SERVICE IN ASSISTANT TO ASSOCIATE PROFESSOR TENURE DECISION FOR FIRST THREE YEARS OF CAREER BY START DATE AND TYPE OF INSTITUTION (ON A 100-POINT SCALE)

		Type of Institution	
Activity	Start Date	Doctoral Granting	Nondoctoral Granting
Teaching	Early	49	65
	Middle	35	64
	Overall	**41**	**64**
Research	Early	39	28
	Middle	56	24
	Overall	**49**	**26**
Service	Early	9	7
	Middle	10	12
	Overall	**10**	**10**

The interaction between type of institution and activity is significant at p<.05. Means relevant to this interaction are highlighted.

TABLE 64
IMPORTANCE OF TEACHING, RESEARCH, AND SERVICE IN ASSOCIATE TO FULL PROFESSOR PROMOTION DECISION BY TYPE OF INSTITUTION FOR FIRST THREE YEARS IN CAREER (ON A 100-POINT SCALE)

	Type of Institution	
Activity	Doctoral Granting	Nondoctoral Granting
Teaching	37	60
Research	45	31
Service	18	9

The interaction is significant at $p < .05$.

for the tenure decision and three-fifths for the promotion decision. In comparison, at ND–G schools the emphasis lags behind at a weighting of less than one-half for both the tenure and promotion decisions.

Faculty versus deans' perceptions. Table 67 presents an overview of the importance of the three activities for business school deans and accounting faculty, type of institution, and type of decision. The same patterns persist between D-G and ND–G schools. It is noteworthy that the faculty and deans tend to agree. The primary area of disagreement is in the importance of research at D-G schools where faculty believe that research receives greater weight and teaching less weight in both tenure and promotion decisions than do deans. Faculty rate service slightly lower in both cases.

One explanation for this difference may be that deans view performances in teaching and research to be positively linked. Table 68 reports the strength of the deans' perceptions of the relationships among the tenure/promotion activities. Although none of the relationships differed significantly by type of institution, the deans did report a strong positive association between teaching and research, as well as between service and teaching. Essentially no relationship was perceived between research and service.

Although this issue was not included on the faculty survey, some accounting academicians would posit that these relationships are quite different. Some faculty seem to be very successful researchers but are regarded as no better than average teachers. Considerable anecdotal evidence also exists regarding faculty members who are good teachers but unsuccessful researchers. In addition, many faculty believe that the reason most promotion requests are denied is due to lack of adequate research and publication activity. Because the failure of a colleague to be promoted or tenured is likely to weigh heavily in faculty memories, they may perceive less relationship between teaching and research than do deans.

Future expectations. Table 69 reflects the expectations of accounting faculty and business school deans about changes in importance of the various criteria related to tenure/promotion decisions between the current time and 1995. As noted in this table, little change in emphasis is expected to occur with regard to the service criterion

TABLE 65

IMPORTANCE OF TEACHING, RESEARCH AND SERVICE IN THE ASSISTANT TO ASSOCIATE PROFESSOR TENURE DECISION BY TYPE OF INSTITUTION AND PHASE OF CAREER (ON A 100-POINT SCALE)

	Type of Institution					
	Doctoral Granting		Nondoctoral Granting		Overall	
Activity	Early Career	Current	Early Career	Current	Early Career	Current
Teaching	41	27	64	47	58 ——	42
Research	49	67	26	43	32 ——	49
Service	10	7	10	8	10	8

Significant at $p < .05$. ____

TABLE 66

IMPORTANCE OF TEACHING, RESEARCH AND SERVICE IN THE ASSOCIATE TO FULL PROFESSOR PROMOTION DECISION BY TYPE OF INSTITUTION AND PHASE OF CAREER (ON A 100-POINT SCALE)

	Type of Institution					
	Doctoral Granting		Nondoctoral Granting		Overall	
Activity	Early Career	Current	Early Career	Current	Early Career	Current
Teaching	37	27	60	42	54 ——	38
Research	45	59	31	45	32 ——	48
Service	18	12	9	12	11	12

Significant at $p < .05$. ____

TABLE 67

IMPORTANCE OF TEACHING, RESEARCH AND SERVICE IN THE TENURE/PROMOTION DECISION BY TYPE OF INSTITUTION AND RESPONDENT GROUP (ON A 100-POINT SCALE)

	Tenure Decision				Promotion Decision			
	Doctoral Granting		Nondoctoral Granting		Doctoral Granting		Nondoctoral Granting	
Activity	Faculty	Deans	Faculty	Deans	Faculty	Deans	Faculty	Deans
Teaching	27	34	47	49	27	33	42	46
Research	66	55	42	37	59	50	44	40
Service	7	10	10	13	12	16	12	14

(i.e., it will remain at about 10 percent). However, increased emphasis is likely to be placed on research and probably will increase more sharply at ND–G schools than at D-G schools. One possible explanation for this shift in emphasis at ND–G schools may result from the fact that the proportion of faculty with doctorates at ND–G schools has increased considerably over time, whereas the proportion at D-G schools has remained substantially unchanged (see Table 15). Thus, new faculty members at ND–G schools are more likely to possess a doctorate than existing faculty, which implies both increased research ability and presumably increased research desire.

As to the change in emphasis on teaching, the dean and faculty respondents disagree. Faculty perceive that teaching will be deemphasized, but deans generally feel it will remain about the same. Note, however, that deans at D-G schools believe teaching will receive greater emphasis by 1995. This view may be justified in two respects. First, these deans believe good research and good teaching are closely related. Second, they probably foresee a lack of significant enrollment growth between the present and 1995. As a result, they may perceive the need for improved teaching and research activities in order to secure tenure/promotion in the future. This increased emphasis on teaching, moreover, may be relevant if these deans wish to control the proportion of their tenured faculty at some maximum.

Influence of organizational levels. Evidence about the extent of control exercised by different organizational levels within the university provides insight into the degree of self-determination that exists for accounting and business units. If control is strictly local (i.e., in accounting units), criteria are largely self-determined. On the other hand, if higher organizational levels exhibit active involvement, criteria are effectively

TABLE 68

DEANS' PERCEPTIONS OF THE RELATIONSHIP BETWEEN TEACHING, RESEARCH AND SERVICE (1 = POSITIVELY CORRELATED TO 7 = NEGATIVELY CORRELATED)

Activities Related	Rating
Teaching/Research	2.0
Research/Service	4.1
Service/Teaching	2.5

TABLE 69

EXPECTATIONS ABOUT CHANGES IN WEIGHTS FOR PROMOTION/TENURE DECISIONS BETWEEN NOW AND 1995 BY ACTIVITY, PROMOTION LEVEL, TYPE OF INSTITUTION, AND RESPONDENT GROUP (1 = INCREASE TO 7 = DECREASE)

	Tenure Decision					
	Doctoral Granting		Nondoctoral Granting		Overall	
Activity	Faculty	Deans	Faculty	Deans	Faculty	Deans
Teaching	4.3	3.6	4.7	4.2	4.6	4.1
Research	2.8	3.0	2.3	2.5	2.4	2.6
Service/Admin.	4.3	4.2	4.3	4.7	4.3	4.6

Significant at $p < .05$. ——

established beyond the accounting unit. To arrive at an estimate of this control, the respondents were asked to give their assessments of the success rates for faculty considered for tenure/promotion at various levels. Above the accounting unit level, they were asked to assume that the candidate had been successful at the lower level(s). By multiplying the success rates at each level, an overall estimate of the success rate was determined.

The interest lies in changes over time not only because they are central to the Committee's charge, but also because they may indicate the extent to which faculty are likely to budget their time commitments to different criteria. For example, if there were either no probability or absolute certainty of promotion then, ceteris paribus, one might expect faculty to perform solely to satisfy their own job satisfaction preferences, ceteris paribus. However, when probabilities lie between these two extremes, different behavior is likely to arise. For example, if the overall probability of success decreases over time, one might expect to see faculty concentrating on the most critical criterion more intensively than those in the past, as less room for variation in behavior would be likely.

Figure 16 conveys the essence of the success rates indicated by the respondents for various time periods, as well as a preview of the extent of control exercised by the various organizational levels. Although the focus in this section is on the tenure decision, it differs only very slightly from the promotion decision. Responses used to generate the means relevant to 1961–66 come from only the early faculty group. Similarly, those for 1971–74 come from only the middle group. Data used in arriving at the current and future figures come from all faculty responses.

The general trend over time is clearly decreasing. For example, the university approval rate drops from nearly 90 percent in 1961–66 to an expected 55 percent by 1995. Moreover, note that between 1961–66 and 1971–74 a sharp drop appears for all organizational levels. Because the 1961–66 figures contain only members of only the early group, some of this decline may be attributable to their optimism vis à vis other faculty. Yet that group's influence is included in both the current and future figures and the temporal declines persist. Thus, according to the respondents, the university and the college currently play active roles roughly equivalent to that played by the accounting unit. Furthermore, both the university and college roles are expected to increase by 1995. The Committee concluded that tenure criteria are set—or at least heavily influenced—by persons situated at higher levels within the organization and that these persons will probably increase the extent of their influence in the foreseeable future.

Figure 17 focuses on the extent of the difference in the exercise of university versus college/accounting unit involvement at D-G institutions over time. To the extent

FIGURE 16

SUCCESS RATES FOR FACULTY SEEKING TENURE BY ORGANIZATION LEVEL AND TIME

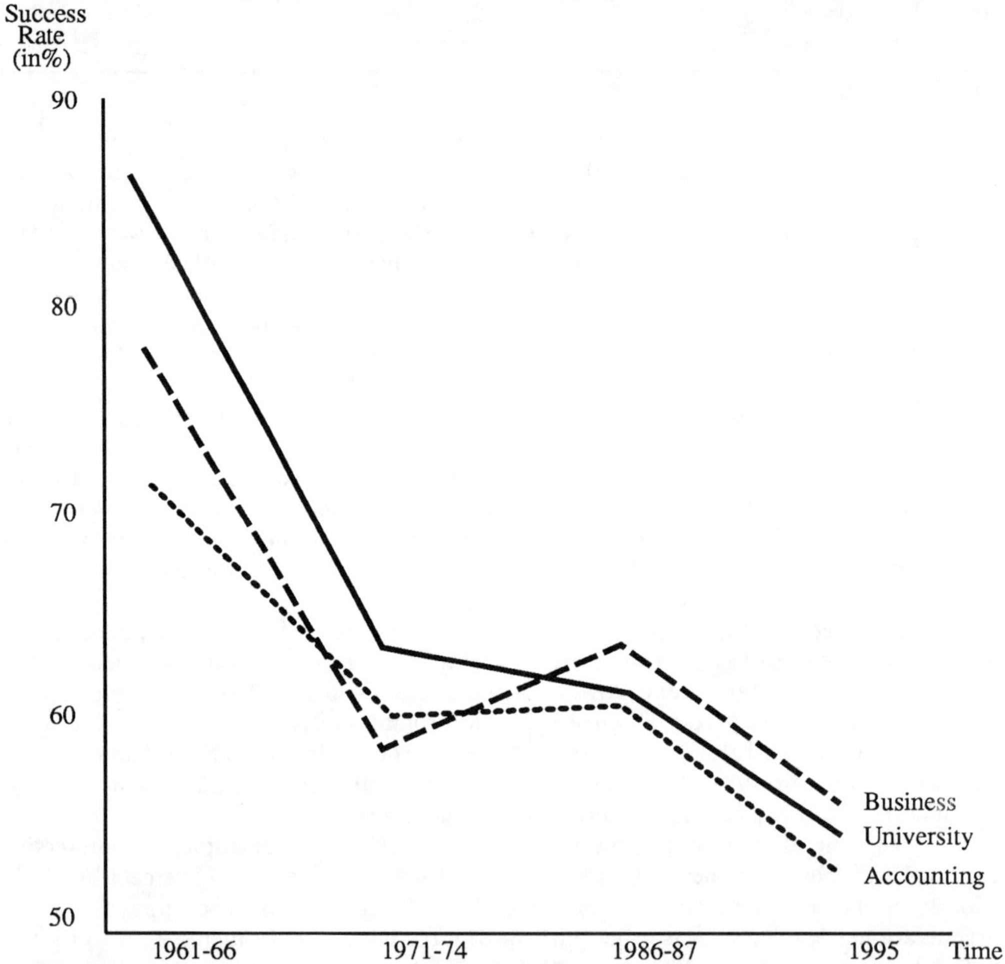

Note: Success rates at the higher organizational levels are conditioned on a favorable recommendation from the lower organizational level(s). A 100 percent reading at the university level should be interpreted as indicating that all faculty seeking tenure who successfully cleared the accounting and college levels would be promoted. This 100 percent reading at the university level would imply *no* exercise of control on tenure decisions at the university level.

that the heights at the same time period differ, the university level is quite involved. That is, the rate at which the university level approves tenure is positively related to the *difference* between the two heights. (No difference in the heights would imply no university control.) It is apparent that the university level became more important over the first three points in time but that its influence is expected to remain about the same or diminish slightly between now and 1995. Nevertheless, its influence makes a significant difference both statistically and practically.

Figure 18, which is the ND–G institution's counterpart to Figure 17, reflects a much greater role on the part of the university relative to the college/accounting unit when

FIGURE 17

SUCCESS RATES FOR FACULTY SEEKING TENURE AT DOCTORAL-GRANTING INSTITUTIONS BY COLLEGE AND OVERALL BY TIME

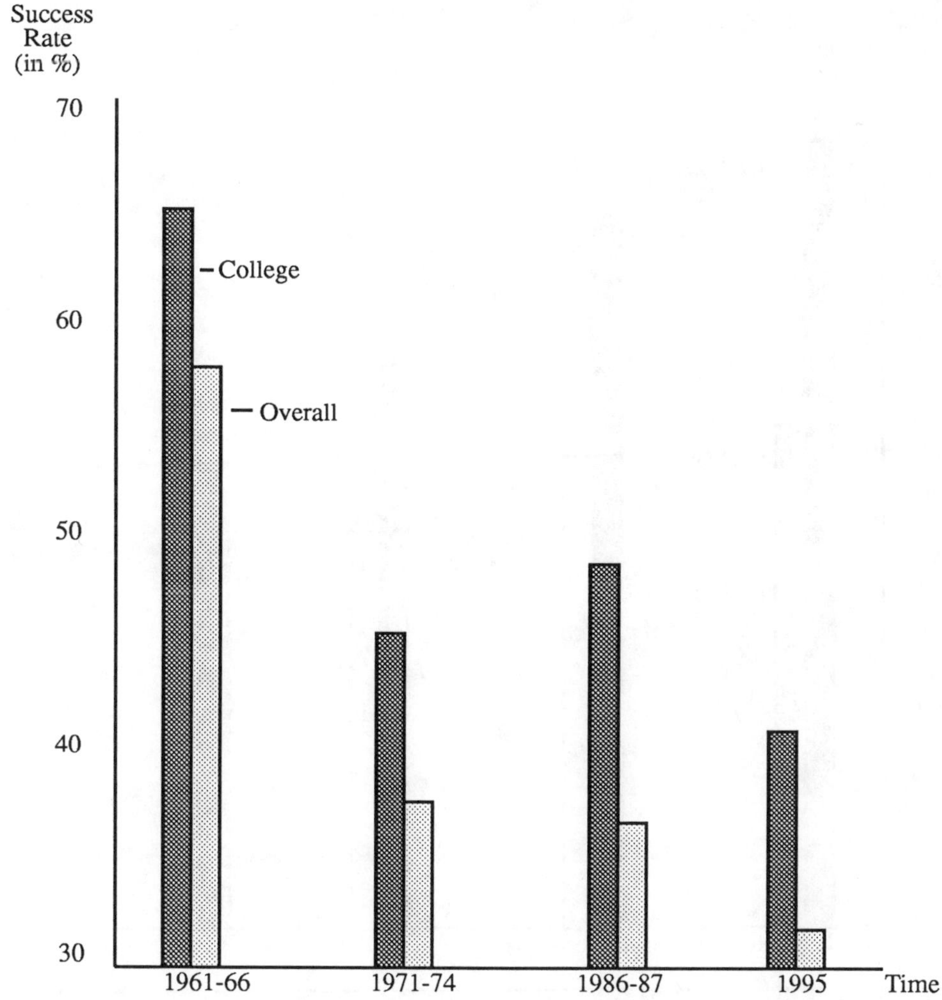

Note: College success rate consistently appears to the left and is taller for each time period.

contrasted with D-G schools. The pattern of the relationship between organizational levels over time is also substantially different from that of the D-G schools. As in several of the areas discussed earlier, the behavior of the ND–G schools appears to lag that of the D-G schools. One possible explanation for the greater relative involvement by the university level at ND–G institutions may well be their generally smaller size and reduced likelihood of having separate college and accounting units. As a consequence, the university may feel the need to play a more active role in controlling the tenure criteria.

FIGURE 18

SUCCESS RATES FOR FACULTY SEEKING TENURE AT NONDOCTORAL-GRANTING INSTITUTIONS BY COLLEGE AND OVERALL BY TIME

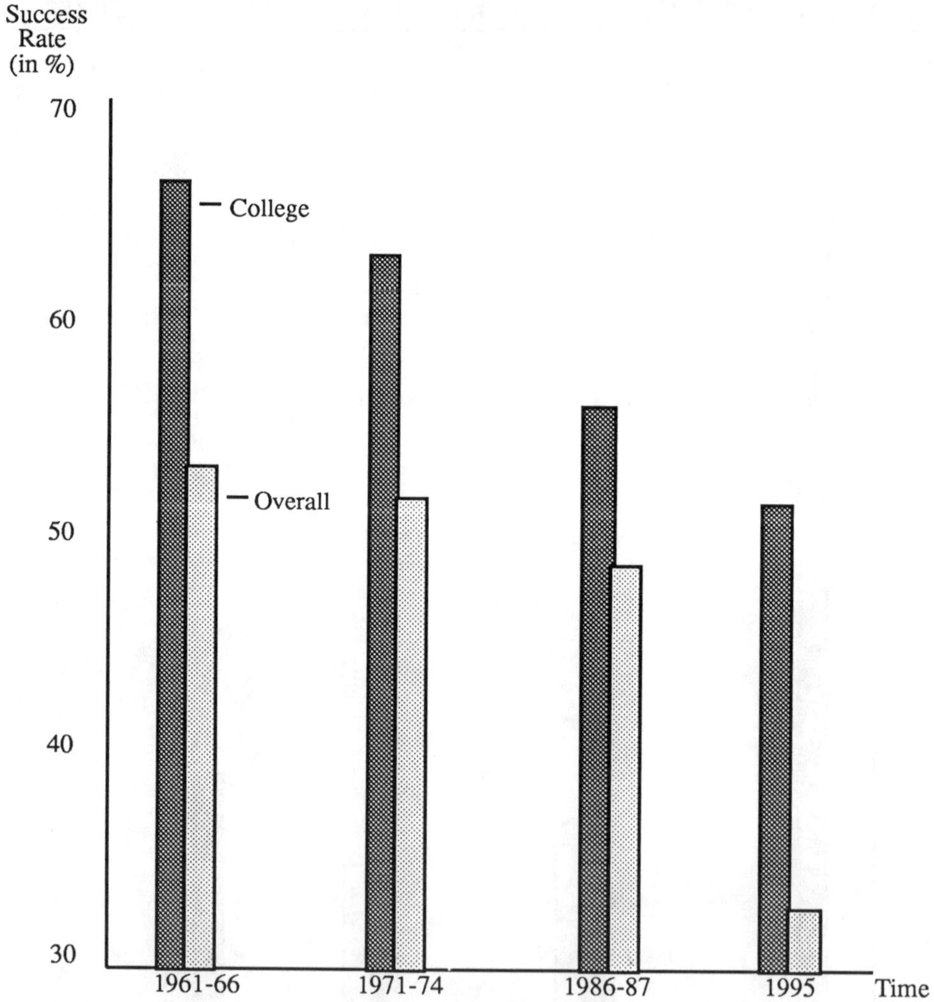

Note: College success rate consistently appears to the left and is taller for each time period.

Figure 19 presents the overall success rates over time by D-G and ND–G institutions. As previously, the sharp decline in the perceived success rates at D-G schools leads the decline at ND–G institutions. But by far the most striking trends are the magnitudes of the declines in overall success rates over time. For D-G schools, the rate plummets from 60 percent in 1961-66 to an expected 32 percent by 1995. Comparable figures for ND–G schools are 53 percent and 31 percent. Unless gross error in the respondents' beliefs exists, there seems to be little doubt that tenure has become far more difficult to obtain over the past 25 years and is likely to become even more difficult in the foreseeable future.

No doubt much of this decline in the success rates for faculty seeking tenure has come as a result of an increase in the supply of doctorally qualified faculty and the decline in the population of college students. In addition, it is likely that economic

FIGURE 19

OVERALL SUCCESS RATES FOR FACULTY SEEKING TENURE BY TIME AND TYPE OF INSTITUTION

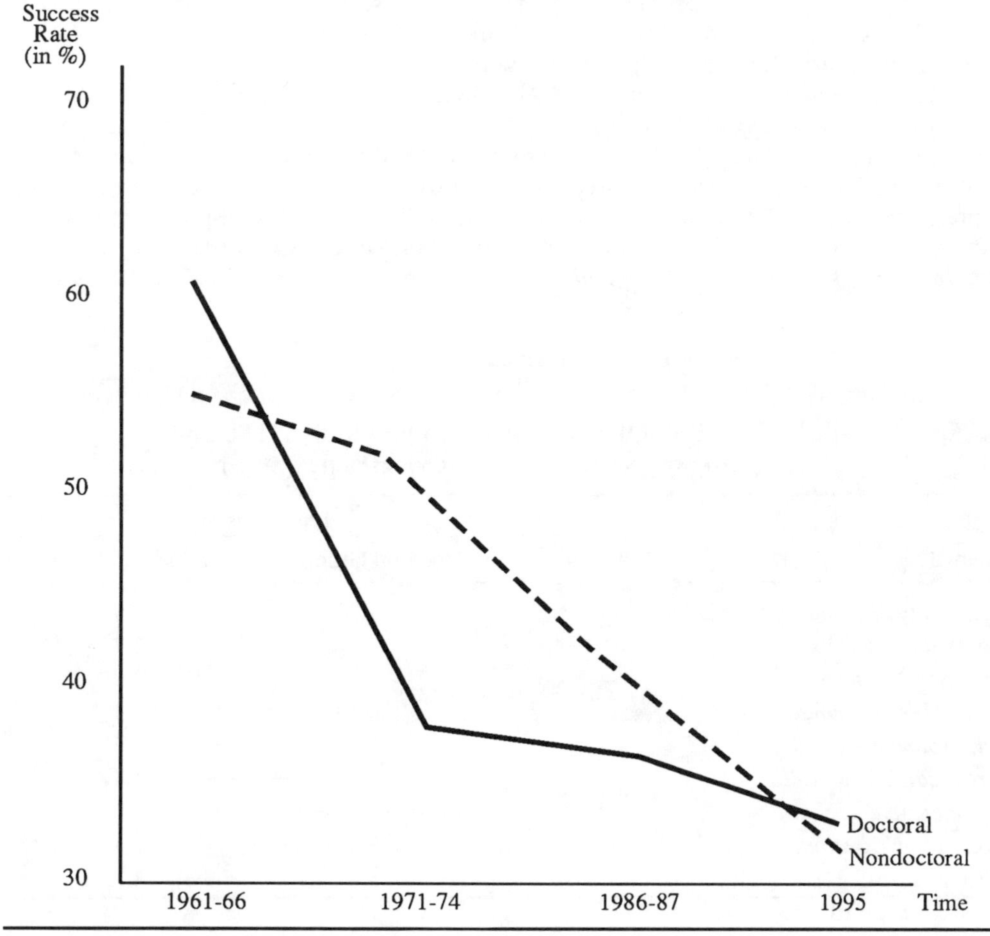

instability beginning with several recessions in the late 1960s has played a role in these trends. Future declines are probably also influenced by the assertion that the population of 18 to 22 year olds in the United States is expected to decrease by 25 percent in the decade ending in 1994 (Pierce-Snyder, 1985). In an earlier section, a forecast that predicted a 6 percent decline in university enrollments was noted.

The trends noted in this section are likely to have substantial consequence on implementation of the recommendations of the American Accounting Association Committee on the Future Structure, Content, and Scope of Accounting Education (1986). That is, if research assumes such a pivotal role in tenure/promotion decisions and if the tenure/promotion success rate falls substantially, from where will the desire to create new curricula and involvement in interactive teaching come? These issues will be revisited later.

Publication outlets. Earlier, evidence was presented that the current editions of the six academic journals studied by Vasarheyli et al. (1986) contain articles that rely almost exclusively (98 percent) on rigorous methodologies. This section presents information that contrasts faculty perceptions of differences between academic and practitioner journals. The latter journals typically do not involve rigorous theoretical formulation supported by sophisticated methodologies. The major purpose here is to determine the perceived importance of these different types of journals in the promotion/tenure decision, especially over time. It is *not* the purpose to make a normative statement as to the quality of these journals.

So that this issue could be studied, the respondents were asked to indicate the positive significance that they perceived to be attached to the various journals listed in Table 70. The selection of journals was not intended to be exhaustive but representative of different types of journals within the academic and practitioner areas. For example, the work of Howard and Nikolai (1983) suggests that the main articles in the *Journal of Accounting Research* are quite similar to those in *The Accounting*

TABLE 70

SIGNIFICANCE OF MAIN ARTICLES FOR PROMOTION AND TENURE DECISIONS BY JOURNAL AND TYPE OF INSTITUTION (1=VERY SIGNIFICANT, 7=NOT SIGNIFICANT)

	Type of Institution		
Journal	Doctoral Granting		Nondoctoral Granting
Journal of Accounting Research	1.2		1.5
Journal of Business	3.1		3.7
Decision Sciences	3.2		3.0
Journal of Accountancy	4.1	—	2.3
CPA Journal	5.1	—	3.6
Practical Accountant	5.9	—	4.4
Management Accounting	3.7	—	3.0
Journal of Taxation	3.4	—	2.5
EDP Auditor	5.0	—	3.7

Significant at $p < .05$. —

Review when compared to all publication outlets available to accounting faculty. Thus both were not included. Referring to Table 70, the first three journals were viewed as academic journals, the next three as general practitioner journals, and the last three as specialized practitioner journals. The questionnaire asked all respondents about the current significance of these journals. In addition, respondents in the early and middle groups also were asked to make similar assessments for the first three years of their academic careers. As with similarly structured questions, MANOVA was used to analyze data in this section.

The data in Table 70 indicate that academic journals are viewed currently as having positive significance at both D-G and ND–G schools. In general the ratings are more favorable for academic journals than practitioner journals although two of the specialized practitioner journals—*Management Accounting* and the *Journal of Taxation*—tend to rate well. One possible explanation for the greater credence of these two journals may be that during the period of the study there were no academic journals in these areas that possessed widespread support. In addition, it may be that because the tax area normally involves more complex codified knowledge than other accounting areas, greater significance is attached to mastering these complexities and writing about them for practitioner consumption.

The most striking difference in Table 70, however, is the marked discrepancy that exists between D-G and ND–G schools with regard to practitioner journals. The practitioner journals are viewed as uniformly more significant for tenure/promotion decisions at ND–G schools. This difference is particularly acute for the *Journal of Accountancy*, by far the premier practitioner journal in terms of circulation. Faculty at nondoctoral schools rank the *Journal of Accountancy* second only to the *Journal of Accounting Research*, but faculty at doctoral schools place it sixth among the nine journals represented.

Table 71 reports the only significant interactions detected in the analysis of the current importance of various publication outlets. The pattern reflected in this table indicates a growing importance of academic journals over start times—particularly at nondoctoral schools. For example, members of the new groups do not register a significant difference for any of the journals. Accordingly, because there are likely to be

TABLE 71

SIGNIFICANT INTERACTIONS INVOLVING JOURNAL, TYPE OF INSTITUTION, AND/OR START DATE

Journal	Start Date	Type of Institution: Doctoral Granting	Nondoctoral Granting
Journal of Business	Early	3.3	4.3
	Middle	3.1	3.6
	New	3.0	3.1
Decision Sciences	Early	3.3	3.9
	Middle	3.4	2.6
	New	2.7	2.8

These interactions are significant at $p < .05$.

more doctorally qualified faculty added to ND–G schools' faculties than D-G schools' faculties in the near future, these journals may play increasingly important roles at these institutions. The analysis between faculty members and deans for the current importance of various journals uncovered no statistically significant differences. It should be noted, however, that the sample size for deans was far smaller than that for faculty.

Tables 72 and 73 support the interpretations noted above. Both tables relate to the importance in tenure/promotion decisions attached to main articles in various journals for the early phase of the respondents' careers. Table 72 indicates approximately the same relationships that existed between academic journals and type of institution noted earlier. Table 73, on the other hand, reinforces the emerging significance of academic journals and the slow diminution of practitioner journals among faculty at various start

TABLE 72

SIGNIFICANCE OF MAIN ARTICLES FOR PROMOTION AND TENURE DECISIONS EARLY IN CAREER BY JOURNAL AND TYPE OF INSTITUTION (1=VERY SIGNIFICANT, 7=NOT SIGNIFICANT)

	Type of Institution		
Journal	Doctoral Granting		Nondoctoral Granting
Journal of Accounting Research	1.3		1.6
Journal of Business	2.8	———	3.2
Decision Sciences	3.1		3.1
Journal of Accountancy	3.5	———	2.1
CPA Journal	4.6	------	3.4
Practical Accountant	5.3	———	3.9
Management Accounting	4.0	———	2.6
Journal of Taxation	3.1	------	2.5
EDP Auditor	4.6	———	3.4

Significant at p < .05. ——
Significant at p < .10. ---

TABLE 73

SIGNIFICANCE OF MAIN ARTICLES FOR PROMOTION AND TENURE DECISIONS BY JOURNAL AND START DATE (1=VERY SIGNIFICANT, 7=NOT SIGNIFICANT)

	Start Date			
Journal	Early		Middle		New
Decision Sciences	3.8	------	2.9		2.8
Journal of Accountancy	2.3		2.1	———	3.2
Management Accounting	2.9		2.7	———	3.3
EDP Auditing	3.6		3.5	———	4.2

(In each row of Table 73, a solid bracket line also joins the Early and New values.)

Significant at p <.05. ___
Significant at p <.10. – –

dates. The impact and timing of the change is especially noteworthy regarding practitioner journals. All three of the practitioner journals that showed substantial declines across the faculty start-date groups showed significant declines only for the middle and new groups. And, as shown in Table 10, the population of doctoral faculty in accounting increased markedly during the time horizon represented by these two groups, with approximately two-thirds of all accounting doctorates currently on faculties produced since 1971.

Although the trend reflects overall significance, there are hints that new faculty at D-G schools take a particularly dim view of the importance of practitioner journals in helping achieve tenure/promotion. For example, new faculty at ND–G schools assigned an average response of 2.7 for the *Journal of Accountancy*, and those at doctoral schools a 4.6. Comparable averages for members of these two groups for *Management Accounting* were 2.9 and 4.6, respectively, and for *EDP Auditing* they were 4.0 and 4.9, respectively.

Figure 20 presents a picture of changes over time in the significance of main

FIGURE 20

SIGNIFICANCE OF MAIN ARTICLES FOR PROMOTION AND TENURE DECISION BY TYPE OF INSTITUTION, JOURNAL, AND TIME (1 = VERY SIGNIFICANT; 7 = NOT SIGNIFICANT)

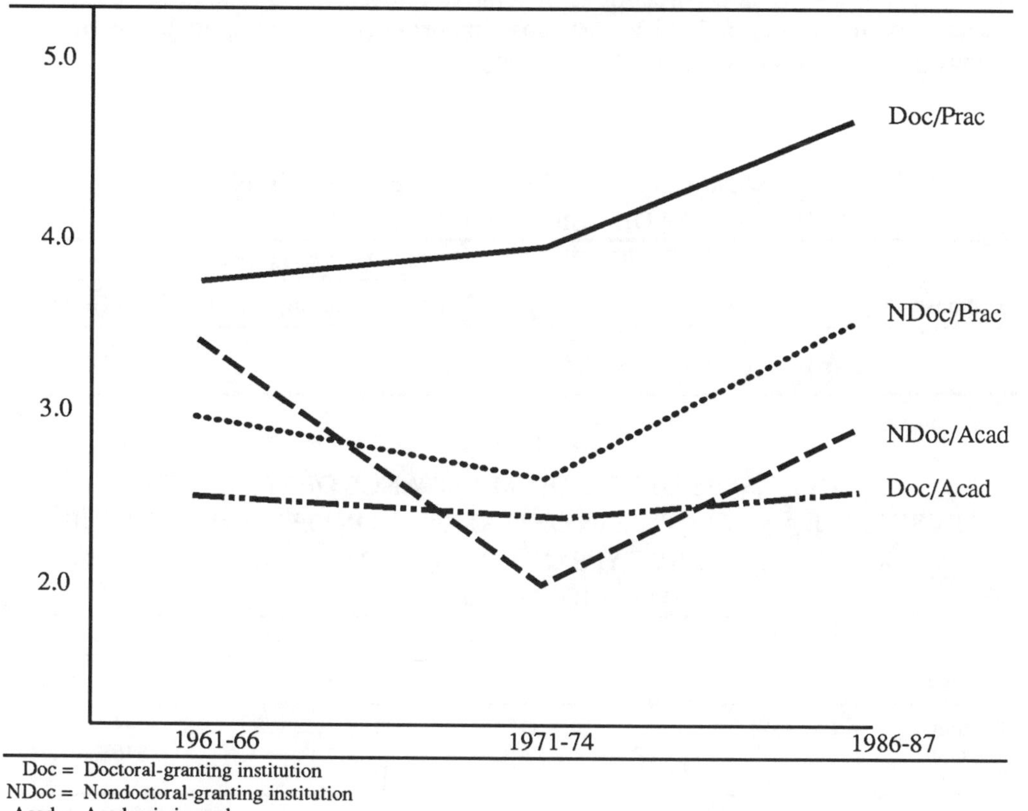

Doc = Doctoral-granting institution
NDoc = Nondoctoral-granting institution
Acad = Academic journal
Prac = Practitioner journal

articles for tenure/promotion decisions. The figures for 1961-66 are based on responses from members only of the early group, for 1971–74 from members of the middle group, and for 1986–87 from members of all groups. The top line shows that practitioner journals have lost considerable significance for tenure/promotion decisions over time at D-G schools. A similar pattern seems to be developing at ND–G schools. This lag pattern between doctoral and nondoctoral schools is consistent with the trends noted in several of the other factors.

Academic journals have remained stable in their importance at D-G schools and have generally gained importance over time at ND–G schools. The trend of decreasing importance at ND–G schools between 1971–74 and 1980–81 probably indicates the impact that members of the early group have on the overall mean for 1980–81 because members of this group do not consider academic journals to be as significant as members of other groups at nondoctoral schools (Table 71).

Market values. The above data suggest a strong case for the importance of research in tenure/promotion decisions. Another variable used by many institutions in arriving at compensation decisions is the perceived market value of the faculty member. Table 74 presents information gathered from the dean respondents; it supports the proposition that this variable is used widely for such decisions.

To determine the extent to which teaching, research, and service entered into the market value assessment, the deans were asked to allocate 100 points among the three areas based on their perceptions of relative importance. Table 75 indicates that research performance tends to be the most important factor, no matter whether the school grants or does not grant doctoral degrees. The weight placed on research in

TABLE 74

DEANS CONSIDERING MARKET VALUE IN COMPENSATION DECISIONS BY TYPE OF INSTITUTION

	Type of Institution	
Response	Doctoral Granting	Nondoctoral Granting
Yes	21	33
No	4	3

TABLE 75

DEANS' ASSESSMENTS OF IMPORTANCE OF TEACHING, RESEARCH, AND SERVICE IN DETERMINATION OF MARKET VALUE BY TYPE OF INSTITUTION (ON A 100-POINT SCALE)

	Type of Institution	
Criterion	Doctoral Granting	Nondoctoral Granting
Teaching	28	39
Research	59	46
Service	10	9

Significant at $p<.05$. ———

the market valuation decision, however, is considerably greater at D-G schools, which is understandable because earlier results indicated that the type of research record is likely to be quite different at the two types of institutions.

One other item that differed between type of institution, but not significantly, was the shift across different ranks. For D-G schools, research was emphasized more heavily at the assistant rank (64 points) and less heavily at the full rank (56 percent). For ND–G schools, the reverse held (44 points for assistants and 49 points for fulls). Teaching remained stable across ranks for D-G schools and decreased slightly (41 to 36) for ascending ranks at ND–G schools. In comparison, service increased slightly across ranks for both types of institutions (6 to 13 for doctoral and 8 to 10 for nondoctoral).

Perhaps the relative weightings of teaching and research are quite arbitrary because many deans believe that performances in the various areas generally tend to be correlated (see Table 67). To emphasize this perception, we point to a recent interview with Dean Thomas A. Bausch (1987), then President of the American Assembly of Collegiate Schools of Business. He stated: "The key element to excellence in teaching—more and more obvious to me—is research. There's no such thing as an excellent teacher over the long run, unless that teacher is solidly research grounded." To a lesser degree, performance in service and teaching are also perceived to be positively related. However, the results indicate that the relationship between performance in the research and service areas tend to be spuriously related.

Salary

The respondents ranked increased salary levels as having the third most favorable effect on the increased quality of accounting education over the past 25 years, assigning it a mean rating of 2.5. In an earlier section dealing with the influence of accreditation—especially the requirement of the doctoral degree for terminal status—the impact that the resulting shortage of accounting faculty had on beginning salary levels was discussed. Figure 14 indicated that accounting faculty have fared well compared to other faculty and that new assistant professors have fared very well. There can be little doubt that the sharp increase in salary levels over time has contributed favorably to the insurgence of new talent into the accounting professorial ranks.

One problem, often discussed by accounting administrators because of its contribution to conflict within the accounting unit, is the resulting salary compression that has occurred during this period of rapid faculty growth. Salary compression can be defined as the relative lack of premium associated with higher academic rank. Figure 14 indicates that the overall relationship of accounting salaries to other faculty salaries has not changed drastically during the 13-year period addressed. In the 1974–75 period this ratio was 1.10 and in the 1986–87 period, only 1.15. The figure also indicates far more dramatic relative growth in the assistant and associate salaries. The change in ratios from the 1974–75 period to the 1986–87 period by rank were (1) assistant, 1.16 to 1.34; (2) associate, 1.12 to 1.26; and (3) full, 1.08 to 1.12.

To arrive at a better comparison, Figure 21, which contrasts accounting professor salaries by rank to full accounting professor salaries, was constructed. As shown in this figure the ratio of assistant to full professor salary for the 1974–75 period was .69 and the ratio of associate to full professor salary was .80. Although the 1986–87 ratio of associate to full professor salary had remained nearly the same (.81), the ratio of

FIGURE 21
RATIO OF ACCOUNTING PROFESSORS' SALARIES TO FULL ACCOUNTING PROFESSORS' SALARIES BY RANK AND TIME (1974-86)

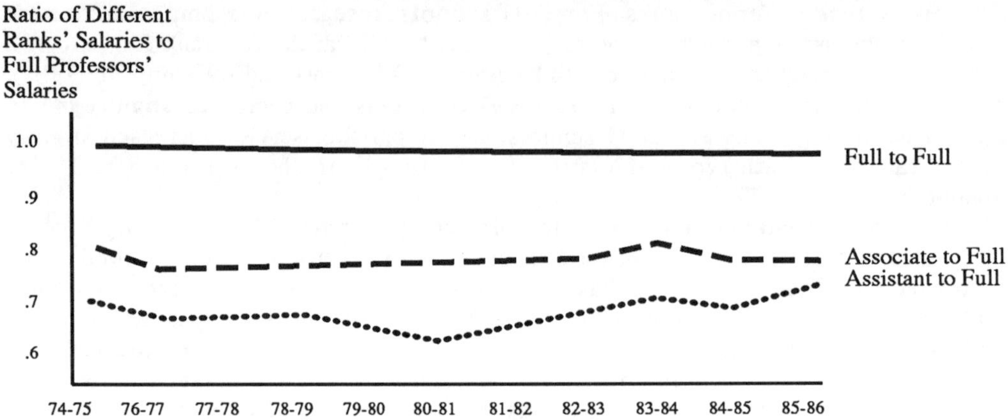

assistant to full professor salary had climbed substantially (to .75). Additional evidence of salary compression is provided by Jacobs and Herring (1987), whose study found the mean differences in the price-level adjusted salaries of assistant to associate and full accounting professors to be statistically significant over the 1979–80 to 1984–85 time horizon.

These data, per se, do not result in overwhelming evidence of serious salary compression. However, other factors bear on the saliency with which salary compression is perceived by faculty. Foremost among these factors is the normal summer salary that is guaranteed to new assistant professors at many schools. The salaries are guaranteed due to market conditions and allow new assistant professors to spend their summer time exclusively on research. The justification for such salaries lies in the belief that establishing a research record is very important to new faculty because it plays such an important role in the tenure decision as discussed earlier. In addition, failure to attain tenure within a set time period (usually six years) nearly always results in termination.

Figure 22 indicates the percentage of schools offering summer research funds to new assistant professors. In general, the temporal pattern has been quite erratic, which may well be attributable to shifts among the sample respondents in the Administrators of Accounting Programs Data Base (AAP). Nevertheless, more than half of all schools responding for the 1986–87 academic year offered guaranteed research support. The relative amount of support has stayed quite stable over the period for which the AAP has existed. That is, the summer support averages one-sixth of the academic year base salary and extends for two summers. However, at more research-oriented schools, it is not uncommon for the package to be two-ninths of the academic year salary for a period of three years. Thus, when assistant salaries reflect this one-sixth salary increase, their adjusted salary becomes greater than that of associate professors, and the ratio of assistant to full professor salary becomes .88.

Another concern is that full professors shoulder the bulk of the service responsibilities during the academic year and that these responsibilities do not enter heavily into the reward structure. The survey data support the conclusion that service activities play a small role in the reward structure compared to teaching and research. However, the data do not support the conclusion that faculty in different start-date groups differ significantly on the time devoted to service or teaching during the academic year. In evaluating this conclusion, it should be remembered that the survey data do not consider the efficiency with which faculty execute duties. The data also cut

FIGURE 22

PERCENT OF NEW HIRES WITH SUMMER RESEARCH SUPPORT—GUARANTEED AND GENERALLY AVAILABLE OVER TIME

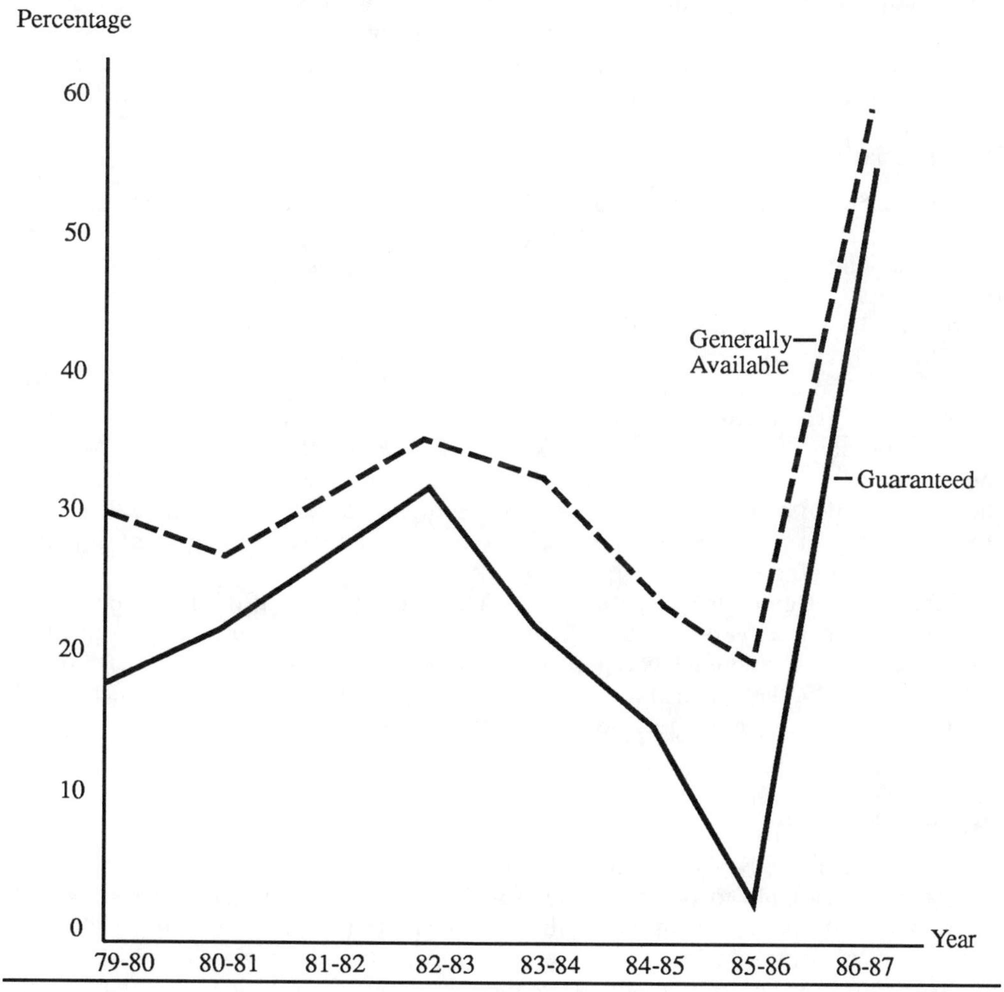

Source: Williams et al., AAP Data Base (1979—80, 1982–86).

across many different types of universities; this may introduce high variation, resulting in the lack of significant differences. Finally, the issue of compression may be most serious at universities undergoing a change in their development. That is, when universities move from a "teaching" university to a "research" university the stress may be especially noticeable.

Faculty in earlier times spent more time on teaching, which played a greater role in the reward structure then. They conducted their research with little or no special financial assistance (e.g., summer research support). The research methodologies presently common in many top accounting journals (see earlier discussion) were not taught in many of their doctoral programs. Those who did not embrace the current methodologies as they came into accounting research find themselves faced with very significant start-up costs to acquire such knowledge. And this demand for significant investments of time and energy comes at a time when members of both the early and middle groups acknowledge that they spend significantly less time on research than they did in their early careers. Now that research plays a heavier role, their mix of talents is not so positively valued as it was in the past. As Jacobs and Herring (1987) note, the full professors who have been least affected by the salary compression trend are those who have continued to be active in research or who have been full-time administrators.

Paid Sabbatical Leaves

Paid sabbatical leaves are another feature of the professorial environment that differs generally from that found in other professions. Nearly four of five (79 percent) of the respondents indicated that they had such leaves available to them at their institutions. On a 7-point scale with 1 equal to very important to 7 equal to not important, the respondents assigned the availability of these leaves a mean value of 3.2. Thus at first look it may seem that paid sabbaticals are not so important.

When asked about the importance of sabbaticals during the early part of their careers, the respondents from doctoral schools assigned them significantly more importance than those at nondoctoral schools (3.2 and 4.0, respectively). Also, the importance of paid sabbaticals for those in the new group was significantly greater than those in the middle and early groups (in chronological order, 4.0, 4.2, and 2.9). Thus the availability of paid sabbatical leaves may be quite important in terms of attracting new assistant professors.

Finally, the Committee detected a significant change among the respondents over the course of their careers. In the early phase of the careers of the faculty in the early and middle groups, respondents reported a mean of 4.1 regarding the importance of this reward. Currently, these same faculty report a mean of 3.3. This may imply that today's environment requires more release time to stay current, perform research, and so on than that of the past.

Additional Matters

Accounting faculty have the opportunity to be rewarded in other ways not generally as available to other members of the academic community. These include favorable options regarding (1) mobility due to the continuing supply-demand imbalance, (2) salary stipends in the form of sponsored faculty fellowships and professorships, (3) consulting, and (4) change of career to a practice environment. The

Committee gathered no data on these matters, but note their favorable nature.

Summary—Rewards

The analysis of the reward structure for accounting professors indicated significant flexibility compared to many other professional pursuits. Tenure/promotion decisions exhibited increasing weight on research and decreasing weight on teaching. This pattern was especially noteworthy between the early/mid-1960s and the early 1970s. This pattern is expected to continue between now and 1995. Obtaining tenure/promotion has increasingly become more difficult and will become substantially more difficult between now and 1995 (near 60 percent success now, expect near 30 percent in 1995). Criteria for successful promotion are very heavily influenced at the business college and university levels and will likely continue.

Academic journal outlets have been well received at all universities over the past 25 years. Newer faculty value them more than other faculty—especially at ND–G schools. And although practitioner journals receive far more importance at nondoctoral schools than at doctoral schools, new faculty rate these journals significantly lower than other faculty.

Deans report that a faculty member's market value is commonly considered in compensation decisions. Research performance plays the heaviest role in determining market value, and teaching plays a secondary role. In terms of relative weights, deans at D-G schools assign values of 60 and 28 percent, respectively, to these two activities. Among deans at ND–G schools, 46 and 39 percent, respectively, are assigned. Deans generally believe research and teaching performance to be quite positively correlated.

Salary levels are significantly higher (about 15 percent) for accounting faculty compared to faculty at large. Lower-ranking accounting faculty are better off than higher-ranking faculty relative to faculty overall in their same ranks. In addition, salary compression problems may be overstated generally and probably are manifest most observably in universities moving from a "teaching" orientation to a "research" orientation.

Paid sabbatical leaves are available to about 80 percent of the respondents. New faculty and faculty at D-G schools value them more heavily than faculty in other groups. The value placed on these leaves has increased over the course of the respondents' careers.

ENDNOTES

[1] Unless noted otherwise, data collected for this section were gathered from the *Statistical Abstract of the United States 1961–1986.*

[2] *Occupational Projections and Training Data* (U.S. Department of Labor, Bureau of Labor Statistics, April 1986).

[3] Z. Palmrose, "Litigation and Independent Auditors: The Role of Business Failures and Management Fraud," *Auditing: A Journal of Practice and Theory* (Spring 1987), pp. 90–103.

[4] Robert Roy and James MacNeill, *Horizons for a Profession* (New York: American Institute of Certified Public Accountants, 1967).

[5] "Blood on the Ledger," *Forbes* (May 18, 1987), pp. 202–204.

[6] *Practicing CPA* (January 1985), pp. 3–5.

[7] Ibid., note 5.

[8] "Controllership and Treasurership: Modern Definitions," *Financial Executive* (June 1964), pp. 3–6.

[9] Data reported in this section, and in the sections devoted to faculty, institutions, and financing, were obtained or compiled from a variety of sources. The primary sources were *The Condition of Education 1985 Edition* (National Center for Education Statistics, Office of Educational Research and Improvement, U.S. Department of Education); *The American Freshman: National Norms for Fall 1971 through 1984* and *The American Freshman: Twenty Year Trends, 1966–1985* (Higher Education Research Institute, University of California at Los Angeles and the American Council of Education); *Giving USA—Annual Report 1985* (American Association of Fund–Raising Council); and *Projections of Education Statistics to 1983-1984*, *Projections of Educational Statistics to 1986-1987*, and *Projections of Educational Statistics to 1992–1993* (National Center for Education Statistics, U.S. Department of Education). Projections presented within the section are based on the intermediate projections provided by the National Center for Education Statistics (thorough explanations of the assumptions and methods underlying the projections may be found within the Center's reports).

[10] If enrollment is expressed in terms of full-time equivalents, the increases prior to 1983 appear less dramatic but post-1983 decreases appear more drastic.

[11] *The American Freshman: Twenty Year Trends, 1966–1985* (Higher Education Research Institute, University of California at Los Angeles and the American Council of Education).

[12] The questionnaire defined *teaching* to include "preparation time, grading and other teaching functions as well as classroom contact time." "Dissertation and master's thesis supervision/ assistance" were also included. *Research* included "activities directly related to preparation of articles." *Continuing education* included "attendance at professional conferences and seminars, participation in formal education classes, and informal activities required to keep current with the accounting and business literature." The other terms were considered self–explanatory.

[13] The information in this section was provided by Deborah Gardner from the executive office of the American Accounting Association, Sarasota, Florida, in

December 1987.

[14] Unless otherwise noted, the data in this section came from private sources accessible to Don Dupont, Managing Director—Personnel at Arthur Andersen & Co., and a member of this committee.

[15] Unless otherwise noted, the data in this section came from AACSB archival sources that were accessible to Jane Rubin, Associate Director of AACSB Accounting Accreditation and a member of this committee.

[16] The statistics reported in this discussion come from the data base of Vasarhelyi et al. This data base utilizes a multiple-taxonomy to classify all articles published in *The Accounting Review, The Journal of Accounting Research, Accounting Organizations and Society, The Journal of Accounting Auditing and Finance, The Journal of Accounting and Economics*, and *Auditing: A Journal of Practice and Theory* from 1963 (or the date of inception) to 1986. For purposes of this discussion, rigorous research was measured as the total number of articles classified as utilizing the statistical modeling school of thought or as employing either empirical or archival—primary (i.e., CRSP and Compustat tapes) research methods.

[17] We assume that full and associate professors are tenured and that assistant professors and instructors/lecturers are not. Undoubtedly this assumption results in some error. However, there is no strong reason to believe that it distorts the pattern over time.

APPENDIX A
DATA AND STATISTICAL PROCEDURES

Using MANOVA in a strictly proper sense requires that certain ssumptions be satisfied. Among these assumptions are multivariate normality and homogeneity of variance between cells. In some cases the data exhibited violations of both of these assumptions. However, numerous simulations have shown that under certain conditions, MANOVA is robust to withstand the effects of such violations. See Timm (1980, pp. 41–87) for a summary of these studies.

With regard to violations of the multivariate normality assumption, simulations indicate that relatively large cell sizes countermand the effects of failing to meet this assumption. Because the cell sizes (22 to 31) generally exceeded the definition of large (20), we do not believe that threats to this assumption represent serious concern as to the robustness of the MANOVA findings.

With regard to the data violating the homogeneity of variance assumption, we were more concerned that MANOVA might give us false signals regarding the significances of the trends than its failing to reject a null hpothesis due to this violation. Various alternatives exist to detect the impact of this violation. Some of the measures that we considered were: (1) converting some of the measures (e.g., time per week) to percentages; (2) discarding outliers; (3) using transformations; and (4) randomly selecting respondents to reduce each of the cells to the same size. All of these techniques have their own limitations.

For example, conversion to percentages would work in some cases. However, such conversion would mask the relative impact of subjects working different amounts of time each week. Moreover, because these individuals are themselves distributed differently within cells, the validity of such a procedure may well provide more harm than help to the validity of the ultimate conclusions.

Discarding outliers has much of the same impact. A particular limitation of this technique is that outliers on one dimension of the dependent variable (e.g., time devoted to teaching per week) may not be an outlier with regard to another dimension (e.g., time devoted to service per week). Thus, this method did not seem attractive in the situation.

Transformations of the raw data directly were also considered. Kirk (1968, p. 64), in writing about univariate transformations, indicates that no transformation is likely to be satisfactory when systematic relationships do not exist between cell means and their respective variances. We investigated the relationship between cell means and their respective variances and noted no systematic pattern of relationships. In addition, we believed the interpretation of transformations would at times present substantial difficulty.

Because of the limitations noted in the above methods, we chose to discard subjects randomly to equalize the cell sizes (22), to repeat the tests and to compare the results of those tests with the original tests. Based on these results, it appears that the violations of the homogeneity of variance assumption had little effect in most of the MANOVAs employed in this study. In several cases significances were lost when this procedure was employed; however, the direction of trends registering significance in the original tests persisted.

Discarding over 15 percent of the sample obviously contributed to the loss of power in reperforming the MANOVAs. Further, the bulk of the original analysis showed little sensitivity to the lack of homogeneity. The sampling frame of reference has limitations that by necessity forced us to work with cruder estimates that we would desire (or, indeed, accept in laboratory conditions). These are discussed elsewhere and in our view represented the only manner in which to attack the charge given us. Presentation of raw data or mere means was deemed inappropriate due to report size limitations and failure to provide us or the reader with a reasonable basis for differentiating between the apparent significance of some trends as compared to others. Thus we elected to use the original results to discuss trends because we believe they represent a reasonable assessment of the movements across time and between different types of institutions.

APPENDIX B
FACULTY QUESTIONNAIRE

Several of the following questions ask you to respond on the basis of your activities over the past three years. If during the past three years, you have moved to a new academic institution, please base your responses on the length of time you have been employed at your current academic institution.

Several of the questions also ask for you to reflect on your *first three years* as a full-time, tenure track faculty member. If you were at more than one institution during this time, please base your response on the institution at which you spent most of your time.

1. Over the past three years, how many hours of work each week, on average, have you devoted to the following activities? (Please respond for the *nine-month* academic year.)

Teaching*	___hours
Research**	___ hours
Service/administration	___ hours
Remunerative outside work	___ hours
Continuing education***	___ hours
Other (e.g., textbook)	___ hours

* Includes preparation time, grading, and other teaching functions as well as classroom contact time. Also includes dissertation and master's thesis supervision/assistance.

** Includes activities directly related to preparation of articles.

*** Includes attendance at professional conferences and seminars, participation in formal educational classes and informal activities required to keep current with the accounting and business literature.

2. Over the past three years, how many hours of work each week, on average, have you devoted to the following activities? (Please respond for the traditional *three-month* summer period.)

Teaching	___ hours
Research	___ hours
Service/administration	___ hours
Remunerative outside work	___ hours
Continuing education	___ hours
Other (e.g., textbook)	___ hours

Note: This questionnaire was sent to members of the early and middle groups and differs in one important respect from that sent to members of our early group. That is, only members of the first two groups were asked to respond to attitudes/behaviors about their first three years (see items 3, 4, 6, etc.).

3. During your first three years as a full-time, tenure track faculty member, how many hours of work each week, on average, did you devote to the following activities? (Please respond for the *nine-month* academic year.)

Teaching	___ hours
Research	___ hours
Service/administration	___ hours
Remunerative outside work	___ hours
Continuing education	___ hours
Other (e.g., textbook)	___ hours

4. During your first three years as a full-time, tenure track faculty member, how many hours of work each week, on average, did you devote to the following activities? (Please respond for the traditional *three-month* summer period.)

Teaching	___ hours
Research	___ hours
Service/administration	___ hours
Remunerative outside work	___ hours
Continuing education	___ hours
Other (e.g., textbook)	___ hours

5. What percentage of your total job satisfaction over the past three years was derived from the following activities?

Teaching	___ %
Research	___ %
Service/administration	___ %
Remunerative outside work	___ %
Continuing education	___ %
Other (e.g., textbook)	___ %
Total	100%

6. During your first three years as a full-time, tenure track faculty member, what percentage of your total job satisfaction was derived from the following activities?

Teaching	___ %
Research	___ %
Service/administration	___ %
Remunerative outside work	___ %
Continuing education	___ %
Other (e.g., textbook)	___ %
Total	100 %

7. How many months of work experience did you have in the following areas *prior to* becoming a full-time, tenure track faculty member?

Public accounting, Big Eight	___ months
Public accounting, Other	___ months
Private sector, Fortune 500	___ months
Private sector, Other	___ months
Government	___ months
Other (please specify)	___ months

8. Of the work experience listed in question 7, how much was in the following specialized fields?

Auditing	__ months
Financial	__ months
Managerial/cost	__ months
Management advisory/systems	__ months
Taxation	__ months
Governmental	__ months
Other (please specify)	__ months

9. What percentage of your instruction time during the past three years was involved in teaching courses in the following areas?

Auditing	__%
Financial	__%
Managerial/cost	__%
Management advisory/systems	__%
Taxation	__%
Governmental	__%
Accounting research/methodology	__%
Other (please specify)	__%
Total	100%

10. During your first three years as a full-time, tenure track faculty member, what percentage of your instruction time was involved in teaching courses in the following areas?

Auditing	__%
Financial	__%
Managerial/cost	__%
Management advisory/systems	__%
Taxation	__%
Governmental	__%
Accounting research/methodology	__%
Other (please specify)	__%
Total	100%

11. Do you hold any degree in a discipline other than accounting?
(Please circle) Yes No

12. If yes to question 11, please list your degree(s).

Bachelor's	_____(please specify discipline)
Master's	_____(please specify discipline)
Doctoral	_____(please specify discipline)

13. How many semesters/quarters were you in residence as a doctoral and/or master's student? (Please consider a summer as equal to one semester/ quarter.)

Doctoral student ___ semesters/quarters (Please circle one)

Master's student ___ semesters/quarters (Please circle one)

14. Of the semesters/quarters listed in question 13, how many did you serve in the following capacities? (If you had mixed assignments, please estimate the equivalent semesters/quarters.)

	Doctoral student	Master's student
Research assistant	___	___
Teaching assistant	___	___
Administrative assistant	___	___
Other (please specify)	___	___

15. In what year did you begin employment as a full-time faculty member?

____

16. Using a 100-point scale, what relative weight do you perceive your academic institution currently places on the following activities with respect to tenure and promotion decisions?

	Assistant to Associate Professor	Associate to Full Professor	Tenure Decision*
Teaching	_	_	_
Research	_	_	_
Service/administration	_	_	_
Other (please specify)	_	_	_
	100	100	100

*If different from assistant to associate, please complete.

17. Assume it is 1995. During the period from 1986 to 1995, the relative emphasis for tenure and promotion decisions in your academic institution for

	Has Increased		Stayed the same			Has Decreased	
Teaching	1	2	3	4	5	6	7
Research	1	2	3	4	5	6	7
Service/administration	1	2	3	4	5	6	7
Other (if used in 16)	1	2	3	4	5	6	7

18. During your first three years as a full-time, tenure track faculty member, what relative weight did you perceive your academic institution placed on the following activities with respect to tenure and promotion decisions?

	Assistant to Associate Professor	Associate to Full Professor	Tenure Decision*
Teaching	_	_	_
Research	_	_	_
Service/administration	_	_	_
Other (please specify)	_	_	_
	100	100	100

* If different from assistant to associate, please complete.

19. What do you perceive as the percentage rate of approval for candidates considered for promotion/tenure at each of the following levels in the decision-making process? (Please fill in your estimate from zero to 100.)

	Currently		By 1995	
	Promotion, Not Tenure	Tenure	Promotion, Not Tenure	Tenure
Accounting Faculty/Unit	___	___	___	___
Business College*	___	___	___	___
University*	___	___	___	___

* In these cases, assume that the candidate has been recommended for promotion/tenure from the lower level(s).

20. During your first three years as a full-time, tenure track faculty member, what did you perceive as the percentage rate of approval for candidates considered for promotion/tenure at each of the following levels in the decision#making process? (Please fill in your estimate from zero to 100.)

	Promotion, Not Tenure	Tenure
Accounting Faculty/Unit	___	___
Business College*	___	___
University*	___	___

*In these cases, assume that the candidate has been recommended for promotion/tenure from the lower level(s).

21. How significant do you currently perceive main articles in the following publication outlets to be, with respect to the positive impact on tenure and promotion decisions? (Please circle the appropriate number or *leave unanswered* if you are unfamiliar with the nature of the publication. The publications noted are samples of various types of journals and are not intended to cover all journals.)

	Very Significant						Not Significant
Journal of Accountancy	1	2	3	4	5	6	7
Management.Accounting	1	2	3	4	5	6	7
EDP Auditor Journal	1	2	3	4	5	6	7
Journal of Business	1	2	3	4	5	6	7
Journal of Accounting Research	1	2	3	4	5	6	7
Journal of Taxation	1	2	3	4	5	6	7
Decision Sciences	1	2	3	4	5	6	7
Practical Accountant	1	2	3	4	5	6	7
CPA Journal	1	2	3	4	5	6	7

22. During your first three years as a full-time, tenure track faculty member, how significant did you perceive main articles appearing in the following publication outlets to be, with respect to their positive impact on tenure and promotion decisions? (Please circle the appropriate number or *leave unanswered* if you are unfamiliar with the nature of the publication. Even though some of the journals named below were not published at this time, please assess the relative significance of a main article in a publication of this type.)

	Very Significant						Not Significant
Journal of Accountancy	1	2	3	4	5	6	7
Management Accounting	1	2	3	4	5	6	7
EDP Auditor Journal	1	2	3	4	5	6	7
Journal of Business	1	2	3	4	5	6	7
Journal of Accounting Research	1	2	3	4	5	6	7
Journal of Taxation	1	2	3	4	5	6	7
Decision Sciences	1	2	3	4	5	6	7
Practical Accountant	1	2	3	4	5	6	7
CPA Journal	1	2	3	4	5	6	7

23. Other types of research/publication activity are noted below. How significant do you currently perceive these types of activity to be, with respect to the positive impact on tenure and promotion decisions? (Please circle the appropriate number.)

	Very Significant						Not Significant
Regional Meeting Proceedings	1	2	3	4	5	6	7
Regional Meeting Paper Presentations	1	2	3	4	5	6	7
National Meeting Proceedings	1	2	3	4	5	6	7
National Meeting Paper Presentations	1	2	3	4	5	6	7
Textbooks	1	2	3	4	5	6	7

24. Other types of research/publication activity are noted below. During your first three years as a full-time, tenure track faculty member, how significant did you perceive these types of activity to be, with respect to their positive impact on tenure and promotion decisions? (Please circle the appropriate number.)

	Very Significant						Not Significant
Regional Meeting Proceedings	1	2	3	4	5	6	7
Regional Meeting Paper Presentations	1	2	3	4	5	6	7
National Meeting Proceedings	1	2	3	4	5	6	7
National Meeting Paper Presentations	1	2	3	4	5	6	7
Textbooks	1	2	3	4	5	6	7

25. During the past three years, how many *different* course *preparations*, on average, have you done each semester/quarter?

____ semester/quarter (Please circle one)

26. During your first three years as a full-time, tenure track faculty member, how many *different* course preparations, on average, did you do each semester/quarter?

____ semester/quarter (Please circle one)

27. During the past three years, how many different course preparations have you done in total?

Undergraduate level ___
Master's level ___
Doctoral level ___

28. During your first three years as a full-time, tenure track faculty member, how many different course preparations did you do in total?

Undergraduate level ___
Master's level ___
Doctoral level ___

29. During the past three years, how many course *sections*, on average, have you taught each semester/quarter?

____semester/quarter (Please circle one)

30. During your first three years as a full-time, tenure track faculty member, how many course *sections*, on average, did you teach each semester/quarter?

____semester/quarter (Please circle one)

31. How important do you currently perceive the availability of a paid sabbatical to be with respect to your professional and academic development? ("Paid leaves" is defined here to be at least 1/2-time pay for one full academic year or full pay for 1/2 academic year. Please circle the appropriate number.)

Very Important						Not Important
1	2	3	4	5	6	7

32. During your first three years as a full-time, tenure track faculty member, how important did you perceive the availability of a paid sabbatical to be with respect to your professional and academic development? (Please circle the appropriate number.)

Very Important						Not Important
1	2	3	4	5	6	7

33. Does your academic institution currently offer faculty members paid sabbatical leaves?

(Please circle) Yes No

34. During your first three years as a full-time, tenure track faculty member, did your academic institution offer faculty members paid sabbatical leaves? (Please use above definition.)

(Please circle) Yes No

35. How important do you feel the following goals are with respect to *undergraduate* accounting education? (Please circle the appropriate number.)

	Very Important						Not Important
To master knowledge in accounting	1	2	3	4	5	6	7
To develop logical reasoning ability	1	2	3	4	5	6	7
To develop sense of professional ethics	1	2	3	4	5	6	7
To increase the desire and ability to undertake self-directed learning	1	2	3	4	5	6	7
To prepare for employment after college	1	2	3	4	5	6	7
To develop communication skills	1	2	3	4	5	6	7
To foster sensitivity to social responsibilities	1	2	3	4	5	6	7
To encourage leadership roles	1	2	3	4	5	6	7

36. How important do you feel the following goals are with respect to *master's level* accounting education? (Please circle the appropriate number.)

	Very Important						Not Important
To master knowledge in accounting	1	2	3	4	5	6	7
To develop logical reasoning ability	1	2	3	4	5	6	7
To develop sense of professional ethics	1	2	3	4	5	6	7
To increase the desire and ability to undertake self-directed learning	1	2	3	4	5	6	7
To prepare for employment after college	1	2	3	4	5	6	7
To develop communication skills	1	2	3	4	5	6	7
To foster sensitivity to social responsibilities	1	2	3	4	5	6	7
To encourage leadership roles	1	2	3	4	5	6	7

37. During your first three years as a full-time, tenure track faculty member, how important did you feel the following goals were with respect to *undergraduate* accounting education? (Please circle the appropriate number.)

	Very Important						Not Important
To master knowledge in accounting	1	2	3	4	5	6	7
To develop logical reasoning ability	1	2	3	4	5	6	7
To develop sense of professional ethics	1	2	3	4	5	6	7
To increase the desire and ability to undertake self-directed learning	1	2	3	4	5	6	7
To prepare for employment after college	1	2	3	4	5	6	7
To develop communication skills	1	2	3	4	5	6	7
To foster sensitivity to social responsibilities	1	2	3	4	5	6	7
To encourage leadership roles	1	2	3	4	5	6	7

38. During your first three years as a full-time, tenure track faculty member, how important did you feel the following goals were with respect to *master's level* accounting education? (Please circle the appropriate number.)

	Very Important						Not Important
To master knowledge in accounting	1	2	3	4	5	6	7
To develop logical reasoning ability	1	2	3	4	5	6	7
To develop sense of professional ethics	1	2	3	4	5	6	7
To increase the desire and ability to undertake self-directed learning	1	2	3	4	5	6	7
To prepare for employment after college	1	2	3	4	5	6	7
To develop communication skills	1	2	3	4	5	6	7
To foster sensitivity to social responsibilities	1	2	3	4	5	6	7
To encourage leadership roles	1	2	3	4	5	6	7

39. Many changes in the accounting education environment have occurred over the past 25 years. How do you perceive the following changes to have affected the quality of accounting education? (Please circle the appropriate number *if* you feel there has been a significant change in the direction indicated. Please leave blank if you feel there has been no change or if the change is opposite the direction indicated.)

	Favorably						Unfavorably
Increased emphasis on research methodology	1	2	3	4	5	6	7
Increased student enrollment	1	2	3	4	5	6	7
Accreditation of accounting programs	1	2	3	4	5	6	7
Increased use of multiple-choice testing formats	1	2	3	4	5	6	7
Reduced faculty teaching loads	1	2	3	4	5	6	7
Increased class size	1	2	3	4	5	6	7
Establishment of terminal degree requirement for faculty	1	2	3	4	5	6	7
Increase in codified accounting/ tax knowledge	1	2	3	4	5	6	7
Increase in codified accounting/ tax knowledge	1	2	3	4	5	6	7
Increased availability of computers	1	2	3	4	5	6	7
Reduced student/faculty interaction outside the classroom	1	2	3	4	5	6	7
Increased faculty salary levels	1	2	3	4	5	6	7
Improved quality of student	1	2	3	4	5	6	7
Increased research support	1	2	3	4	5	6	7
Stability of the four-year accounting curriculum course of study	1	2	3	4	5	6	7

40. During your first three years as a full-time, tenure track faculty member, what academic institution did you spend the majority of your time? ________________

41. What is your current age? ___

42. What is your gender?
(Please circle) Male Female

If you would like to receive a frequency analysis of the responses to this questionnaire, please complete your name and address below, and mail this page (in a separate envelope from your questionnaire) to Professor Joseph J. Schultz, Jr., School of Accountancy (BA 223), Arizona State University, Tempe, AZ 85287.

Name ______________
Address ______________
____
____

APPENDIX C
CURRENT
DEANS' SURVEY

1. Using a 100 point scale, what relative weight do you perceive your academic institution currently places on the following activities with respect to tenure and promotion decisions?

	Assistant to Associate Professor	Associate to Full Professor	Tenure Decision*
Teaching	_	_	_
Research	_	_	_
Service/administration	_	_	_
Other (please specify)	_	_	_

* If different from assistant to associate, please complete.

2. Assume it is 1995. During the period from 1986 to 1995, the relative emphasis for tenure and promotion decisions in your academic institution for

	Has Increased		Stayed the same		Has Decreased		
Teaching	1	2	3	4	5	6	7
Research	1	2	3	4	5	6	7
Service/administration	1	2	3	4	5	6	7
Other (if used in 16)	1	2	3	4	5	6	7

3. Does your academic institution consider an individual faculty member's market value when making compensation decisions?

(Please circle) Yes No

4. Irrespective of your answer to question 3, what relative weight do you perceive the following factors to have in determining an accounting faculty member's market value? (Please assume that the faculty member's high level of performance will continue in the future.)

	Assistant Professor	Associatel Professor	Full Professor
Teaching	_	_	_
Research	_	_	_
Service/administration	_	_	_
Other (please specify)	_	_	_
	100	100	100

5. Based on your experience, how do you perceive the following traditional academic performance dimensions to be related?

	Positively Correlated		No Correlation		Negatively Correlated		
Teaching/Research	1	2	3	4	5	6	7
Research/Service	1	2	3	4	5	6	7
Service/Teaching	1	2	3	4	5	6	7

6. How significant do you perceive main articles in the following publication outlets to be with respect to the positive impact on tenure and promotion decisions? (Please circle the

appropriate number or *leave unanswered* if you are unfamiliar with the nature of the publication.)

	Very Significant						Not Significant
Journal of Accountancy	1	2	3	4	5	6	7
Management.Accounting	1	2	3	4	5	6	7
EDP Auditor Journal	1	2	3	4	5	6	7
Journal of Business	1	2	3	4	5	6	7
Journal of Accounting Research	1	2	3	4	5	6	7
Journal of Taxation	1	2	3	4	5	6	7
Decision Sciences	1	2	3	4	5	6	7
Practical Accountant	1	2	3	4	5	6	7
CPA Journal	1	2	3	4	5	6	7

7. Other types of research/publication activity are noted below. How significant do you perceive main articles appearing in the following publication outlets to be with respect to their positive impact on tenure and promotion decisions? (Please circle the appropriate number.)

	Very Significant						Not Significant
Regional Meeting Proceedings	1	2	3	4	5	6	7
Regional Meeting Paper Presentations	1	2	3	4	5	6	7
National Meeting Proceedings	1	2	3	4	5	6	7
National Meeting Paper Presentations	1	2	3	4	5	6	7
Textbooks	1	2	3	4	5	6	7

8. What do you perceive as the percentage rate of approval for candidates considered for promotion/tenure at each of the following levels in the decision making process? (Please fill in your estimate from zero to 100.)

	Promotion, Not Tenure	Tenure	Promotion, Not Tenure	Tenure
Accounting Faculty/Unit	___	___	___	___
Business College*	___	___	___	___
University*	___	___	___	___

* In these cases, assume that the candidate has been recommended for promotion/tenure from the lower level(s).

9. What degrees do you hold and in what year did you receive them?

Degree	Major Field of Study	Year Received
___	___	___
___	___	___
___	___	___

10. How many years have you served as Dean of the Business College?

___

APPENDIX D
ACCOUNTING DEPARTMENT ADMINISTRATOR QUESTIONNAIRE

1. Approximately how many students (total undergraduate and graduate) are enrolled in the Business College at your academic institution? ____

2. Approximately how many accounting majors are enrolled in the undergraduate accounting program at your academic institution? ____

3. Approximately how many students are enrolled in a program leading to a master's degree in accounting at your academic institution? ____

4. Approximately how many faculty members are employed by the Accounting Department at your academic institution? ____

5. How many full-time, tenure track faculty members are employed by the Accounting Department at your academic institution? ____

6. Approximately what percentage of the Business College faculty is tenured? ____

7. Approximately what percentage of the Accounting faculty is tenured? ____

8. What is the name of your academic institution? ____

CHANGES IN ACCOUNTING EDUCATION COMMITTEE
1986-87

Jay M. Smith
Chairman
Brigham Young University

Richard Boley
Georgetown University

Bruce Budge
University of Montana

Alan Johnson
California State University, Hayward

David Luthy
Utah State University

Robert Strawser
Texas A&M University

Milton F. Usry
The University of West Florida

REPORT OF THE CHANGES IN ACCOUNTING EDUCATION COMMITTEE 1986–87

INTRODUCTION AND AAA CHARGE

CHARGE TO COMMITTEE

The charge to the Changes in Accounting Education Committee (hereafter referred to as the Changes Committee) appointed by then AAA President Ray M. Sommerfeld was as follows:

To document, in as much detail as possible, the most significant changes in accounting education that have occurred during the past 25 years so that we might better anticipate the near-term difficulties inherent in implementing the 1986 (AAA) Report of the Committee on the Future Structure, Content, and Scope of Accounting Education. President Sommerfeld amplified the charge by indicating that the work of the committee should include, but not be limited to, documenting the following changes:

1. The number of accounting programs available.
2. Enrollment trends and class sizes, in both absolute and relative terms.
3. The content of and diversity in "accounting programs."
4. Changes in teaching/learning methods, including textbooks.
5. The role of the computer in accounting education.
6. The professional school movement.
7. Accreditation issues.

The Report of the Committee on the Future Structure, Content, and Scope of Accounting Education (hereafter referred to as the Futures Committee) briefly discussed the current state of accounting education in Part II. In general, the Futures Committee believed that very little had changed in accounting education over the past 25 to 50 years.

The Committee has noted that the basic content of most university accounting educational programs has remained relatively unchanged for many years and has not fully adapted to the changing scope of accounting practice (AAA, 1986, p. 176).

After briefly discussing the curriculum, the teaching process, accounting in the university, and continuing professional education, the Committee report concluded:

This overview of the current state of accounting education indicates that future accountants are not receiving the preparation they need to meet the increased demands of the expansive, more complex profession that is emerging (AAA, 1986, p. 178).

Using this conclusion as a basis, the Futures Committee made 28 specific recommendations for change in accounting education. Change of a widespread nature is generally difficult to achieve. This is especially true in education, with widely divergent types of institutions, faculties, resources, and student bodies. In order to facilitate change, it is necessary to define more clearly and to study the forces impacting it. By studying past changes in accounting education, a group, such as the American Accounting Association, may be able to serve as a catalyst to achieve future changes. It is hoped that this report, which documents changes in accounting education since 1960, will be of value in implementing further changes in the 1990s and beyond.

COMMITTEE STRUCTURE

The Changes Committee consisted of a chairman and six members. An attempt was made to include a faculty member from each of the major specialty areas within the discipline. The following members served the Committee in these capacities:

Richard Boley—Georgetown University—Taxation
Bruce Budge—University of Montana—Financial Accounting
Alan Johnson—California State University, Hayward—Auditing
David Luthy—Utah State University—Accounting Information Systems
Jay M. Smith, Chairman—Brigham Young University—Intermediate Accounting
Robert Strawser—Texas A&M University—Auditing and Financial Accounting
Milton F. Usry—The University of West Florida—Cost/Managerial Accounting

Other important areas, such as governmental, not-for-profit, and international accounting were covered through contact with specific specialists. Two committee meetings were held during the year. This report is an outgrowth of those meetings.

COMMITTEE APPROACH TO CHARGE

Several sources were used to document the changes in accounting education that have occurred since 1960. Educational research results have been published over the 25-year period in *The Accounting Review*, AAA Committee Reports, the AAA education monograph series, *Collegiate News and Views*, and more recently in the *Journal of Accounting Education* and *Issues in Accounting Education*. Special statistical analyses of supply and demand of accounting graduates and curriculum requirements have been published by the AICPA. National education committees and associations are continually publishing material that relates to movements in education. We have reviewed these documents and will refer to several of them in this report.

Another source of information about accounting education can be found by studying accounting textbooks. It is not clear whether the market demand changes the textbooks or the textbooks create the demand. Studies do show, however, that the content and structure of an accounting textbook parallels very closely the content and structure of a typical accounting course. Authors have a responsibility to be aware of the needs of the marketplace and to produce textual materials that meet those needs. Study of textbooks clearly indicates that radical change in an established approach is rarely successful. Publishers and authors are, therefore, reluctant to initiate all of the changes they may feel pedagogically inclined to include. Over 25 years, however, some change patterns have emerged, especially with some courses. These will be identified as the different courses are discussed.

Another source solicited by the Committee was faculty whose teaching experience spans much of the 25-year period. Five to ten professors were identified in each major course area, and a standardized questionnaire was sent to these "experts" to solicit their views as to the changes that have occurred in their course areas. In most instances, the experts were contacted by letter or telephone in advance of mailing the questionnaire to determine their willingness to assist us. Most of those we solicited agreed to answer our questionnaire. Analysis of the completed questionnaires disclosed some general trend changes that seem to span the individual courses. These will be identified as "accounting education trends" and discussed in a general way. Specific comments regarding individual courses are presented in later sections of this report including the appendices. It is hoped that the material gathered will be of value in the specific recommendations arising from this Committee report.

SUMMARY OF REPORT AND RECOMMENDATIONS

The report that follows includes several summary observations and recommendations. To assist readers in focusing on these points, a summary of the report with specific committee recommendations is included in this section. Elaboration and support for these recommendations are found in the report.

Contrary to the statement made by the AAA Futures Committee that little has changed in accounting education during the past 25 years, we find that the curriculum has changed significantly as well as teaching methodology and the length of the accounting program. The changes, however, have not occurred evenly across the accounting areas. Introductory accounting, intermediate accounting, and advanced accounting courses have not experienced significant changes. Because these courses have traditionally been recognized as the core of the accounting curriculum, their relative stability has overshadowed the significant changes in systems, auditing, and taxation. The introduction of five-year professional degrees during this period at many universities has had a considerable influence on graduate accounting education.

Although there have been significant accounting education changes, the Committee identified six pervasive influences that in many cases have inhibited change, or even caused changes that have weakened accounting education. These influences are briefly summarized in the following paragraphs.

TEXTBOOK DEPENDENCY

Most accounting courses are too dependent on textbooks. Because texts typically change slowly, courses that rely too heavily on the text do not adapt to new conditions efficiently.

Recommendation

Teachers should be encouraged to use textbooks as only one source of information for students. Course syllabi should be developed as textbook independent as possible, with outside reading assignments from current literature recognized as the norm for acceptable performance.

LACK OF FACULTY REWARD STRUCTURE

Curriculum development and experimentation are not adequately rewarded in the academic environment. Everyone seems to recognize this deficiency, but very few schools are doing anything about it. Time spent in noneducational research is still rewarded more richly than is educational research.

Recommendation

This pervasive problem must continue to be addressed at individual schools. Doctoral programs in accounting must increase attention to the teaching aspect of their students' future career.

CPA EXAMINATION

The CPA examination has become a significant influence on the overall accounting curriculum and on individual courses at most institutions. Decisions as to courses to teach, topics to cover, and type of evaluative examinations to give are affected directly by the content and approach of the CPA examination. The results of the examination are now published by the National Association of State Boards of Accountancy (NASBA) by school, by graduate and undergraduate degree, and by first-time exam takers and repeats. Schools are thus being evaluated by the results of their students on the examination. The examination was never intended to be used in this way; it is only one factor governing entrance into the profession.

Recommendation

The Committee strongly believes that accounting education and sitting for the CPA examination should be separated. University review courses should be discontinued. Teachers should refrain from overuse of CPA questions on quizzes and examinations. The Committee would like to see pressure brought on NASBA to discontinue publishing examination results by school. We also recommend that a secured examination be considered by the AICPA Board of Examiners. This would enable the AICPA to develop a better testing instrument and thus not have to start over on each examination.

ACCREDITATION

Perhaps the greatest influence on the overall accounting curriculum comes from accreditation requirements. The Committee believes that although accreditation can be positive in its emphasis upon certain specified changes, it can also be negative by acting as a deterrent to experimentation in overall curriculum development. The Committee is concerned by the fact that present accreditation bodies are controlled by deans of business schools who are often not in touch with the needs of the accounting profession.

Recommendation

The Committee believes that the American Accounting Association has an obligation to continue strong efforts to influence the accreditation process because of its significant impact on what happens to the curriculum at a given institution.

FASB, CONGRESS, AND SEC INFLUENCE

Several external bodies have exerted considerable pressure on the accounting curriculum during the past 25 years. The proliferation of accounting and auditing standards has led to an attempt to include most of the standards somewhere in the courses. One of the results of this expansion has been the recommendation by many groups that accounting education be a five-year program. It does not seem wise to insulate the classroom from these external forces.

Recommendation

Professors should broaden their courses to incorporate the external forces wherever appropriate. Case material, outside guest speakers, and executives-in-residence programs represent excellent ways to achieve this breadth.

BUSINESS ENVIRONMENT

An increasingly complex business environment, which is closely related to the external organizations identified in the previous section, has also had an impact on accounting curricula. The complexities of international trade, foreign exchange, international politics, emerging Third World powers, and increasing trade and national deficits all impact accountants in carrying out their professional responsibilities. Accounting students must study business and economics in increasing depth. The Futures Committee recognized this need and incorporated a business philosophy in its recommendations.

Recommendation

Curriculum committees at each university must be aware of the need to avoid deleting breadth while adding depth through more specialized accounting courses. The Committee believes that an undergraduate degree must remain broad in nature and that specialized courses should be left for the graduate year.

The AAA Futures Committee made 28 recommendations in its report. Some of these recommendations dealt with curriculum, some with structure, some with accreditation, some with economics of accounting education, and some with faculty incentives. Members of the Changes Committee did not evaluate these recommendations but accepted them as "given." The Committee analyzed the recommendations to determine whether our study indicated the direction of any trend relative to each recommendation over the 25 years studied. Exhibit 7 (page 175) summarizes this analysis. In some cases the Committee found very little change in any direction relative to the recommendation (i.e., these years have neither worsened nor improved the conditions that gave rise to the Futures Committee's recommendation). In some cases action was already under way to meet the recommendations, either in a moderately or extensively positive way. The most troublesome condition involved the cases in which the movement was in a negative or opposite direction to the recommendation. It is the Committee's recommendation that immediate attention be directed to these areas by the educational community so that accounting education does not move further away from the Futures Committee recommendations while implementation programs are initiated. Where there has been little change, study is necessary to determine how a positive start can be made. Where there has already been a positive start, additional encouragement should be given.

GENERAL QUANTITATIVE ACCOUNTING EDUCATION TRENDS 1961–85

To understand the changes in accounting education over the past 25 years, it is important to examine the change in numbers of students, programs, and faculty resources that have occurred over this time. For example, some of the curriculum changes have been stimulated by the sheer change in numbers over the past two decades. The following sources of quantitative information were found most useful by the Committee in documenting these trends.

Doyle Z. Williams, *Accounting Education—A Statistical Survey*, AICPA. 1967–68; 1972–73; 1977–78; 1982–83 (Curriculum content of accounting programs)

U.S. Department of Education. Annual (Number of college graduates by degree and by specialty)

AACSB Membership Directory. Annual (Number of business schools with accounting programs; accreditation information)

James R. Hasselback, *Prentice-Hall Accounting Faculty Directory*. Annual (Number of business schools with accounting programs and accreditation information by year)

AICPA, *Supply and Demand of Accounting Graduates*. Annual (Number of graduating accounting majors with bachelor's and master's degrees)

Due to the different sources used, the numbers varied somewhat. Where possible, we relied on statistics from the U.S. Department of Education because of its thoroughness over the entire 25-year period studied.

STUDENT TRENDS

A dramatic change in student mix and numbers has occurred.[1]

	1961	1985	% Increase
Bachelor's degrees—total	402,000	979,000	143
Bachelor's degrees—accounting	10,632	47,005	342
Percentage of accounting to total	2.6	4.8	
Master's degrees—total	78,000	286,000	265
Master's degrees—accounting	469	3,207	584
Percentage of accounting to total	.6	1.1	

As the trend shows, both accounting undergraduates and graduates as a percentage of total graduates have almost doubled. The increase in degrees awarded to women has been much more dramatic than for men, as indicated in the following summary exhibit.

	1961	1985	% Increase
Bachelor's degrees accounting—men	10,171	23,955	136
Bachelor's degrees accounting—women	461	23,050	4,900
Percentage of women to men	4.5	96.2	
Master's degrees accounting—men	440	1,948	343
Master's degrees accounting—women	29	1,259	4,200
Percentage of women to men	6.6	64.6	

The quantitative change in the mix of men and women graduates in accounting must be considered in analyzing the change in accounting education over the last 25 years. Most of the change has occurred since the mid-1970s as revealed by these computations of accounting degrees as a percentage of total awarded bachelor's and master's degrees combined.

	1961	1965	1970	1975	1980	1985
Total	2.3	2.4	2.2	2.7	3.8	4.0
Men	3.4	3.7	3.5	4.1	4.8	4.1
Women	.3	.4	.5	1.1	2.7	3.8

It is interesting to note that the percentage of women graduating with an accounting degree as compared to those with all other degrees increased rapidly during the years when the total women college graduates as a percentage of total college graduates was also increasing. Since 1982, more women than men have graduated from college in the United States. This means that the continued increase in the number of accounting graduates can be attributed to the significant movement of women into accounting. Without such movement, accounting graduates would have declined during the last five years. Indeed, accounting undergraduate degrees awarded to men have been decreasing since reaching a high level in 1977, and accounting graduate degrees awarded to men have been decreasing since 1979. In total, accounting degrees conferred increased every year in the period 1961–85 except for the last year, 1985. Because there is a four- to six-year lag between college entrance and college degrees awarded, the decline in enrollment in accounting programs probably began in the early 1980s. Figures 1–4 graphically show these trends for both total educational degrees and accounting degrees awarded during the period 1961–1985.

FIGURE 1
BACHELOR'S DEGREES BY SEX—TOTAL UNITED STATES
1961–85

FIGURE 2
TOTAL U.S. DEGREES BY SEX
1961–85

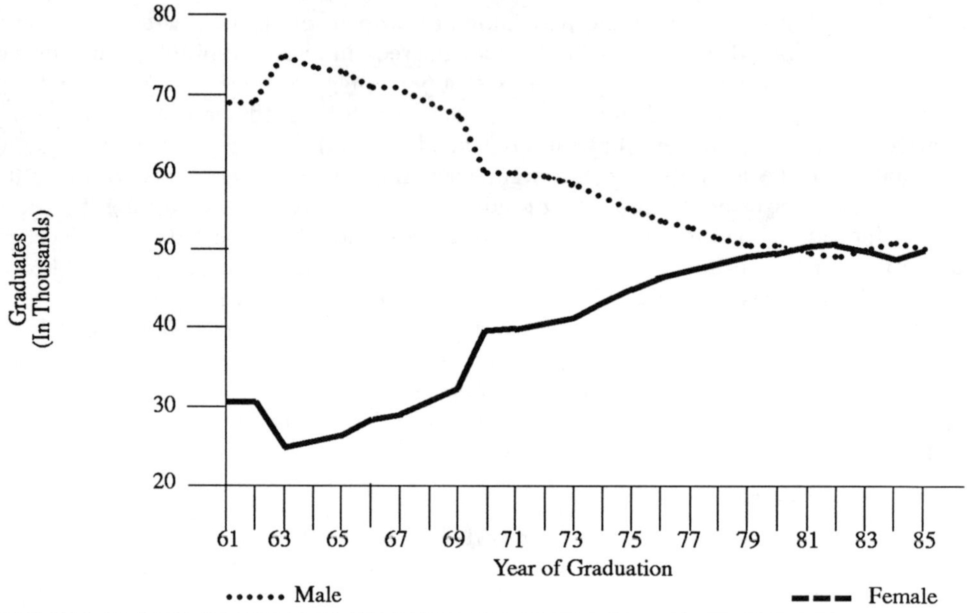

FIGURE 3
ACCOUNTING BACHELOR'S DEGREES BY SEX
1961–85

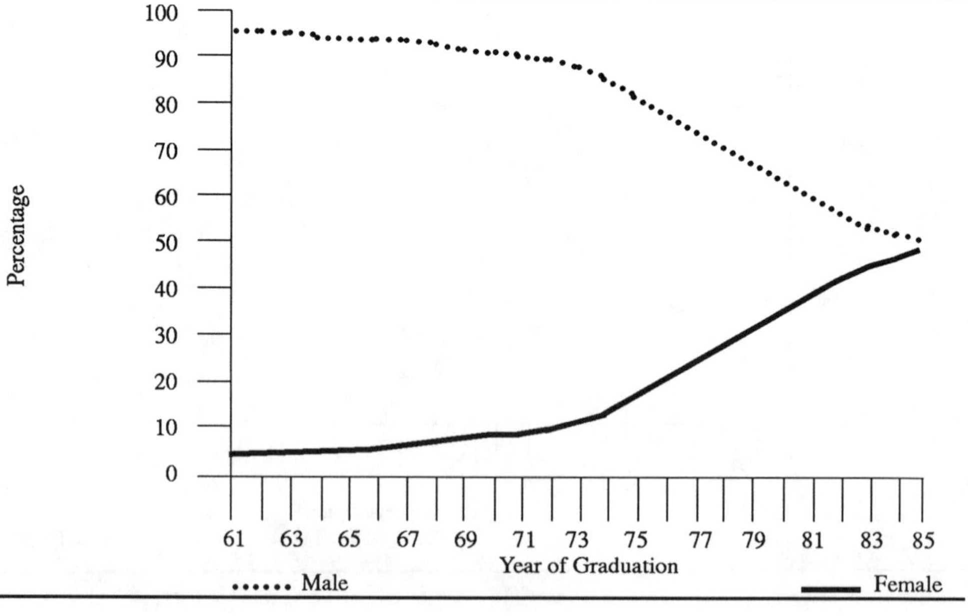

FIGURE 4
ACCOUNTING MASTER'S DEGREES BY SEX
1961–85

ACCOUNTING PROGRAM TRENDS

The increase in student graduates in accounting during the last 25 years has been reflected in two ways on accounting programs: (1) established accounting programs have been graduating larger numbers of students, and (2) more accounting programs have been established at both new and established institutions. The increase in students in the mid- and late 1970s caused such a strain on resources that many programs were forced to establish entrance criteria to restrict the number of students majoring in accounting.

Exhibit 1 summarizes statistical data concerning the number of two- and four-year schools in the United States and the number that have accounting programs. Although the data are not available for all 25 years, sufficient data exist to determine the trend. Although the number of four-year schools increased by 34 percent between 1960 and 1984, the number of four-year schools with a bachelor's degree in accounting increased by 117 percent. During this same period, the number of two-year schools increased by 210 percent, and the number with accounting programs apparently increased similarly, although no figures are available until 1966. Accreditation statistics disclose a 165 percent increase in business schools accredited by the AACSB in the 25-year period, less than a third of those being offered at four-year schools. Sixty-six schools' accounting programs have been accredited as of June 1987.

EXHIBIT 1

STATISTICAL DATA ON U.S. COLLEGES AND U.S. COLLEGES GRANTING ACCOUNTING DEGREES 1959–87

Year	U.S. Total Number of Four-Year Schools	U.S. Total Number of Two-Year Schools	Two-Year Schools with Accounting Programs	Four-Year Schools with B.S. Accounting Programs	Four-Year Schools with M.S. Accounting Programs	Number of Business Schools Accredited by AACSB	Number of Schools with Accounting Programs Accredited by AACSB	Number of Two-Year Schools Closing	Number of Four-Year Schools Closing
59/60	1,422	582		361		96			
60/61	1,431	598		365		99		7	1
61/62	1,443	598		386		105		1	1
62/63	1,468	625		373		109			
63/64	1,499	633				113		6	1
64/65	1,521	654		403		117		7	1
65/66	1,551	679		425		120		6	2
66/67	1,577	752	486	449	115	126		7	2
67/68	1,588	786		469		130		8	6
68/69	1,619	864		490		139		10	11
69/70	1,639	886	518	521	119	147		10	8
70/71	1,665	891		541		152		23	9
71/72	1,675	931	443	546	127	157		9	3
72/73	1,701	964				162		7	12
73/74	1,717	1003		581		170		7	11
74/75	1,744	1003	442	525	138	178		4	13
75/76	1,767	989	497	570	144	189		2	6
76/77	1,783	1,002				199		3	5
77/78	1,808	1,018	523	634	153	204		3	9
78/79	1,843	1,111				211		5	4
79/80	1,863	1,112	533	685	166	217		1	5
80/81	1,861	1,195				224		1	3
81/82	1,883	1,200				231	18	1	6
82/83	1,887	1,224	539	726	186	238	24	3	4
83/84	1,914	1,203	546	782	187	241	44		4
84/85	1,911	1,235				245	53		4
85/86		1,222	611			247	61		
86/87						254	66		

Sources:

U.S. Department of Education, National Center for Education Statistics, Fall Enrollment in Higher Education.
The College Blue Book, Degrees Offered by College and Subject (Macmillan Publishing Co.)
1959–73 Department of Health, Education, and Welfare, "Earned Degrees Conferred"; 1974–84, *The College Blue Book*.
Jane Rubin at the American Assembly of Collegiate Schools of Business

Textbook sales are another means to demonstrate growth in the number of accounting students. Although publishers' estimates vary somewhat as to the total market, the following number of textbooks sold annually represents information obtained from several publishers.

	1986	1960
Introductory accounting	1,000,000	500,000
Intermediate accounting	210,000	70,000
Cost accounting	250,000	70,000
Auditing	75,000	25,000

As the student numbers decrease in the 1980s, there may be pressure to alter the admission restraints in order to maintain established accounting programs. Even with the increased admission requirements, however, some evidence suggests that the quality of accounting graduates has deteriorated over the past decade. Usry (1987) reports that since 1975, the average SAT and ACT scores of CPA candidates have decreased more than the average decrease for all students during that period. Because most CPA candidates must have a degree in accounting, this study seems to indicate a quality deterioration. The Committee was not able to establish an explanation for this seeming inconsistency.

The 1982-83 Statistical Survey (Williams, 1983) reported the following accounting class size statistics in Table 23:

Principles Courses	44
Other Undergraduate Courses	32
Graduate Courses	24

Earlier surveys had not gathered this information, so the Committee was unable to identify a trend in class size during the 25-year period. Committee members believed that a gradual decline in class size overall had occurred during this period but could not substantiate this belief with documentation. Introductory accounting is probably an exception to this observation.

CURRICULUM MIX TRENDS

Accounting programs can be generally described by the mix of general, business, and accounting courses that are required. The best source of information for the average mix comes from the five-year statistical studies prepared for the American Institute of CPAs by Doyle Williams, Dean of the School of Accounting at the University of Southern California (Williams, 1968, 1973, 1978, 1983). The number of schools participating in this survey has varied over time from 61 schools in the first study in 1967-68 to 365 schools in 1982-83. Exhibit 2 is a condensed summary of Table 31 from the 1982-83 survey (Williams, 1983). These surveys show the number of *required* hours for accounting students. The number of identified hours apparently does not include the elective hours needed to equal the 128 semester hours normally required for graduation. We have inserted this information as a "plug" in the exhibit to equal 128 semester hours.

As indicated in Exhibit 2, the required nonbusiness subjects declined significantly from 1967-68 to 1977-78. The 1982-83 survey indicated a reversal of this trend, although with numbers still lower than the first two survey years. During the 15-year period the number of accounting hours required has increased slightly, and EDP and

EXHIBIT 2
ACCOUNTING CURRICULUM MIX—HOURS
FIFTEEN-YEAR PERIOD

Required Classes	1967/1968	1972/1973	1977/1978	1982/1983
Mathematics	5.5	6.0	5.9	6.6
Statistics	3.6	4.0	4.3	4.3
Economics	8.7	8.2	8.0	8.1
Business Law	5.1	4.9	4.5	5.4
Systems/EDP	1.5	2.6	3.5	3.4
Business, inc. EDP	13.2	15.0	21.3	26.0
Nonbusiness	42.3	41.9	29.8	35.4
Accounting	26.3	28.3	28.0	29.5
Total Required	106.2	110.9	105.3	118.7
Nonrequired and NA	21.8	17.1	22.7	9.3
Four-Year Total	128.0	128.0	128.0	128.0

NA : Not Available
Source : Adapted from Doyle Z. Williams, *A Statistical Survey of Accounting Education 1982/83*, Table 31 (AICPA).

computer courses have also increased. Williams observed ". . .it appears that schools have not moved a significant number of their accounting courses to the fifth year to make room for increased emphasis in quantitative methods, economics, and EDP." Indeed, as the curriculum becomes more crowded with courses, some areas have to be deemphasized. In most cases, the general education courses have suffered the most, and specialized computer, accounting, and general business courses have benefitted.

It was the belief of the Committee that accounting offerings have increased significantly during the 25-year period. A cursory review of college catalogs in 1960 and 1986 indeed does indicate a significant increase in the number of accounting courses listed. A summary of accounting courses from 20 college catalogs for the 1986/87 school year is included in Exhibit 3. Tax and computer courses and accounting seminars are listed separately from the rest of the accounting courses. It was difficult to separate graduate and undergraduate courses by number because many classes are open to both groups. We therefore arbitrarily categorized all courses with a 500 or higher number as graduate courses. As can be seen, a wide disparity exists among the schools in the number of courses listed. Of course, catalog listings have the weakness of not indicating which courses are currently being offered. Some schools keep their course listings current, but others may leave courses in the catalog even though they are no longer being offered.

A similar listing for 1960 would require obtaining catalog data from individual schools. Although this was not completed in sufficient detail to include a similar exhibit for 1960, comparison of selected schools did indicate a proliferation of accounting offerings. As an example of this change, Exhibit 4 contains a comparison in detail from the catalogs of Brigham Young University for 1960 and 1986. The most significant change is in graduate offerings as a result of the strong professional school program initiated in the mid-1970s.

EXHIBIT 3
NUMBER OF CLASSES AVAILABLE IN ACCOUNTING PROGRAM
1986–87 SCHOOL YEAR

	Undergraduate				Graduate			
School	Accounting	Tax	Computer	Seminar	Accounting	Tax	Computer	Seminar
Arizona State	13	2	1	0	7	5	1	2
Univ. of Arizona	12	2	1	0	9	5	0	3
Brigham Young Univ.	21	3	3	1	10	13	4	5
Cal State Hayward	12	10	10	8	9	10	3	4
Univ. California-Berkeley	18	4	2	0	NA	NA	NA	NA
Univ. of Southern Calif.	9	3	1	0	21	16	2	0
Univ. of Florida	9	1	1	1	17	7	1	6
Univ. of West Florida	16	3	5	1	6	4	0	0
Georgetown Univ.	16	2	1	1	1	10	0	0
Univ. of Maryland	10	2	2	0	15	2	10	1
Univ. of Minnesota	19	4	1	2	12	14	0	6
Univ. of Montana	17	2	1	6	1	0	0	6
Univ. of North Carolina	11	2	1	1	12	4	0	2
Pennsylvania State Univ.	16	3	0	5	NA	NA	NA	NA
Texas A&M	17	3	1	2	NA	NA	NA	NA
Univ. of Texas	15	3	1	3	6	2	1	3
Utah State Univ.	14	2	1	4	17	6	1	4
Univ. of Utah	12	3	3	2	26	7	6	8
Washington State Univ.	10	2	0	2	7	1	0	3
Univ. of Washington	15	4	1	1	20	2	2	1
Average	14.1	3	1.9	2	11.5	6.4	1.8	3.2

Sources: Class Catalogs from each school
Note: All classes with 500 number or above are assumed to be graduate level.
At the University of California–Berkeley, the University of Maryland, and the University of North Carolina, accounting classes are listed under Business Administration rather than accounting. As a result, some nonaccounting business classes typically listed with the accounting classes, such as business law, are not included in the totals for these three schools.

PROFESSIONAL SCHOOL MOVEMENT

One of the most significant accounting education trends of the period studied by the Committee is the emphasis upon integrated five-year accounting programs and the movement of some universities to schools of accountancy.[2] Events in the late 1960s led to the recommendation in 1968 by the AICPA Committee on Education and Experience Requirements for CPAs that, because of the great expansion of knowledge and skills necessary to be a successful accountant, five years of education should be required. In 1973 the Council of the AICPA endorsed this recommendation. As an outgrowth of these recommendations, a new association was organized in 1977 known as the Federation of Schools of Accountancy (FSA). The 20 universities that banded together to organize this federation had as their objective a program that would facilitate the adoption of five-year accounting programs in schools of accountancy. In the decade since its organization, 33 schools have become fully accredited members of the association, having achieved a sufficient level of autonomy and curriculum development to warrant inclusion. Although the format of these programs has varied from institution to institution, the integrated five year program that provides for admission in the third or fourth year into an accounting program has been most popular. Students take a mix of undergraduate and graduate courses leading to both a bachelor's and master's degree in accounting, sometimes awarded at the same time.

EXHIBIT 4
BRIGHAM YOUNG UNIVERSITY
ANALYSIS OF COURSE OFFERINGS
1960 AND 1986

Classes by Category	1960	1986
Auditing	0	1
Financial	2	3
Government	0	0
Introductory	3	4
Management	2	2
Systems	2	2
Tax	1	3
Other	1	4
Total	11	19
Undergraduate or Graduate Classes by Category		
Auditing	1	0
Financial	6	2
Government	0	1
International	0	1
Management	1	0
Systems	3	1
Tax	1	1
Other	2	2
Total	14	8
Graduate Classes by Category		
Auditing	0	3
Financial	0	0
Management	0	5
Systems	0	4
Tax	0	13
Other	1	7
Total	1	32
Overall Program Total	26	59

Many other schools have moved to a five-year program even though they have not chosen to be recognized as separate professional schools and thus not part of the FSA organization.

In 1983 Shimerda and Lewis published survey results indicating the extent of movement to five-year programs at that time. This survey was made of 201 accounting departments or professional programs listed in the 1980–81 AACSB Directory and to 44 schools that had been identified as having changed to professional school status or as being in the process of changing. At that time 26 percent of the responding institutions had adopted or were adopting integrated five-year accounting programs, 31 percent were still evaluating the possibility of a change, and 23 percent had considered and rejected the change. The remaining 20 percent had not yet considered the issue.

Although many groups have advocated five-year programs, at the time of this writing only four states, Florida, Utah, Hawaii, and Tennessee, have legislation requiring postbaccalaureate course work to sit for the CPA examination. Recruiters continue to hire heavily at the undergraduate level, especially for staff auditors. The marketplace has not yet placed sufficient emphasis on graduate education through higher salaries or limited undergraduate hiring to indicate strong professional support. This has resulted in a slower than anticipated growth in professional schools of accountancy and professional graduate accounting programs.

ACCREDITATION

PROFESSIONAL ACCREDITATION

Accreditation in professional schools began in 1904 when the council on Medical Education was established by the American Medical Association (Allyn, 1966). This initial accreditation was followed by Business in 1916, Dentistry in 1918, Law in 1929, and Engineering in 1936 (Allyn, 1966). Accounting accreditation has historically been accomplished only as a part of the accreditation performed by the American Assembly of Collegiate Schools of Business (AACSB) of entire business schools. In the 1960s and 1970s, the accounting academic community was concerned by the limited specialization permitted under AACSB guidelines. Although AAA and AICPA reports on accounting education all recommended that the total course load should comprise 20-25 percent of accounting courses, the AACSB placed a limit of 15 percent specialization in any undergraduate business program (Allyn, 1966, p. 309). Concern over this disparity was a factor in the significant interest that arose for the creation of professional schools of accounting.

ACCOUNTING ACCREDITATION

During the 1970s the discussion of separate accreditation standards for accounting received attention by most segments of the academic and professional community. In 1974 the AICPA formed the Board of Standards for Programs and Schools of Professional Accounting (Campbell, 1983). As indicated in the previous section, in 1977 a group of schools organized the Federation of Schools of Accountancy. In 1975 and 1976 the AAA formed committees on accreditation (AAA, 1977). These groups considered the benefits and costs of accounting accreditation. When it became apparent that some accreditation was going to occur, the principal issue was who would assume the responsibility for it. After lengthy negotiations, and with less than a unanimous view, the AACSB, under the direction of business school deans, was recognized as the organization responsible for the development and administration of accounting accreditation standards. In June 1980, the AACSB adopted these standards, and accreditation began in 1981. As of the summer of 1987, 66 schools had received separate accounting accreditation by the AACSB.

Three different types of accreditation are available: Type A—baccalaureate programs with a concentration in accounting, Type B—MBA with a concentration in accounting, and Type C—master's of accounting. As of 1987, 65 schools had accredited their A program, 15 their B, and 36 their C (AACSB, 1986–87; AICPA, July 1987). A school with an accredited baccalaureate program and a master's program must obtain accreditation of the latter program as well.

The accreditation standards currently applied by the AACSB include standards for faculty credentials, resource availability, and curriculum content. The latter requirement relates most directly to the work of this Committee. The standards for an undergraduate accounting degree are as follows:

1. At least 40 percent of courses in general education.
2. At least 25 percent in the following five areas included in the common body of business knowledge.
   a. Production, marketing, and finance.
   b. Economic and legal environment, ethical issues.
   c. Quantitative methods, MIS, and computer systems.
   d. Organizational theory and interpersonal communications.
   e. Integrative analysis and policy determination.
3. More than 15 percent but less than 25 percent in the following accounting topics.
   a. Financial accounting.
   b. Accounting theory.
   c. Management/Cost accounting.
   d. Managerial information and computer systems.
   e. Financial and operating auditing.
   f. Taxation.

Accreditation of accounting master's programs shall provide for greater depth and breadth in professional accounting courses. A minimum program shall include

a. All of the baccalaureate degree requirements
b. At least 30 semester hours beyond the bachelor's requirement in financial accounting, accounting theory, management accounting, computerized management information systems, audit, and tax, including 15 semester credit hours of courses restricted to graduates only (AACSB, 1988–89).

In a study of AACSB-accredited business schools conducted in 1982, 84 percent of the respondents indicated that they were planning to seek accreditation for at least one of their accounting programs (Brown and Balke, 1983).

CHANGES IN SPECIFIC ACCOUNTING COURSES

Changes in accounting education over time can be viewed either as macro changes that in turn affect the individual courses, or as micro changes in specific courses that in total tend to affect the entire accounting curriculum. The Committee attempted to look at education change from both perspectives. The resources used to analyze the change in specific courses and specialties included textbooks in the courses and a questionnaire distributed to several course experts. The courses and/or areas included in this approach were the following:

1. Introductory accounting.
2. Cost/Managerial accounting.
3. Intermediate accounting.
4. Taxation.
5. Auditing.
6. Advanced accounting.
7. Accounting theory.
8. Accounting information systems.
9. Not-for-profit accounting.

EXPERT RESPONSES

Questions were asked of the experts related to changes in the following 12 specific items:

1. Movement from undergraduate courses to graduate courses.
2. Number of credit hours to cover the area.
3. Topics in basic course in area.
4. Type of learning activities used.
5. Treatment of behavioral accounting material.
6. Inclusion of computer applications.
7. Conceptual versus procedural coverage.
8. Ethics.
9. International coverage.
10. Quantitative methods
11. Information systems approach.
12. Open versus closed-end problems.

SUMMARY MATRIX OF EXPERT RESPONSES

A matrix that summarizes the responses received from the experts for these nine courses/areas relative to the 12 specific items is included in Exhibit 5. The matrix represents change, not level of inclusion. Thus if an item is covered in a course, but its coverage has changed very little in the 25-year period being investigated, the matrix will report an "L," meaning little change. Detailed results of the questionnaire may be obtained from the American Accounting Association.

ACCOUNTING EDUCATION TRENDS

Review of the matrix and of textbooks demonstrates some general patterns over all courses studied. Very few extensive changes were noted. A notable exception is taxation. Tax education has changed extensively in several ways. The treatment of taxation as a graduate discipline has emerged as a widely accepted change during the period studied. A high demand exists for graduates of master's-level tax programs. The number of graduate tax credit hours has expanded greatly at many institutions. The integration of the microcomputer into tax classes has been more widespread than in most other courses. Because of the great volume of tax law, a more conceptual approach to teaching taxes has evolved as an alternative to the traditional, detail-rule-dominated approach. Another area that has changed extensively is accounting systems. In 1961, systems courses were few in number and generally were included as an elective in the curriculum. By 1985, entire graduate and undergraduate programs of management information systems had become more common.

Computer integration is very spotty. Many applications are very superficial in content. Relatively few complement and assist the learning process. Other applications may even impede learning because they involve only number insertions to a spreadsheet program rather than development of analytical or conceptual understanding. Much experimentation needs to be done, but inherent deterrents to change in accounting education impede progress.

An information systems approach to accounting education is not occurring. Systems courses are generally not popular. Only 17 percent of introductory auditing courses require as a prerequisite a systems course, even though over 50 percent of auditing courses have adopted a systems-cycle approach to the course as opposed to a balance sheet, account-oriented approach. Introductory accounting courses have become disclosure oriented, not systems oriented. Although the elimination of detailed

EXHIBIT 5
SPECIFIC ACCOUNTING COURSE CHANGE MATRIX

Course Area	Move to Grad. Ed	Number of Hours	Topics—Basic Course	Learning Activity	Behavioral	Computer	Conceptual/ Procedural	Ethics	Int'l.	Quantitative Methods	Int'l. Systems	Open / Closed Prob.
Introductory	L	L	M	L	L	M	L	L	L	M	L	L
Cost/ Managerial	M	L	M	M	M	E	M	L	M	M	L	M
Intermediate	L	M	M	M	L	L	M	L	L	L	L	M
Taxation	E	E	L	L-Basic M-Advanced	L	E	E	L	L-Basic M-Advanced	L	L	L-Basic E-Advanced
Auditing	M	M	E	M	L	M	M	M	L	M	L	M
Advanced	M	L	L	L	L	M	L	L	L	L	L	L
Theory	U	L	M	L	L	L	L	L	L	L	L	L
Systems	M	E	E	M	M-Basic E-Advanced	M	M	M	L	L-Basic M-Advanced	L	E
Not-for-Profit	L	L	M	L	L	U	M	L	L	L	L	M

L = Little change
M = Moderate change
E = Extensive change
U = Uncertain

bookkeeping approaches to accounting does allow courses to stress concepts over procedures, several Committee members felt we had gone too far. Where is the systems cycle taught? Where do students obtain a feeling for how information is generated, controlled, and summarized to provide useful input to decision making?

There is very little integration of behavioral research or ethical considerations in accounting courses. Some behavioral material is included in the managerial courses, especially in budget-setting topics. Ethics is considered in auditing courses, but usually only in relation to the AICPA code. A primary reason for the lack of this integration seems to be a proliferation of topics that "must be covered because they are on the CPA examination." This is especially noted in the intermediate accounting course. Although textbooks have included more case material, class time and class assignments tend to move quickly to the more structured exercises and problems that focus on specific FASB standards. Cases that stress behavioral and ethical considerations require significant class time to be effective. There seems to be an attitude that there is simply too much material to cover to take time for this luxury. The Committee expresses great concern over this condition and assigns a high priority to identifying the variables that contribute to this development.

The replies from the experts seemed to confirm the view held by Committee members that the education delivery system has not changed much during the past 25 years. Accounting courses are still dominated by problem-solving lecture/discussions in class. There seems to be individual creativity in some courses, but it is not widespread. Some reasons for this lack of innovative change are explored in the last section of this report.

SPECIFIC COURSE CHANGES

Although the matrix captures a general overview of how specific courses have changed over the past 25 years, the comments of the experts are much richer than can be captured in a single category. Furthermore, incorporating impressions derived from textbook content analysis is needed. In the following pages, each of the nine course/areas covered is briefly discussed, incorporating these various sources.

Introductory Accounting

Only moderate change has occurred in introductory accounting during the past 25 years. Most programs offer one year of introductory accounting, either two semesters or three quarters. The introduction of separate financial and managerial textbooks, as contrasted with one book covering both areas, has changed the mix of content to 50 percent in each area in semester programs. Where a single text is used and in schools on a quarter basis, the mix is more likely to be 60 percent financial and 40 percent managerial. The financial portion of introductory accounting has become more "authoritative pronouncement" oriented, and less coverage is given to theory and system orientation. The managerial portion of the course has become more cost and economics oriented with less managerial emphasis. The Price Waterhouse–sponsored project in the late 1960s to make a major shift in the content and direction of introductory accounting courses was adopted at only a few schools.

The integration of the computer into introductory courses has proceeded slowly. Lack of computer facilities sufficient to meet the high enrollments in introductory courses is a limiting factor. Much of the available material is "input oriented" and does little to enhance the learning of introductory accounting. Some increase in quantitative tools, such as inventory models, break-even analysis, and present value, has been observed in the courses. Time constraints are a major problem in dealing adequately with these topics, and concern over redundancy with later courses exists.

The increased emphasis on authoritative rules and the movement of the CPA examination to objective-type questions concerned the experts as well as the Committee. So much material could be covered that introductory courses tend to stress the procedures and the cookbook approach, thus stultifying learning and leading to an inadequate preparation for both accounting and business students. An uneasiness with the current status of introductory accounting exists. The courses should deemphasize mechanical procedures, and the content should be directed more toward developing skills in the use of financial information for business majors in general. It appears difficult to change significantly the direction partly because of the widespread use of graduate teaching assistants to cover this level of course. Such teachers have little incentive to adopt a more difficult teaching assignment that would incorporate conceptual and broad issues in the courses.

Cost/Managerial Accounting

Moderate to extensive change has occurred in many aspects of the cost/managerial courses in the accounting curriculum. Despite this change, much more still needs to be done. The principal need for further change is to increase the relevance of the courses by relating them more directly with what management accountants actually do.

With the increase in coverage in introductory accounting, most programs offer two cost/managerial courses at the undergraduate level and at least one additional course at the graduate level. A movement to less emphasis on the mechanics and more emphasis on the role of accounting data for decision making was noted. This movement has included the use of quantitative techniques utilizing mathematical models and regression analysis. Although the big movement to these tools occurred about 25 years ago, the availability of computers in the classroom has greatly enhanced the opportunity to use these models in the courses. The cost course is still heavily manufacturing oriented, although less so than in 1960.

The computer has been integrated more extensively in cost/managerial courses than in most other accounting courses. The use of the personal computer has made it possible to deal with more complex, and thus more realistic, problems. A strong movement to more comprehensive cases was noted, with less use of simplified and stylized problems. It is likely that this movement will occur with even greater emphasis during the next 10 years. The expansion of cost/managerial courses in the graduate programs has been accompanied by more coverage of current research results in the advanced courses.

The cost/managerial courses are the only ones noted that report an increase in behavioral coverage. The behavioral impact of such matters as goal congruence, individual and group behavior, and long-term versus short-term goals are now stressed, where 25 years ago they were seldom included.

Intermediate Accounting

The most significant change that has occurred in intermediate accounting during the past 25 years has been related to the explosion in financial accounting standards.

EXHIBIT 6
NUMBER OF TEXT PAGES DEVOTED TO EACH TOPIC IN INTERMEDIATE ACCOUNTING

Topics	Average 1972/74 Editions	Average 1986 Editions	Change	Percent Change
Fundamental Processes	59	62	3	4.7
Financial Statements	95	112	17	17.8
Corporations and Equity	141	147	6	4.3
Cash & Temporary Investments	40	44	4	9.4
Receivables	35	42	7	19.3
Inventories	106	108	2	2.1
Tangible Fixed Assets	93	100	7	7.2
Intangible Assets	39	41	2	5.8
Funds and Investments	56	50	–5	–9.5
Current Liabilities	34	44	10	29.4
Long-term Liabilities	55	56	1	1.4
Analysis of Financial Statements	57	47	–10	–16.8
Actuarial	25	47	22	87.0
Statement of Change in Position	52	60	8	15.9
Correction of Errors	21	25	4	17.9
Theory	40	57	17	42.2
Price Level Statements	38	58	21	54.3
Pensions and Leases	40	112	72	180.6
Income Tax	23	44	21	90.2
Accounting Changes	17	25	8	45.6
Revenue Recognition	13	48	35	272.5
Other	28	0	–28	—
	1,104	1,327	223	

The many pronouncements of the APB and the FASB have added numerous topics to the area of financial accounting. A majority of these have been added to intermediate accounting. The most dramatic result of this emphasis has been in the size of intermediate accounting textbooks. After adjusting for the change in number of words per page, most intermediate texts increased in size by 40 to 50 percent in the period between 1972 and 1986. For example, the leading textbook in terms of sales, Kieso and Weygandt, had 1,151 pages in its 1974 edition and 1,274 in its 1986 edition. However, through change in page size and print lines per page, the number of words per page increased from 513 in 1974 to 676 in 1986. On a 1986 page size basis, therefore, the 1974 edition was only 873 pages in length, and the increase in words between the two editions was 46 percent. Other texts showed similar increases. An analysis was made by the Committee of the topic-area coverage in four leading intermediate textbooks. The result of this analysis is summarized in Exhibit 6. Pensions, leases, revenue recognition, income tax, and actuarial material account for much of the increase. Only two topical areas reveal a decrease: analysis of financial statements and funds and investments.

The increased coverage has resulted in an increase in hours devoted to intermediate accounting. Most schools still offer a year of intermediate; however, many programs are moving to four-hour rather than three-hour classes. Concern with the great increase in material to be covered in this course is justifiable. Some selectivity of topics was noted, but there was a belief that the courses were too heavily textbook dependent, and that if a text covered a topic, even in an appendix, the student would feel cheated if the topic were not included in the course.

Commentators on the bulging intermediate textbooks, such as Stephen Zeff (1979, 1980), have suggested that a new approach to intermediate texts is needed. A special conference dealing with the problem was held at Ohio State University in 1982 at which textbook authors, practitioners, and nontextbook academicians were present (Jensen, 1982). Although most participants recognized that a problem exists, the realities of the marketplace dampened any expectation that a change would occur. Indeed, all intermediate texts are very similar in approach, and attempts to deviate have either resulted in the discontinuation of the texts or movement to the more traditional approach.

This proliferation of material has made it difficult for teachers to include conceptual issues and open-end questions and cases. These items take more class time and thus compete with coverage of specific topics.

There has been little integration of behavioral, ethical, or international topics into intermediate courses. The use of the computer has also been spotty. Its primary use could come in specific problem areas that have been highly standardized by the standard-setting bodies with specific rules that can be placed into formulas and used to solve a variety of problems. Care must be taken that solution in this manner does not become so mechanical that concepts are not seen. This problem exists regardless of whether the computer is used, but its use could free up time to discuss conceptually what is occurring. The tendency, however, is to cover more topics with the extra time.

Intermediate accounting is still considered to be the central core of most accounting programs. A general feeling that the course is being drowned with an attempt to cover all the pronouncements exists. Intermediate accounting instructors might do well to follow the change in taxation courses noted below that stresses a conceptual approach and does not attempt to cover all the rules and regulations established by rule-making bodies. Also noted is the heavy influence of the CPA examination on what is covered in intermediate. Unless a change in this influence occurs, the increasing movement to an all-objective–question CPA examination may lead to an even greater procedural rather than conceptual emphasis.

Taxation

A substantial increase in the number of master's-level tax or tax concentration programs, computer integration, and a more conceptual approach in teaching represent the three most extensive and significant changes in tax education over the past 25 years. Although such changes certainly have not taken place in every university (and perhaps not even in a majority), they have been pervasive enough to represent a definite trend.

The number of master's-level tax or tax concentration programs has increased substantially since 1960. Growth in the number of graduate tax programs and profiles of such programs are well documented in Broden and Lubell (1986), which also includes copies of their earlier (related) studies, Broden and Lubell (1979), and Lubell and Broden (1975). In 1960, three graduate tax programs (all in New York City) existed, up from one in 1950. Since 1960 the progression has been to 11 in 1970, 30 in 1980, 71 in 1983, and 86 in 1985. Current enrollment and annual graduation numbers also reflect this increase. In 1973 approximately 1,500 students enrolled in graduate tax programs and approximately 200 graduated. In contrast, in 1985 approximately 7, 800 enrolled and about 1,600 graduated.

Computers are currently used in tax education and practice for return preparation, research, and planning. All respondents to the expert survey indicated that computers have been introduced into their tax courses in the 1980s. The widespread availability of microcomputers since 1980 has been the impetus for this important development. For a perspective on the significance and recency of the "computer revolution," consider that a 1978 survey of undergraduate tax courses as to course content, instructional materials, and teaching methods does not mention computers (Heller et al., 1981). In contrast, a 1985 survey of American Taxation Association members found that one-third was currently using the computer in tax classes and an additional third intended to incorporate the computer into tax classes in the near future. In the order of frequency of responses, the types of software reported were spreadsheets, tax planning, tax compliance, word processing, and data bases (White et al., 1987)

It is generally agreed that today's tax courses are more conceptual than those offered in 1960. There is still some concern as to whether tax courses remain too rule oriented and whether there has, in fact, been a shift back toward a rule- orientation in recent years. The character of the CPA examination and the massive changes in the tax law in recent years were cited as factors that are working against further conceptualization in undergraduate tax courses. At the master's level, student demand for very practical courses (particularly in part-time, evening programs) is seen as an impediment.

Changes in texts and the type of instructors teaching taxes are largely responsible for the increased conceptualization that has occurred. Although the substantial number of tax texts on the market today differ greatly in the extent of conceptual orientation, as a group they stand in marked contrast to the cookbook-of-rules approach that dominated in 1960. The conceptual focus of Sommerfeld, Anderson, and Brock (1969) and the business decision focus of Raby (1964) are early examples of significant departures from the 1960 norm.

In 1960 much of tax instruction was by non-terminal degree individuals, many of whom were also part- or full-time practitioners. Such individuals are perceived to have a more rule-oriented (less conceptual) approach than full-time, terminal degree faculty. Few, if any, accounting doctoral programs at that time provided for tax concentrations. Thus the full-time, terminal degree person may have also tended toward a course based on the available texts. Evidence of a change in the educational background of individuals teaching taxation is provided by a recent study that identified 27 accounting doctoral programs with a concentration in taxation. The same study showed that, in 1982, the total pre-1970 degree group teaching taxation included 30 percent doctoral degree holders, but the total post-1980 degree group comprised 54 percent of doctoral degree holders (Boley and Outslay, 1983).

In summary, three different "forces"— market, technology, and intellectual— have significantly influenced the major changes that have occurred in tax education over the past 25 years. The strong demand, principally by public accounting firms, for graduates of master's-level tax or tax concentration programs has driven the increase in such programs. The widespread availability of microcomputers and related software since 1980 and their rapidly developing use in tax practice have been the impetus for computer integration in the classroom. Finally, the intellectual product of key educators in the creation of tax textbooks and doctoral programs has encouraged and spread the shift to more conceptually based tax education.

Auditing

Perhaps the most significant change in auditing education over the past 25 years occurred at the very beginning of this period. In 1961 Mautz and Sharaf published their seminal work *A Philosophy of Auditing*. Prior to this time, no conceptual foundation for the practice of auditing had been organized and accepted. Auditing courses tended to be procedural in nature, with an emphasis on financial statement verification following a "balance-sheet" approach to the study. Standish reported in *The Accounting Review* (1964) that between 50 to 65 percent of the leading auditing textbooks' coverage dealt with financial statement verification. Most chapters of these 1960 auditing textbooks included lists of audit program steps that should be followed by auditors to perform their duties. Audit practice cases were popular and were often used in an "advanced auditing course" that stressed the practical audit processes.

The plea of Mautz and Sharaf for a recognized discipline of auditing similar to the discipline of accounting struck a responsive chord with many educators. However, not much change occurred in the auditing courses until the 1970s. Two events in this time period significantly affected auditing education. Audit research, stimulated by significant monetary grants by Peat Marwick Mitchell & Co., became more popular among educators and resulted in papers that questioned some of the accepted tenets of auditing. Technology changes, particularly related to the computer, enabled practitioners to change the manner in which audits were being conducted. Increased emphasis on internal control review, risk analysis, the theory of evidence, analytical review, and transaction flows became common among practitioners. A changing legal environment raised serious questions as to the auditors' role and responsibility in the financial marketplace. The importance of independence and ethical conduct became important topics for consideration. Many conceptual issues were discussed by standard-setting bodies, and a body of auditing standards emerged to help auditors evaluate their work.

Auditing textbooks and courses tend to follow audit practice at many institutions. About half of the auditing textbooks used changed from the financial statement verification approach to the transaction cycle approach. In the last 10 years, introductory auditing textbooks and introductory auditing courses have emphasized the conceptual topics, leaving the audit detail to training programs of accounting firms or advanced auditing courses. For example, in Arens and Loebbecke's 1984 edition, the first half of the text is related to conceptual topics, and only one-third of the book discusses the approach to auditing transaction cycles.

As audit standards, audit technology, audit research, and audit procedures have expanded, audit professors report the same dilemma faced by intermediate accounting professors: too much material to cover in one course. Some schools have introduced second audit courses to meet the problem. Other schools have recognized that auditing is a specialty that should be reserved for graduate or integrated five-year programs.

With few exceptions, audit courses still are directed to external auditing as opposed to internal auditing. A limited number of schools have introduced internal auditing courses in their curriculum. Attempts to integrate internal audit topics into the introductory courses have usually resulted in only token attention. Time constraints are usually recognized as the major deterrent to internal audit coverage.

The introduction of the personal computer is having a dramatic impact on the manner in which audits are being conducted. Audit courses are being affected by the computer, but usually more in advanced courses than in the basic course. Again, time to cover everything is a principal stumbling block. Because audits are increasingly being approached on a systems basis, it is important that students have a good understanding of business systems. Frakes (1986) reports that only one-sixth of auditing courses in 1986 required a systems course as a prerequisite to introductory auditing. If a student does not have the systems background, some time must be devoted in the auditing course to systems topics. This has tended to cause even further frustration for students and teachers alike.

A significant change in who teaches the auditing classes has occurred in the 25-year period. Frakes reports that 65 percent of auditing professors in 1985 have their doctorates and that 94 percent of them are CPAs. Although 1960 statistics were not available, auditing teachers in that year were often part-time practitioners who brought to the classroom their particular firm's approach to auditing and its procedures. The increased academic qualifications for auditing professors has resulted in a broader approach to the introductory course. The use of cases with open-end answers seems popular with auditing professors; however, the time requirements for such material is of concern. Some of the respondent experts indicated they were using fewer cases now than 10 years ago and cited the time constraint as the principal reason.

Because auditing is directly related to real-world activities, teachers of auditing have always relied on their own personal "war stories" to enliven class discussion. Because of limited current exposure for many professors, the need for good case or example material is acute. Some teachers have attempted the use of role-playing and video presentations. CPA firms have increasingly made available material for audit education, and professors have the challenge to integrate these materials into their courses.

The behavioral and international areas appear to receive little attention in auditing courses. There is really no such thing as international auditing. Consideration of auditing applications in multinational environments is usually left for graduate programs.

In summary, the introductory auditing course has changed significantly in the 25-year period, and the nature of advanced auditing courses has changed to cover areas often included in earlier introductory courses. Less attention is being paid to audit details and procedures, and more time is spent in helping students to understand the philosophy of auditing. Most teachers find auditing very difficult to teach. There are fewer specific answers than in traditional accounting courses, and that makes accounting students uneasy. Recognition that auditing is indeed a discipline separate from accounting seems to have increased, but the popularity of graduate programs for auditors is much less than for those in taxation.

Advanced Accounting

The advanced accounting course has traditionally been a one-semester or one-quarter course dedicated to financial accounting topics not covered in intermediate accounting. The course has consistently had consolidations as its core topic with a potpourri of other specialized topics surrounding it. This course is often listed as an elective course and is not required of all accounting majors, especially at the undergraduate level. This course has changed very little in its basic nature over the 25-year period. Time value of money topics that were included in the advanced accounting textbooks 25 years ago have worked their way into introductory accounting and business courses. Realization and liquidation accounting is gone, and in their place has come an expanded treatment of foreign currency transactions and translation.

The complex adjustments of consolidation accounting have been simplified through microcomputer applications. The computer is just beginning to make an impact on the course. It is still largely a detail, procedure-oriented course with little attention paid to conceptual issues or open-end case presentations except in some specialized topical areas where few rules exist. Very little behavioral or ethical integration has occurred.

Most of the new, more complex financial accounting topics have been included in intermediate accounting textbooks. This is one of the explanations for the greatly expanded size of intermediate accounting textbooks and the crowding of intermediate accounting courses. The expert respondents indicated that the CPA examination has had a strong impact on the topics emphasized in advanced accounting. As the AICPA Board of Examiners has changed its coverage of traditional advanced accounting topics, the advanced accounting course has also changed, although on a lagged basis.

Accounting theory. The accounting theory course in most schools is an elective course at the undergraduate level and a required course at the graduate level. In some schools a separate theory class has been replaced by an integration of theory into intermediate accounting, and the addition of an accounting research class at the graduate level.

As part of the research into the theory area, the Committee examined the table of contents for several theory texts between the period 1962 and 1987. The Committee also reviewed the theory course descriptions contained in *Accounting Trends*, an annual Prentice-Hall publication containing selected course syllabi. The course descriptions included in this publication are not a random selection but rather a collection of "innovative or particularly effective accounting courses." The following trends in topical coverage were noted:

1. Theory in the mid-60s focused more on the then-current issues such as (a) funds flow, (b) combinations, (c) income determination, (d) price-level changes, and (e) inventory valuation.
2. In the late 1960s, there was a trend toward accounting history and historical influence.
3. By the mid-1970s, the more popular topics were (a) political, institutional, and social forces shaping accounting, (b) objectives of financial reporting, and (c) disclosure.
4. The late 1970s and early 1980s were characterized by an emphasis on (a) standards, (b) standard-setting process, (c) price-level changes or inflation accounting, and (d) the FASB conceptual framework project. These topics reflect the change from data preparation as an end in itself to a recognition of using accounting to improve the overall well-being of an organization.

As can be observed, the theory class has tended to be fluid in its content. Its emphasis is conceptual, with outside assignments usually involving library research papers. Theory usually comes at the end of a student's academic preparation; consequently, it is sometimes difficult to shake earlier, more rule-oriented conceptions of accounting knowledge.

Accounting Information Systems

The area of accounting information systems (AIS) has undergone extensive change in the past 25 years. For example, one university reports that it offered two AIS courses ("accounting machine wiring" and "procedure development") in 1960 but currently offers complete undergraduate and graduate programs in AIS including such courses as "data base concepts" and "auditing of AIS." A number of forces at work have contributed to this growth and change (AAA, 1987D; Kneer, 1986). Some of these forces include (1) the advances in hardware and software technology that have resulted in the widespread use of powerful, inexpensive computers with relatively user-friendly computer software, (2) the expanding role of accounting and auditing in industry and government, (3) the changing mix of services provided by public accounting firms, and (4) the changing accreditation requirements of the AACSB.

During the past 25 years, AIS has become a recognized applied academic discipline. However, only within the past six or seven years has AIS gained recognition as a necessary curriculum component. AIS now exists with its own educational and research identity. Manifestations of the maturation of AIS as an academic discipline include (1) the organization and growth of an American Accounting Association (AAA) special interest section, (2) proliferation of AIS research and publication, (3) continuing efforts at AIS curriculum development by the AAA and other associations, (4) the emergence of a number of graduate and undergraduate courses and programs in AIS, (5) the increasing number of topics covered in the AIS curriculum, (6) the level of sophistication of computer tools used in the AIS curriculum, and (7) the increasing number of support courses in management information systems and computer science.

Developments in information processing technology have significantly affected course content in recent history. AIS courses have changed from emphasizing data manipulation procedures that focused on the chart of accounts, structure of journals, and flows of paperwork to emphasizing the development of an understanding of contemporary information processing technology, including microcomputers and their application. Also, advanced information concepts associated with financial modeling and decision support systems are now found in many AIS courses. In addition, developments in areas such as cognitive psychology, artificial intelligence, and expert systems are beginning to be included in AIS courses, especially at the graduate level.

The typical AIS course appears to contain a mix of concept and technique even though the diffusion of microcomputers in both education and practice has tended to encourage a more procedural approach with an emphasis on spreadsheet preparation. However, there appears to be an effort to have AIS instruction be reality based with the use of the case approach, system design projects, and field studies by student teams.

Some concern that the full capabilities of modern technology are not being utilized in AIS instruction seems to exist. There is a belief that modern technology has been adapted to what has already been done for the past 20 years. This has resulted in an increase in the speed of processing without fully utilizing the capabilities of modern technology for AIS instruction.

One member of the AIS expert panel made the following observation that concerns the future of both AIS instruction and accounting education. This expert comments that he sees "the future role of accountants as not to 'account' but rather to 'analyze and interpret'":

> Large volumes of economic, financial, and operating data will be collected, processed, and made available to users automatically. That is, accounting will become a less relevant, perhaps even trivial, task. Instead, understanding how to use the information will become critical. Prescribed information formats such as conventional financial statements will become increasingly irrelevant as information technology affords us with opportunities to analyze information in multiple formats. (There is a real question whether] accounting will survive as an academic discipline, but there will be a need for specialists in the analysis and interpretation of information relevant to economic decision-making.

The concern of this expert, along with the admonition of the AAA Committee on the Future Structure, Content, and Scope of Accounting Education, represents one of the challenges of the future, which is to ". . . approach accounting education as an information development and distribution function for economic decision making" (Bedford et al,, p. 169).

Certainly great changes have taken place in AIS education in the past 25 years. The impact of this area on accounting practice and education is just beginning to be felt. The Committee was impressed that the acceleration of change in this area will continue in the decade ahead, and care must be taken to assure a useful integration of these concepts throughout the specific areas being discussed in this portion of the Committee report.

Not-for-Profit Accounting

Accounting in the not-for-profit area has changed dramatically in the past 25 years. Most university courses in this area 25 years ago were devoted to governmental accounting and were based upon the standards as promulgated by the Government and Municipal Officers Association. Course material was detailed, with emphasis on the various recommended funds and the way in which transactions affected the various funds and groups. The course was usually an elective undergraduate course, and in many schools was included as part of the advanced accounting course. In the 1960s and 1970s, the AICPA issued several Audit Guides dealing with various non-profit entities (e.g., hospitals, colleges and universities, state and local governments, and voluntary health and welfare organizations). The CPA examination began to include questions dealing with other than government entities, and the fund-oriented textbooks began to include separate chapters for each of these distinctive non-profit entities. When the Government Accounting Standards Board (GASB) was formed, another source of accounting standards was established. There is currently more activity in standard-setting for the not-for-profit area than has ever occurred.

Fund accounting, as a separate conceptual system, began to be stressed in the 1970s as something separate from the detailed discussion of different funds, accounts, and financial statements. The inclusion of these other types of entities added greatly to the content of not-for-profit courses and made it more difficult to cover this material in a chapter or two of advanced accounting. As the amount of money being spent by government and other not-for-profit-entities has increased, the need for accountants and auditors trained to understand and work with fund accounting systems has also increased.

The computer has been indispensable to entities engaged in fund accounting. However, university classes have apparently not used this tool as much as might be done.

PERVASIVE INFLUENCES THAT IMPACT ACCOUNTING EDUCATION

Six influences appear essential to any analysis of accounting education, whether retrospective or prospective:

1. Textbook dependency.
2. Lack of faculty rewards.
3. CPA examination.
4. Accreditation requirements.
5. FASB, Congress, and SEC influence.
6. Business environment.

Each, in turn, is discussed in the ensuing paragraphs. The order of discussion is not intended to convey a rank ordering.

TEXTBOOK DEPENDENCY

Most accounting courses are textbook dependent. Radical departures from popular textbooks are seldom successful in the marketplace. This means that course structure and content changes slowly. The Price Waterhouse experience in trying to change introductory accounting texts and courses is an example of a radical change that was not successful. Intermediate accounting texts have grown in size significantly, however, their basic structure and approach have not changed. Texts that started out differently have moved back in later editions to a more standard look. Many of the basic taxation texts have changed from the Prentice-Hall/Commerce Clearing House cookbook-of-rules approach to a broader, more conceptual direction. Taxation appears to be the area where texts, such as *An Introduction to Taxation* (Sommerfeld, Anderson, and Brock, 1969) most significantly affected the direction of course structure and content.

LACK OF FACULTY REWARD STRUCTURE

Curriculum development and experimentation is not adequately rewarded in the academic environment. At schools having doctoral programs in accounting, much of the undergraduate teaching is assigned to doctoral students whose primary objective is to earn their degrees. Their incentive is to meet minimal requirements to meet their assistantship provisions. Usually that means "teaching the text." Tenure and promotion decisions seldom reward curriculum efforts in the same way they do research and publications. Release-time financial grants for curriculum change receive a lower priority at most institutions than do research projects that could lead to refereed articles in leading accounting journals.

CPA EXAMINATION

The CPA examination has become a significant influence on the overall accounting curriculum and on individual courses at most institutions. Because student success and failure on the examination can be measured objectively, many schools and many legislatures have used success rates on the CPA examination as a surrogate measurement of the success of a particular accounting program. The availability of examination results by state and by school has accentuated the use of this measure. The

Committee strongly believes that this influence has been, and continues to be, principally negative. Decisions as to courses to teach, topics to cover, and type of evaluation examinations to give are affected directly by the content and approach of the CPA examination. The belief of students and faculty alike at many institutions is "if it isn't on the CPA examination, it's not important." Such an attitude ascribes to the CPA examination something never intended by the AICPA in administering the examination. It is intended to be used as one factor governing entrance into the profession. Its content is influenced by grading considerations, prior examinations, actions of standard-setting bodies, and so on. As evidenced by the current recommendations of the AICPA Board of Examiners to move to an entirely objective examination, the large number of examinees has become a driving force in shaping the examination content.

The Committee strongly believes that accounting education needs to be separated from sitting for the CPA examination. Legal education with its the bar examination represents a desirable model to follow. Candidates for the bar examination almost universally plan to sit for a nonuniversity-related review course after graduation from law school. The examination is scheduled so that there is usually time after graduation to take the four- to five-week course. This relieves law schools from concentrating on the bar examination. As an academic community, we should be less concerned about what the examination contains, including the present discussion of the Board of Examiners' recommendations, and more concerned about making it clear that accounting education cannot and should not be evaluated by citing pass rates on this entrance examination. CPA review courses for credit are still offered at many schools. The Committee recommends strongly that such courses be deleted from the accounting curriculum.

The Committee also notes with concern the recent publication by NASBA of the examination results by school attended. Although readers are warned that many factors other than school affect the results, and that the results are being published for interest only, 75 percent of the annual statistical publication is devoted to school information. There has been increased reference to these statistics, and the lead article in the September 1987 issue of *New Accountants* highlights the top 10 schools for the 1986 examinations. These statistics are assuredly going to be misused and will further heighten the negative influence of the CPA examination on accounting education. We recommend that the AAA Executive Committee take immediate action to urge strongly that NASBA discontinue publication of CPA exam results by school attended.

ACCREDITATION REQUIREMENTS

Perhaps the greatest influence on overall curriculum comes from accreditation requirements. Generally, curriculum accreditation requirements are related to subjects and courses as contrasted with methodology and specific course content. The current AACSB accreditation of undergraduate and graduate accounting programs is having a significant impact on such courses as systems, computers, and general business courses. The Committee believes that accreditation has often been a deterrent to experimentation in overall curriculum development because it emphasizes a broad status quo. We are also concerned that present accreditation bodies are controlled by deans of business schools who are often not in touch with the needs of the accounting profession. The Committee believes that the American Accounting Association has an obligation to continue strong efforts to influence the accreditation process because of its significant impact on what happens to the curriculum in a given institution.

FASB, CONGRESS, AND SEC INFLUENCE

The accounting profession has had strong external pressures exerted on it during the past 25 years, especially by Congress and the SEC. These bodies have been instrumental in affecting the setting of accounting and auditing standards, in modifying at least twice the profession's accepted code of ethics, and in establishing and enforcing quality control standards, such as peer review. The AICPA-controlled Accounting Principles Board (APB) gave way to a more independent Financial Accounting Standards Board in the early 1970s. As these external forces have affected the profession, so have they affected accounting education. The proliferation of standards has led to an attempt in many curricula to include most of the standards somewhere in the courses. Because the sheer number of these standards has made such an effort impossible to achieve, some selectivity has been necessary. The importance of education has not been overlooked by these external forces. For example, the Treadway Commission, which has been studying the issues surrounding management fraud, included a separate chapter on accounting education in its 1987 exposure draft. It included in its recommendations references to exposing students early to the reality of management fraud in corporate America. It also suggested that more than four years of education may be needed if accountants are to fulfill their responsibility to the general public.

It does not seem possible, nor does it seem wise, to insulate the classroom from the external forces affecting the profession. Students should understand that accounting is a discipline that has significant impact on the economy both of our country and the world. Professors should broaden their courses to incorporate these influences wherever appropriate. The use of case material that includes these forces in the write-up is one way to assure consideration of those issues. Invitation of individuals exerting this external influence to address the students, participate in executives-in-residence programs, and prepare course materials are all excellent ways to incorporate this material into a student's school experience.

BUSINESS ENVIRONMENT

The last influence identified by the Committee is related to the one just discussed. However, it recognizes that business in a compressed world has become infinitely more complex that it was a quarter of a century ago. Most national companies have become international companies with offices and affiliates located all over the world. The complexities of international trade, foreign exchange, international politics, emerging Third World powers, and increasing trade and national deficits all impact accountants in carrying out their professional responsibilities. Students studying accounting must study business and economics in increasing depth. Many accounting programs, especially graduate programs, have added general business subjects to an increasing degree. Where feasible, master of accountancy students are being enrolled in graduate MBA courses. Even though many graduate accounting programs are specialized in emphasis, most of them do not ignore the need to address business complexities while students are studying the proliferation of standards.

A recognition of this influence seems to have motivated the members of the AAA Futures Committee, chaired by Professor Bedford, to recommend some significant modifications to accounting education in the years to come. The Changes Committee recognizes the increasing influence of the business environment and recommends that curriculum committees at all universities consider this influence in its curriculum studies and revisions.

CONCLUSIONS

Contrary to the statement made in the Futures Committee report that little has changed in accounting education during the past 25 years, the Changes Committee finds that there have been many significant changes in most areas. These have occurred primarily in curriculum topics related to the fringe topics of accounting. Introductory, intermediate, and advanced accounting courses have not changed significantly during the period. The major change occurred in the volume of material included in the texts, and thus in the courses. Many of the professional five-year programs have introduced significant changes to the requirements for a master's of accountancy degree.

The AAA Futures Committee made 28 recommendations in its report. Some of these recommendations dealt with curriculum, some with structure, some with accreditation, some with economics of accounting education, and some with faculty incentives. The Changes Committee did not evaluate these recommendations but accepted them as "givens." The report of the 1986–87 AAA Follow-Up Committee on the Future Structure, Content, and Scope of Accounting Education should be reviewed for the extent of agreement on the Futures Committee's recommendation. In general, however, discussions among the Committee members seemed to indicate general agreement with them. Exhibit 7 compares the Futures Committee's recommendations with the Changes Committee's conclusions as to the direction and extent of any trend relative to the recommendation over the 25 years studied. Some of the recommendations dealt with areas not studied, and in those cases "No information" is indicated. In some cases very little change seems to have occurred in any direction relative to the recommendation (i.e., these years have neither worsened nor improved the conditions that gave rise to the Futures Committee recommendation). In some cases action is already under way to meet the recommendations, either in a moderately or extensively positive way. The most troubling condition observed involved the cases in which movement was made during the period but in the opposite direction to the recommendation, again either moderately or extensively negative. The Committee recommends that immediate attention is necessary in those areas identified as negative trends so that no further movement away from the Futures Committee recommendations occurs while implementation programs are initiated. Where there has been little change, study is necessary to determine how a positive start can be made. Where there has already been a positive start, additional encouragement should be given.

In many cases, the pervasive influences discussed in this report have the negative trends. If some of the recommendations made by the Committee could be implemented, a reversal of the trends may be possible.

This report has not explored in detail the internal and external environments facing accounting professorial faculty. Change in accounting education can come only as these factors are better understood and modified to encourage change in the direction of the Futures Committee's recommendations to assist in formulating policy that will facilitate implementing the 28 recommendations.

EXHIBIT 7
CHANGES COMMITTEE ANALYSIS
OF FUTURE COMMITTEE RECOMMENDATIONS

Number	Recommendation	25-Year Tremd
1	View accounting as broad information system.	Little change
2	Broad general education—avoid premature specialization.	Negative (E)
3	Expand liberal arts and sciences.	Negative (M)
4	Accounting education—emphasize skills for life-long learning.	Positive (M)
5	Design learning objectives to help students learn, think, and be creative.	Little change
6	Establish high expectations for students. Adjust curriculum to match professional skills, capacities, and knowledge needed.	Positive (M)
7	Flexible accounting programs.	Negative (M)
8	Broad educational accounting structure	Negative (M)
9	Specialized education only at graduate level.	Negative (E)
10	Comparative advantage study to determine type of specialization.	Negative (M)
11	Design courses so students can be active independent learners.	Negative (M)
12	Design learning technologies to increase faculty contact with students.	Little change
13	Change in textbooks to realize these objectives.	Little change
14	Faculty rewards should be broad.	Negative (E)
15	Encourage basic and applied research.	Positive (M)
16	High standards of admission to accounting programs.	Positive (M)
17	Faculty involvement in introductory and intermediate. Increased student advisement.	Little change
18	Resources for complementary programs.	No information
19	Extend peer review of faculty by nonaccounting faculty.	No information
20	Encourage interaction among faculty members in accounting and liberal arts.	No information
21	University action to encourage graduate study.	Positive (M)
22	University action to emphasize use of arts, sciences, and humanities resources.	No information
23	University action to allow more autonomy to accounting programs.	Positive (M)
24	Minimize procedural accounting in courses required for accreditation.	Little change
25	Base curricula on accounting practice and research and multidisciplinary research.	Little change
26-28	Economic dimensions of accounting education.	No information

M = Moderately
E = Extensively

ENDNOTES

1. The detailed statistics for the 25 years are included in Appendix A. The source of the data is the U.S. Department of Health, Education and Welfare and the U.S. Department of Education. The specific references are included in the Appendix 1, Appendix 2, and Appendix 3.

2. The recommendation for professional schools of accountancy is as old as the profession itself. For a discussion of the history of this movement, see Bloom (1986) and Langenderfer (May 1987).

APPENDIX A-1

ACCOUNTING DEGREES CONFERRED BY DEGREE AND SEX
1960–85

	Bachelor's Degrees			Master's Degrees		
School Year	Total	Men	Women	Total	Men	Women
60/61	10,632	10,171	461	469	440	29
61/62	11,344	10,748	596	603	568	35
62/63	11,869	11,260	609	604	572	32
63/64	13,000	12,250	750	683	650	33
64/65	14,874	13,969	905	755	720	35
65/66	15,101	14,203	898	862	834	28
66/67	15,692	14,664	1,028	1,024	973	51
67/68	17,922	16,672	1,250	1,137	1,073	64
68/69	20,032	18,460	1,572	1,333	1,254	79
69/70	21,183	19,343	1,840	1,083	1,004	79
70/71	22,099	20,036	2,063	1,097	994	103
71/72	24,801	22,307	2,494	1,377	1,269	108
72/73	27,947	24,710	3,237	1,621	1,480	141
73/74	29,341	25,313	4,028	1,798	1,610	188
74/75	31,116	25,601	5,515	2,227	1,948	279
75/76	35,806	28,161	7,645	2,730	2,252	478
76/77	39,183	29,241	9,942	3,278	2,642	636
77/78	40,145	28,345	11,800	3,354	2,633	721
78/79	41,393	27,907	13,486	3,571	2,744	827
79/80	42,712	27,295	15,417	3,456	2,499	957
80/81	43,344	26,298	17,046	3,449	2,415	1,034
81/82	45,542	26,213	19,329	3,246	2,160	1,086
82/83	45,732	24,961	20,771	3,046	1,997	1,049
83/84	47,692	25,276	22,416	3,297	2,090	1,207
84/85	47,005	23,955	23,050	3,207	1,948	1,259

Sources:
60/61 to 63/64: U.S. Department of Health, Education and Welfare, "Earned Degrees Conferred."
After 63/64: U.S. Department of Health, Education and Welfare and U.S. Department of Education, "Digest of Educational Statistics."
66/67: Estimated. No statistics were published that year.

APPENDIX A-2

INDEX 1960 = 100

RELATIVE NUMBER OF ACCOUNTING DEGREES CONFERRED BY DEGREE AND SEX

1960–85

	Bachelor's Degrees			Master's Degrees		
School Year	Total	Male	Female	Total	Male	Female
60 /61	100.0	100.0	100.0	100.0	100.0	100.0
61 /62	106.7	105.7	129.3	128.6	129.1	120.7
62 /63	111.6	110.7	132.1	128.8	130.0	110.3
63 /64	122.3	120.4	162.7	145.6	147.7	113.8
64 /65	139.9	137.3	196.3	161.0	163.6	120.7
65 /66	142.0	139.6	194.8	183.8	189.5	96.6
66 /67	147.6	144.2	223.0	218.3	221.1	175.9
67 /68	168.6	163.9	271.1	242.4	243.9	220.7
68 /69	188.4	181.5	341.0	284.2	285.0	272.4
69 /70	199.2	190.2	399.1	230.9	228.2	272.4
70 /71	207.9	197.0	447.5	233.9	225.9	355.2
71 /72	233.3	219.3	541.0	293.6	288.4	372.4
72 /73	262.9	242.9	702.2	345.6	336.4	486.2
73 /74	276.0	248.9	873.8	383.4	365.9	648.3
74 /75	292.7	251.7	1,196.3	474.8	442.7	962.1
75 /76	336.8	276.9	1,658.4	582.1	511.8	1,648.3
76 /77	368.5	287.5	2,156.6	698.9	600.5	2,193.1
77 /78	377.6	278.7	2,559.7	715.1	598.4	2,486.2
78 /79	389.3	274.4	2,925.4	761.4	623.6	2,851.7
79 /80	401.7	268.4	3,344.3	736.9	568.0	3,300.0
80 /81	407.7	258.6	3,697.6	735.4	548.9	3,565.5
81 /82	428.3	257.7	4,192.8	692.1	490.9	3,744.8
82 /83	430.1	245.4	4,505.6	649.5	453.9	3,617.2
83 /84	448.6	248.5	4,862.5	703.0	475.0	4,162.1
84 /85	442.1	235.5	5,000.0	683.8	442.7	4,341.4

Sources:

60/61 to 63/64: U.S. Department of Health, Education and Welfare, "Earned Degrees Conferred."

After 63/64: U.S. Department of Health, Education and Welfare and U.S. Department of Education, "Digest of Educational Statistics."

66/67: Estimated. No statistics were published that year.

APPENDIX A-3
TOTAL DEGREES CONFERRED IN THE UNITED STATES
BY DEGREE AND SEX
1960–85

	Bachelor's Degrees			Masters Degrees		
School Year	Total	Men	Women	Total	Men	Women
60/61	401,784	255,900	145,884	78,269	54,158	24,111
61/62	420,485	262,015	158,470	84,889	58,705	26,184
62/63	410,421	239,108	171,313	131,589	98,586	33,003
63/64	460,467	263,121	197,346	142,759	105,704	37,055
64/65	492,984	279,777	213,207	158,141	116,104	42,037
65/66	524,117	301,051	223,066	172,268	123,255	49,013
66/67	575,000	325,000	250,000	192,000	135,000	57,000
67/68	632,289	357,682	274,607	211,170	146,344	64,826
68/69	728,845	410,595	318,250	229,096	155,316	73,780
9/70	792,316	451,097	341,219	208,291	125,624	82,667
70/71	839,730	475,594	364,136	230,509	138,146	9,363
71/72	887,273	500,590	386,683	251,633	149,550	102,083
72/73	922,362	518,191	404,171	263,371	154,468	108,903
73/74	945,776	527,313	418,463	277,033	157,842	119,191
74/75	922,933	504,841	418,092	292,450	161,570	130,880
75/76	925,746	504,925	420,821	311,771	167,248	144,523
76/77	919,549	495,545	424,004	317,164	167,783	149,381
77/78	921,204	487,347	433,857	311,620	161,212	150,408
78/79	921,390	477,344	444,046	301,079	153,370	147,709
79/80	929,417	473,611	455,806	298,081	150,749	147,332
80/81	934,640	469,383	465,257	295,739	147,043	148,696
81/82	952,998	473,364	479,634	295,546	145,532	150,014
82/83	969,510	479,140	490,370	289,921	144,697	145,224
83/84	974,309	482,319	491,990	284,263	143,595	140,668
84/85	979,477	482,528	496,949	286,251	143,390	142,861

Sources:

60/61 to 63/64: U.S. Department of Health, Education and Welfare, "Earned Degrees Conferred."

After 63/64: U.S. Department of Health, Education and Welfare and U.S. Department of Education, "Digest of Educational Statistics."

66/67: Estimated. No statistics were published that year.

APPENDIX A-4
ACCOUNTING DEGREES AS A PERCENTAGE OF TOTAL DEGREES BY DEGREE AND SEX 1960–85

	Accounting Degrees—Percentage of				
	Total B.S. Degrees		Total M.S. Degrees		Total M.S. and B.S. Degrees
School Year	Male	Female	Male	Female	Male and Female
60/61	4.0	0.3	0.8	0.1	2.3
61/62	4.1	0.4	1.0	0.1	2.4
62/63	4.7	0.4	0.6	0.1	2.3
63/64	4.7	0.4	0.6	0.1	2.3
64/65	5.0	0.4	0.6	0.1	2.4
65/66	4.7	0.4	0.7	0.1	2.3
66/67	4.5	0.4	0.7	0.1	2.2
67/68	4.7	0.5	0.7	0.1	2.3
68/69	4.5	0.5	0.8	0.1	2.2
69/70	4.3	0.5	0.8	0.1	2.2
70/71	4.2	0.6	0.7	0.1	2.2
71/72	4.5	0.6	0.8	0.1	2.3
72/73	4.8	0.8	1.0	0.1	2.5
73/74	4.8	1.0	1.0	0.2	2.5
74/75	5.1	1.3	1.2	0.2	2.7
75/76	5.6	1.8	1.3	0.3	3.1
76/77	5.9	2.3	1.6	0.4	3.4
77/78	5.8	2.7	1.6	0.5	3.5
78/79	5.8	3.0	1.8	0.6	3.7
79/80	5.8	3.4	1.7	0.6	3.8
80/81	5.6	3.7	1.6	0.7	3.8
81/82	5.5	4.0	1.5	0.7	3.9
82/83	5.2	4.2	1.4	0.7	3.9
83/84	5.2	4.6	1.5	0.9	4.1
84/85	5.0	4.6	1.4	0.9	4.0

Sources:

60/61 to 63/64: U.S. Department of Health, Education and Welfare, "Earned Degrees Conferred."

After 63/64: U.S. Department of Health, Education and Welfare and U.S. Department of Education, "Digest of Educational Statistics."

66/67: Estimated. No statistics were published that year.

FOLLOW-UP COMMITTEE ON THE FUTURE STRUCTURE, CONTENT, AND SCOPE OF ACCOUNTING EDUCATION 1986–87

Marcos F. Massoud
Chairman
Claremont McKenna College

Ernest Bartholomew
Arthur Young & Co.

Gary A. Luoma
University of South Carolina

Jerry M. Daily
Touche Ross & Co.

Mohamed Onsi
Syracuse University

Nabil Hassan
Wright State University

Larry Rittenberg
University of Wisconsin-Madison

Clark Johnson
Johnson & Johnson Co.

Bill N. Schwartz
Temple University

Edward L. Summers
University of Texas-Austin

REPORT OF THE FOLLOW-UP COMMITTEE ON THE FUTURE STRUCTURE, CONTENT, AND SCOPE OF ACCOUNTING EDUCATION 1986–87

EXECUTIVE SUMMARY

Strong support apparently exists for changing the scope of accounting education from the traditional transaction model to that of a broad economic information developmental model. However, evidence suggests that this change will be difficult to achieve. The causes and sources of this difficulty must be addressed in future efforts.

In the structure area, evidence supports the Committee perception of the importance of the liberal arts component (not as a random selection, but as a well-structured support for accounting education), the general business component, and the general professional accounting component. The respondents believe, however, that the introductory-level material relating to specialized areas (such as tax, auditing, MIS) is a part of the general professional accounting foundation rather than an element to be taught only at the graduate level.

Based upon consideration of all the elements in the structure of accounting education, major support exists for the need to have five years in which to achieve this academic coverage.

Support also exists for the Committee's recommendations that the learning process should involve more faculty participation to enhance the quality of the educational process. However, existing systems do not reward such faculty involvement. The present reward structure does not provide for changing the nature of faculty involvement to reflect the recommendations of the Committee.

INTRODUCTION

ORIGINAL COMMITTEE REPORT

In February 1986 the American Accounting Association Committee on the Future Structure, Content, and Scope of Accounting Education (the Bedford Committee) issued its report titled "Future Accounting Education: Preparing for the Expanding Profession." That Committee addressed the expanding profession and discussed the implications for accounting education. Following a presentation of the current state of accounting education, the Committee concentrated upon the future, concluding with a set of 28 recommendations and a plan to implement these recommendations by the year 2000.

The report of the Committee on the Future Structure, Content, and Scope of Accounting Education was published in *Issues in Accounting Education* (Spring 1986).

AMERICAN ACCOUNTING ASSOCIATION EXECUTIVE COMMITTEE RESPONSE

At its meeting in April 1986 the Executive Committee of the American Accounting Association considered the report of the Committee on the Future Structure, Content, and Scope of Accounting Education. The Executive Committee concluded by stating:

> The Executive Committee expresses appreciation for the significant efforts of the Bedford Committee and their very thoughtful recommendations which deserve careful consideration by members of the Association as well as its external constituencies. The Executive Committee, in endorsing the general thrust of these recommendations, urges all members to participate in the discussions to be held at the spring regional meetings of the Association and to provide input to the 1986–1987 committees formed to develop details of the educational implications of the report.

Then-President Ray Sommerfeld appointed three committees to continue the work of the Bedford Committee. These committees are the following:

- Changes in Accounting Education
- Professorial Environment
- Future Structure Follow-Up

The following is the report of the Future Structure Follow-Up Committee.

COMMITTEE CHARGE

Sommerfeld charged this Committee:

1. To work with the regional vice presidents in scheduling and staffing, at each 1987 spring regional meeting, one discussion session on the more important issues inherent in the 1986 (AAA) Report of the Committee on the Future Structure, Content, and Scope of Accounting Education.
2. To prepare a survey instrument to poll those attending the regional discussion sessions to determine their degree of agreement with and support for the 1986 Report.
3. To summarize the findings of the regional surveys and to present these findings at a concurrent session of the 1987 annual meeting in Cincinnati.

COMMITTEE PROCESS

The organizational meeting of this Committee was held in August 1986. As a result of that meeting, the Committee members set out to gather the information necessary to respond to the charge.

Representatives of the Committee scheduled sessions at each of the regional meetings of the American Accounting Association. In some cases the involvement was as part of a plenary session. In other cases it was through a concurrent meeting. An effort was made at these meetings to gather information relating to the general reaction to the Bedford Committee report, and to assess the support or lack of support that might exist for specific elements of the Committee recommendations.

Two questionnaires (see Appendixes A and B for copies) were prepared, one for academicians and the other for practitioners. After the questionnaires were developed, some members of the Bedford Committee reviewed them to ascertain whether the questions captured the spirit of the 1986 report and its recommendations. The questions asked were not matched directly to the 28 recommendations of the Bedford Committee but accomplished the objectives detailed in our charge.

The President of the AAA and the Chairman of the Committee individually wrote letters to the administrators of accounting programs to solicit their support of the process by holding meetings with their faculty members and encouraging them to respond to the questionnaires. Also faculty members were encouraged to discuss the Bedford Committee report and to give serious consideration to that Committee's recommendations for the future of accounting education.

Members of the Committee attended a meeting of the Administrators of Accounting Programs Group to discuss the Committee's efforts and to gain an understanding of the possible concerns and potential responses to the original Committee recommendations. In addition, the Committee contacted representatives of the American Institute of CPAs, the Financial Executives' Institute, the National Association of Accountants, the Securities and Exchange Commission, the AAA Two-Year College Group, and other professional organizations. The Committee had formal responses from the American Institute of CPAs and the Financial Executives' Institute. The responses from these two organizations were incorporated into this report. In the analysis of the data, responses from individual members of the National Association of Accountants, the Two-Year College Group, and the American Institute of CPAs were also included.

OBSERVATIONS AND RECOMMENDATIONS

The presentation and analysis of the data gathered through attendance at AAA regional meetings, through the two questionnaires, and through contact with various individuals and organizations is included in a separate section of this report. This section contains the Committee's observations and recommendations organized on the same basis as the Bedford Committee report.

SCOPE

Observations

It appears that the majority of academic and practitioner professionals agree that the accounting profession is expanding and that the expectations of performance within the profession are changing. In addition, most agree that this changing environment will impact upon the future of accounting education.

Academicians believe that it will be difficult to shift accounting education to a new format and a new approach to the classroom. Practitioners believe that it will be difficult to shift accounting practice to a new mode of service. Thus it appears that the *transformation* will create problems for the profession, even though most agree that the transformation will be beneficial.

Recommendations

1. The American Accounting Association should give serious consideration to the organization and presentation of workshops and seminars in learning theory,

teaching methods, and classroom concepts.

2. The American Institute of CPAs, the National Association of Accountants, the Financial Executives' Institute, and other practicing professional bodies should give serious consideration to the organization and presentation of workshops and seminars directed to the practitioners. Preferably, the younger practitioners could be the starting point because of the potential for greater benefit from such education.

STRUCTURE AND CONTENT

Observations

It appears that the academicians and practitioners agree that a more structured approach to the selection of liberal arts and sciences courses is advisable, that more general business knowledge is desirable, that a broad base of general professional accounting education is essential, and that specialized professional accounting areas should be a part of a student's education. Combining all of these elements of an education, the academicians and practitioners conclude that a minimum of five years of education is required.

Academicians appear to believe that the introduction of specialized areas (tax, audit, etc.) is an important element of the broad introductory knowledge/skills that span the accounting discipline. Practitioners apparently support this position.

Although there is not universal support for a five-year education in preparation for the practice of accounting, the majority of respondents from both sectors support it. Thus it appears that less time need be devoted to convincing the profession of the need for the five-year preparation and more time devoted to the implementation of such a requirement.

Regarding the importance of the CPA and other professional examinations, it appears that academicians and practitioners *do not* consider the passing of such examinations to be a measure of the quality of an accounting program. However, many representatives of both groups believe that preparation for current practice is an important consideration in guiding the content of accounting courses. It does appear that the nature and content of the CPA examination have an impact upon the structure and content of the upper-level accounting courses, whether by design or by default.

Recommendations

1. The American Accounting Association should take a firm stand on the need for a five-year educational preparation for the profession. Implementing guidelines should be presented to the academic community.
2. Alternative approaches to a five-year education must be supported. An integrated five-year professional program may be one way to accomplish this education. Four years plus some practical experience plus additional education at the graduate level may be another approach.
3. Employer support of the five-year educational requirement is essential. This may be accomplished through tuition-support programs or through a two-tier employment program, with those holding a higher education being the employees who are designated as being on a professional track within the organization.

4. A model curriculum for a five-year program of education, incorporating the recommendations of the Bedford Committee, should be prepared by the American Accounting Association and/or other professional bodies. This curriculum must include specific courses and course content, rather than just areas of concern.
5. In the design of a model curriculum, consideration must be given to the appropriate placement of specialized accounting areas (tax, auditing. . .) in the sequence of courses.
6. The structure and content of courses in the model curriculum should not be influenced by the current format or content of the qualifying examinations.

FACULTY, ADMINISTRATIVE, AND PROFESSIONAL

The Teaching Process

Observations. Practically all respondents (96 percent) agree that educational experiences should be designed to require students to be active, independent learners and problem solvers rather than passive recipients of information. However, when the academicians are asked whether the learning objectives of current accounting courses are designed to help students to learn, to think, and to be creative, a smaller number (65 percent) indicate that their courses provide the means to accomplish such objectives.

Recommendations.

1. Doctoral programs should require a seminar in teaching methodology.
2. All existing faculty members should participate in a workshop on teaching methodology.
3. Outstanding teaching should be recognized in the same way as outstanding research and publishing.

Faculty Responsibilities

Observations. Faculty respondents are willing to accept the Bedford Committee's recommendations regarding the development of student capabilities, senior faculty teaching introductory courses, small class sizes, involvement with the profession, and so on. Current administrative policies and the reward structure do not appear to be flexible enough to accommodate the necessary increase of faculty involvement embodied in these recommendations.

Recommendation.

1. The successful implementation of the Committee recommendations in this area requires additional faculty involvement with students and with the profession. The value of such involvement must be communicated to deans and university administrators, and an appropriate reward structure must be created.

Evaluation of the Accounting Program

Observations. Support appears to be marginal for peer review of accounting programs. There is lack of support for limiting accreditation to graduate programs only.

DEMAND FOR ACCOUNTING GRADUATES

Observations

This section does not relate to any specific recommendations made by the original Committee. The questions were asked of practitioners to determine the mix of undergraduate/graduate hires and the knowledge/skills expected of future employees. The questions were also intended to test the receptiveness of the profession to the employment of those with an advanced education.

Practitioners have expressed the need for more knowledge in the four basic areas of education (liberal arts and sciences, business, general professional accounting, and specialized accounting). They also have indicated their expectation that this will take a five-year education program to accomplish. When asked here if they anticipated hiring more persons with graduate degrees and fewer with undergraduate degrees, the answer, at best, was a *marginal* "yes."

Recommendation

1. Given the acceptance by the practitioners of the need for additional education and the recognition of the time needed to accomplish this education, the practitioners must be willing to commit the necessary resources to hiring employees with graduate degrees.

GENERAL OBSERVATIONS AND CONCLUSION

As can be observed from the results of the Committee's effort, there is no doubt that both academicians and practitioners agree that change is needed to meet the demands of an expanded profession. Change is not easy, however, and it requires the complete cooperation of many different parties, including the American Accounting Association, professional practitioner associations (AICPA, FEI, NAA), and university administrators. Only with cooperation can meaningful change occur.

We now have two committee reports, and we understand that another committee will be appointed to follow the follow-up. The Committee believes the time has come to take action that will go beyond the preparation of reports.

AN ANALYSIS OF THE RESPONSES OF ACADEMICIANS AND PRACTITIONERS

In this section, the responses from the accounting academicians and practitioners are analyzed and contrasted to the items on the questionnaires. Most of these items are based on the recommendations of the Bedford Committee report. Some items are included in both questionnaires, and others are unique to each group. A copy of each questionnaire is attached (Appendixes A and B), and the interrelationships among the Bedford Committee recommendations and the two questionnaires are described in Appendices C through E.

The following analysis begins with items on both questionnaires grouped under certain factors in the spirit of the recommendations stated in the Bedford Committee report. Then the unique items, mainly for the practitioner group, are analyzed and discussed. Numbers in parentheses refer to questionnaire items.

SCOPE

Main Objective

Of the academicians who responded, 85.6 percent agree/strongly agree with the statement that "the accounting profession is expanding, entering new areas with new functions within organizations, within society and with new expectations for those who enter it" (#27). For the practitioner group, 85 percent agree/strongly agree compared with 4.7 percent who disagree/strongly disagree with the above statement (#22).

Although the answers to this question indicate that agreement exists on the future of the accounting profession and the expectations for it and its new members, the question does not address the relationship between the environment and accounting education.

Accounting Discipline

The Bedford Committee report characterizes "accounting [as] a total information system of which financial reports is a part" (#1). Of the academicians, 86.6 percent agree/strongly agree with this description of the accounting discipline, 8.1 percent disagree/strongly disagree. For the practitioners, 87.6 percent agree/strongly agree, and 8.6 percent disagree/strongly disagree with that description (#1).

When the educators were asked about the scope of accounting as a "broad economic information development and distribution process based on the design, implementation and operation of multiple types of information systems" (#2), 74.7 percent agree/strongly agree with this assessment. For the practitioner group, 75.5 percent agree/strongly agree versus 9.4 percent disagree/strongly disagree with this description of accounting (#2).

Implementation

As to whether academicians believe there is "difficulty with shifting accounting education from the traditional model of transaction recording to a broad economic information development" (#3), 66.1 percent agree/strongly agree that difficulties hinder the transformation process, but 17.2 percent did not perceive any difficulties. At one regional meeting some educators said that they feel comfortable teaching the material they learned during their education, but that the new expectations make them uncomfortable. This opinion is worth investigation because it indicates that educating academicians for the proposed shift in the scope of accounting education may be quite important.

Another, more sensitive, issue relating to the changing educational environment is a "political" consideration. Presently, in many educational institutions, departments of accounting and information systems are separate. If the recommendation of the Bedford Committee that accounting should be viewed as a "broad economic information development. . . process" is to become a reality, those who teach in information system departments might not be as receptive to this consideration as are the accounting educators.

For the practitioners, 63.8 percent agree/strongly agree versus 15.6 percent disagree/strongly disagree that it will be difficult to shift *accounting practice* from the traditional transaction model (#3). Thus significantly changing accounting to conform to the scope called for by the Bedford Committee report is seen as difficult by both academicians and practitioners.

STRUCTURE AND CONTENT OF THE ACCOUNTING PROGRAM

Liberal Arts Courses

Academicians were asked whether "liberal arts and science courses that aim to develop students' capabilities for analysis, synthesis, problem-solving, and communication are required" (#5). The issue here is not the requirement of courses in liberal arts and sciences per se, at random, but rather, the articulation of such courses with the development of students' personal and analytical skills that augment accounting requirements. Of the educators, 77.4 percent agree/strongly agree, 11.7 percent disagree/strongly disagree. For the practitioner group, 90.6 percent agree/strongly agree, but 5.7 percent disagree/strongly disagree with a corresponding statement (#5).

Accounting versus Liberal Arts (Ratio of Total and Content)

Although the Bedford Committee recommendations relating to liberal arts courses in the curriculum did not specify hours, the Committee believed it advisable to include a question on the number of hours required in existing programs. The questions specified "60 semester hours in liberal arts and science." As such, the question is very restrictive, and the responses are difficult to analyze. However, additional questions were asked that allowed the analysis to proceed to some meaningful conclusions.

When academicians were asked about the number of credit hours required in liberal arts and sciences (#6), 64.5 percent stated their programs require 60 credit hours. The 21.3 percent who disagree/strongly disagree may be at schools that require either greater or fewer credit hours. The accreditation of business schools allows a range between 54 to 66 semester hours in liberal arts and sciences courses. However, some states require 60 hours for a student to take the CPA exam.

Accounting educators were asked whether "accounting undergraduate programs should be structured to include general education (i.e., Humanities, Arts and Sciences) and general professional accounting education" (#11). Of this group, 93.2 percent agree/strongly agree. For the practitioners, 90.3 percent agree/strongly agree compared with 4.4 percent who disagree/strongly disagree with this requirement (#9). When academicians were asked if "the accounting undergraduate program should emphasize the broad introductory knowledge and skills *spanning* the entire spectrum of the accounting discipline," (#12) 90 percent agree/strongly agree. For the practitioner group, 89.5 percent agree/strongly agree, whereas 4.7 percent disagree/strongly disagree (#10).

Role of Specialized Courses in the Undergraduate Program

The issue of specialty was addressed by asking respondents to consider whether the "accounting undergraduate program should *not* cover in depth the specialized accounting areas (i.e., Tax, Auditing. . .)" (#13). Of the academicians 36.8 percent agree/strongly agree, but 50.9 percent disagree/strongly disagreed. For the practitioner, 38.9 percent agree/strongly agree, and 48.7 percent disagree/strongly disagree with this position (#11).

To follow up on this position, academicians were asked if "specialized professional accounting areas should be taught only at the graduate level" (#14). Of the educators 31.8 percent agree/strongly agree with this position and 53.4 percent disagree/strongly disagree. In the case of practitioners, 34.4 percent agree/strongly agree, and 49.7 percent disagree/strongly disagree (#12).

The message here is that many accounting academicians and practitioners consider some of the specialized areas to be a part of the broad introductory knowledge/skills that span the accounting discipline. How, then, can this be reconciled with the high level of agreement that the structure of the undergraduate program include a broad general professional accounting education? Can all of this be accomplished within a four-year requirement?

Time Requirement—The Fifth Year

Academicians responded that to cover all three levels of education (i.e., general education, general professional accounting education, and specialized professional education), a minimum of five years is required (#15). Responses indicate that 71 percent agree/strongly agree as compared with 16.1 percent who disagree/strongly disagree. For the practitioner group, 66.4 percent agree/strongly agree and 17.3 percent disagree/strongly disagree with this position (#13).

This collective response reveals that a substantial majority of accounting educators and practitioners believes in the need for a five-year program to attain the broad knowledge/skills that span the entire spectrum of the accounting discipline.

The Role of the CPA Exam

The discussion regarding the impact of the CPA exam on the structure, content, and method of delivery of accounting education is debated in other papers.

Accounting academicians were asked to respond to the following: "The quality of an accounting program can be inferred from the percentage of its graduates passing the CPA exam on the first sitting" (#9). The interest here is to test the perception and importance of this examination. Although 18.1 percent agree/strongly agree with this position, 50.5 percent disagree/strongly disagree.

In the case of the practitioners, 24.5 percent agree/strongly agree versus 48.6 percent who disagree/strongly disagree with this position (#7).

To explore the impact of the CPA exam on the content of the accounting curriculum, academicians were asked, "In preparing students for the future, accounting faculty rely on accounting practice and research. . . in establishing curriculum content *rather than* merely preparing them to qualify for current practice" (#10). The response was that 48.6 percent agree/strongly agree, but 26.6 percent disagree/strongly disagree. For the practitioners, 72.3 percent agree/strongly agree and 12.2 percent disagree/strongly disagree with this position (#8).

There is little doubt that the CPA exams have become an important element in structuring the content of accounting curricula, whether by design or by default. Interestingly, accounting academicians are not willing to admit that higher percentage pass rates on this exam at the first sitting is one surrogate for the quality of the program.

DEVELOPING STUDENTS' PERSONAL SKILLS

Advising

When asked whether undergraduate accounting students should be advised that "a rigorous general accounting education and the development of broad personal capacities and skills are preferable to premature specialization in accounting" (#4), 59 percent of the educators agree/strongly agree and 17.6 percent disagree/strongly disagree. This result may reflect the attitude of the responding accounting educators regarding the role of specialization, within the broad accounting education program. Within the practitioner group, 85.6 percent agree/strongly agree and 6.4 percent disagree/strongly disagree with this position (#4). The practitioners evidence more support for this recommendation than the academicians.

Student Personal Capabilities

1. Does "the content of [the] accounting program induce students to develop higher levels of professionalism, leadership, and work ethics" (#8)? Of the educators, 71 percent agree/strongly agree, and 9 percent disagree/strongly disagree. For the practitioner group, 93.9 percent agree/strongly agree, and 2 percent disagree/strongly disagree (#6).
2. Only educators were asked to assess the proposition that "a student's ambition, work ethics, and leadership potential are derived from within rather than taught" (#23). Responses indicated that 42 percent agree/strongly agree, and 31 percent disagree/strongly disagree.

Learning Method/Experience

In another educator-only question regarding whether learning objectives of accounting courses are developed to help students develop learning, thinking, and creative skills (#7), 65 percent agree/strongly agree, whereas 18 percent disagree/strongly disagree.

Regarding whether accounting faculty should design educational experiences for students that require them to be active, independent learners and problem solvers rather than passive recipients of information (#16), 97 percent of the educators agree/strongly agree and 1 percent disagree/strongly disagree. In the case of the practitioners, 94.9 percent agree/strongly agree and 1.6 percent disagree/strongly disagree (#14).

This apparently indicates the following:

1. Although accounting educators generally believe that educational experiences should be developed to nurture the personal skills of accounting students, there is no easy answer to the question of *how* this can be accomplished.
2. There is belief that although a student's ambition, work ethic, and potential leadership depend considerably on him or her, accounting programs can "add value" to develop, strengthen, and nurture these personal values.

The Role of Senior Faculty and Class Size

How can accounting educators develop these personal skills in their students?

Role model—The senior professor (#21)—"Senior faculty members should teach introductory courses." Of the educators, 68 percent agree/strongly agree, but 12 percent disagree/strongly disagree.

Class size to facilitate personal exchange/development of ideas (#22)— "Introductory accounting courses should not be taught in sections larger than 40 students." Of the educators, 64 percent agree/strongly agree, and 22 percent disagree/strongly disagree.

Accounting educators appear to prefer the role model, within a small class, to accomplish the development of those personal skills in their students. The economics of accounting education suggest that this development may not soon be realized.

Impact of Administration Policies

Can organizational policies hinder faculty delivery in the development of a student's personal skills?

The reward structure

- "My school rewards accounting faculty who work with students on intellectual issues emphasizing their personal development" (#17). Of the educators, 19 percent agree/strongly agree, but 55 percent disagree/strongly disagree.
- "At my school, the promotion and tenure decisions are based mainly on research" (#19). Of the educators, 64 percent agree/strongly agree, and 26 percent disagree/strongly disagree.
- "Accounting research grants are awarded by my university to support only theoretical research" (#20). Of the educators, 20 percent agree/strongly agree, and 57 percent disagree/strongly disagree .

We caution the interpretation of what constitutes "theoretical research." In retrospect, the term could have been more clearly defined because it is subject to (mis)interpretation.

For the practitioners, 14.7 percent agree/strongly agree versus 47.4 percent disagree/strongly disagree with the position that accounting research grants be awarded only for applied research (#16). Although a difference in perception of what constitutes applied research could exist, there appears to be a strong attitude in support of theoretical research that may not have immediate impact on the practicing profession.

- "My school rewards accounting faculty who serve the profession and the public through involvement in various professional activities" (#18). Of the academicians, 42 percent agree/strongly agree, but 36 percent disagree/strongly disagree. In the case of the practitioners, 86.6 percent agree/strongly agree, and 3.4 percent disagree/strongly disagree with the position for faculty involvement in the profession (#15).

Autonomy

- "Our university should allow decentralization, giving accounting faculties more autonomy regarding student admission and retention, budget and promotion" (#26). The responses indicate that 56 percent agree/strongly agree, and 21 percent disagree/strongly disagree.

In spite of moderate support for more autonomy for the accounting program, the Committee believes that acceptance within the institution is not promising. Only with the strong support of practitioners can progress toward that end be achieved.

EVALUATION OF THE ACCOUNTING PROGRAM

How should accounting programs be evaluated?

- "To maintain quality, the accounting department/school should implement educational peer reviews of its progress by accounting faculty from other schools and by practitioners" (#24). Of the educators, 53 percent agree/strongly agree, and 22 percent disagree/strongly disagree. For the practitioners, 71.5 percent agree/strongly agree and 8.8 percent disagree/strongly disagree with this position (#17).
- "Ultimately, only graduate programs in accounting should be subject to accreditation" (#25). Of the educators, 16 percent agree/strongly agree, and 65 percent disagree/strongly disagree. Apparently accreditation of undergraduate programs has a value and/or image attached to it, and it will continue for the foreseeable future.

DEMAND FOR ACCOUNTING GRADUATES (PRACTITIONERS ONLY)

The practitioners were asked certain questions to determine the future demand for accounting graduates and the degrees they should possess. By question, the responses are as follows:

- (#18)—46.6 percent agree/strongly agree and 16.1 percent disagree/strongly disagree with the statement that "in the future, more students with *graduate degrees* will be recruited by my organization."
- (#19)—56.3 percent agree/strongly agree and 15.5 percent disagree/strongly disagree with the statement that *"students with an accounting specialty"* (e.g., Tax, MIS. . .) will be more in demand."
- (#20)—18.7 percent agree/strongly agree but 30.8 percent disagree/strongly disagree with the statement that "over the next five years, the numbers of undergraduate new appointments will *decrease*."

It appears that, in the future, those with graduate degrees in a specialty area will be more in demand than those without, and the demand for those with an undergraduate degree will stay about the same (30.8 percent disagree/strongly disagree that hiring this group will decrease over the next five years).

ASSESSMENT OF EXISTING ACCOUNTING PROGRAMS

The practitioners were asked two questions to determine their attitudes toward the knowledge level of recent accounting graduates. A summary of their responses follows:

(#23)—25 percent agree/strongly agree and 31 percent disagree/strongly disagree with the statement that "recent accounting graduates are equipped with the knowledge and skills needed for an expanding profession." This raises a question as to where in the accounting curriculum more coverage is deemed necessary. We asked the following (#21), "Future accounting graduates should possess *more* basic knowledge/skills *in*:

1. Liberal arts and sciences (#21.a), 77.7 percent agree/strongly agree, and 10.4 percent disagree/strongly disagree.

2. General Business (21.b), 90.0 percent agree/strongly agree, 4.2 percent disagree/strongly disagree.
3. General Accounting (#21.c), 77.3 percent agree/strongly agree, and 8.7 percent disagree/strongly disagree.
4. Specialized Accounting (#21.d), 54.5 percent agree/strongly agree, 24.6 percent disagree/strongly disagree.

Interestingly, practitioners want more knowledge of general business. Although they want more in all areas, it is revealing that the relative desire for more specialized accounting is not high. This could be consistent with the observations at one regional meeting that the profession could train/educate the graduates in the very specialized areas, leaving basic general concepts to be covered in the formal institutional curriculum.

It should be emphasized that only 25 percent agree/strongly agree that recent accounting graduates are equipped with the knowledge/skills needed for an expanding profession. This requires a reexamination of the relationship between what is to be taught at the universities and what can be reserved for continuing education programs.

RESPONDENTS' UNSTRUCTURED COMMENTS

Some of the respondents from the practitioner group made comments questioning the perception that the Committees were equating "the profession" with those practicing CPAs in public accounting, and they questioned the emphasis in the accounting curriculum on topics covered by the CPA exam at the expense of other topics. They believe that a strong case can be made for the accounting curriculum to prepare students also for the CMA and CIA exams and for accounting generally. They also believe that the curriculum does not give proper weight to the information needs of nonprofit organizations to emphasize efficient and effective use of resources. Given the fact that many institutions offer an undergraduate track in managerial accounting as well as in public accounting, the content and the structure of both tracks is very similar. Coverage of the broad knowledge of the accounting discipline does not leave credit hours available to attend to the needs of speciality tracks within the traditional 120 semester hours. This could be an explanation for the strong support for the fifth year, with full knowledge of the constraints within which the accounting education system operates. An *undergraduate* accounting degree cannot require a meaningful increase above the 120 semester hours limitation. The practitioner response in favor of hiring more junior members with graduate degrees, as discussed earlier, provides support for the fifth year. The desired structure and content of the fifth year can be inferred from practitioner responses regarding the additional knowledge/skills needed from future graduates.

AN ANALYSIS OF SUBSAMPLE RESPONSES

In the previous section the analysis presented was based on the total response of each group. This section examines whether the total response is consistent with that of each group's subsample characteristics. Responses for the academic group are compared with responses for those in private and in public schools; for those from schools offering undergraduate programs only versus graduate only versus both; for those from accredited versus not accredited programs; for those who are full versus associate versus assistant professors; for those whose primary teaching area is financial, cost, tax, auditing, and so on. These characteristics may provide an in-depth analysis of whether there is homogeneity in responses.

In the practitioner group comparisons are made on the basis of where the respondents work (public accounting, industry, or nonprofit organizations, and on years of service.

For each group the response of each subsample for a given characteristic was analyzed for each item on the questionnaire. To conserve space, discussion is limited to only those items that exhibit different results from the total response. In most cases, major differences did not exist. The following are those that suggest differences in responses.

DIFFICULTY IN SHIFTING ACCOUNTING PRACTICE/EDUCATION (#1, #2, #3)

Although the practitioners agreed that accounting is a total information system of which financial accounting is a part (#l) and that accounting should be viewed as a broad economic information development. . . (#2), 63.8 percent expressed that it will be difficult to shift *accounting practice* from the traditional transaction model (#3). The academicians expressed the same concern relating to a shift in *accounting education.*

Analysis of the responses for (#3) by the number of years of practice reveals a difference: those with less than 10 years agree/strongly agree by 53.07 percent; those by 63.40 percent for those with 10-20 years; and by 66.67 percent those with more than 20 years.

Examination of the responses for (#3) by type of organization (public accounting, industry, nonprofit) indicates no major difference (65.54 percent versus 59.88 percent versus 63.27 percent). All of the subsamples on this dimension apparently agree that the shift will be difficult.

The analysis of the academicians' subsample for the same question reveals the following:

Response by Type of School (in percentages)

	Agree	Disagree
Private		
Bachelor	55.27	23.68
Mix	65.29	13.23
Graduate	46.15	42.31
Public		
Bachelor	69.75	16.81
Mix	67.58	16.89
Graduate	68.75	14.29

Public school respondents perceive greater difficulty in shifting than do those in private schools, although both agree it will be a problem.

Response by Primary Teaching Area

No major differences were noted in responses by grouped primary areas of teaching, such as financial, cost, tax, or auditing. All agree that it will be difficult to shift.

SPECIALIZED AREA (#11)

Of the practitioners, 38.9 percent agree on *not* covering specialized areas at the undergraduate level, and 48.7 disagreed. The subsample results reveal the following:

Response by Number of Years of Service (in percentages)

	Agree	Disagree
Less than 10	29.89	58.76
10–20	33.68	55.44
20 years	43.70	42.93

Those with more than 20 years are divided on the issue. However, those with less than ten years disagree/strongly disagree with the position of not including specialized areas at the undergraduate level.

Response by Type of Organization (in percentages)

	Agree	Disagree
Public Accounting	41.12	47.20
Industry	35.46	49.42
Nonprofit	35.42	54.16

The disagreement with the position of *not* covering, in depth, the specialized areas at the undergraduate level is strong. Respondents from the nonprofit sector and industry generally believe that specialized knowledge should be taught at the undergraduate level.

Also, there is strong disagreement, based on type of organization for practitioners, as to teaching specialized accounting areas *only* at the graduate level (#12).

Response by Type of Jobs (in percentages)

	Agree	Disagree
Public Accounting	36.32	46.49
Industry	31.40	59.65
Nonprofit	31.25	54.17

For academicians there was no basic difference in response based on primary teaching area, rank, or other classifications regarding their disagreement with the position that the undergraduate program should not cover in depth specialized areas or that they should be taught only at the graduate level.

FIVE-YEAR PROGRAM

There is agreement for the need for five years of education among respondents classified by years of service and by type of organization for the practitioner group. The response from the academicians classified by primary teaching area, by rank, or by other characteristics did not reveal different responses for the support for the fifth year.

THE ROLE OF THE CPA EXAM (ACADEMICIANS)

(#10)—Private and Public Schools

Of the respondents from private schools, 55.83 percent agree/strongly agree on not limiting curriculum content to subject matter intended to help the student pass the CPA exam; 45.56 percent expressed the same attitude from public schools. The responses indicated that 22.50 percent from the private schools versus 28.37 percent from the public schools disagree/strongly disagree with this position.

The message seems to be that public school respondents see CPA exams as having slightly more impact on accounting course content.

(#10)—Types of Program and School (bachelor only, graduate only, and both, by private and public school)

There is a more pronounced difference in response patterns between private schools and public schools when type of program is considered (in percentages).

	Agree	Disagree
Private		
Bachelor	58.11	18.92
Mix	45.91	28.69
Graduate	72.00	16.00
Public		
Bachelor	34.74	38.14
Mix	43.05	30.55
Graduate	52.94	22.17

The respondents from private schools offering only bachelor's or graduate degrees indicate that the impact of the CPA exam on the content of accounting courses is less than those from the public schools offering the same degrees.

APPENDIX A
FACULTY QUESTIONNAIRE

Dear Colleague:
This questionnaire is based on the AAA Committee report, "Future Accounting Education: Preparing for the Expanding Profession." Please return this questionnaire, after checking your choice on the described scale, to your chairperson.

Please circle your response:

1) My school is (a) Private (b) Public
2) The accounting degrees offered by our school:
   (a) bachelor
   (b) bachelor, M.S., MBA-accounting
   (c) bachelor, M.S., MBA-accounting, Ph.D.
   (d) graduate school only—MBA Ph.D.
3) The number of accounting graduates with bachelor's degrees per year:
   A. Undergraduate B: Graduate
   (a) less than 100 (a) less than 50
   (b) 101-200 (b) 51-100
   (c) above 200 (c) above 100
4) The majority of our graduates are hired by
   (a) CPA firms (b) others, industry, government., etc.
5) Our accounting program is accredited by AACSB
   (a) yes (b) no
6) Our business school is accredited by AACSB
   (a) yes (b) no
7) I have been teaching:
   (a) less than 5 years (b) 5–10 years (c) above 10 years
8) My academic rank is
   (a) Full Professor (b) Associate Professor (c) Assistant Professor
9) My primary area of teaching is:
   (a) Financial Accounting (b) Cost/Managerial (c) Tax
   (d) Auditing (e) System (f) Other
10) I have read the AAA report "Future Accounting Education...."
   (a) yes (b) no

Please circle your choice on the following scale:

1	2	3	4	5
strongly agree	agree	not sure	disagree strongly	disagree

1) Accounting is a total information system of which financial reporting is a part.	1	2	3	4	5
2) Accounting should be viewed as a broad economic information development and distribution process based on the design, implementation, and operation of multiple types of information systems.	1	2	3	4	5
3) It will be difficult to shift accounting education from the traditional model of transaction recording to a broad economic information development model.	1	2	3	4	5
4) Our accounting faculty advises students that a rigorous general accounting education and the development of broad personal capacities and skills are preferable to premature specialization in accounting.	1	2	3	4	5
5) Our accounting program requires students to take liberal arts and science courses that aim to develop their capacities for analysis, synthesis, problem-solving, and communication.	1	2	3	4	5

6) Our undergraduate accounting program requires students to take 60 semester hours in liberal arts and science.	1	2	3	4	5
7) Learning objectives of our accounting courses are developed to help students learn to learn, to think, and to be creative.	1	2	3	4	5
8) The content of our accounting program induces students to develop higher levels of professionalism, leadership, and work ethics.	1	2	3	4	5
9) The quality of an accounting program can be inferred from the percentage of its graduates passing the CPA exam on the first sitting.	1	2	3	4	5
10) In preparing students for the future, our accounting faculty relies on accounting practice and research, and on multidisciplinary research, in establishing curriculum content, rather than merely preparing them to qualify for current practice.	1	2	3	4	5
11) An accounting program should structure its undergraduate requirements to include humanities, arts and sciences (general education) and the general conceptual information development and reporting knowledge required of all accountants (general professional accounting education).	1	2	3	4	5
12) The undergraduate accounting program should emphasize the broad introductory knowledge and skills spanning the entire spectrum of the accounting discipline.	1	2	3	4	5
13) The undergraduate accounting program should not cover in depth the specialized accounting areas (i.e., Tax, Auditing,...)	1	2	3	4	5
14) Specialized professional accounting areas should be taught only at the graduate level.	1	2	3	4	5
15) A complete accounting curriculum covering all three levels of education (i.e., general education, general professional accounting education, and specialized professional accounting education) will require a minimum of five years.	1	2	3	4	5
16) Accounting faculty should design educational experiences for students that require them to be active, independent learners and problems solvers rather than passive recipients of information.	1	2	3	4	5
17) My school rewards accounting faculty who work with students on intellectual issues emphasizing their personal development.	1	2	3	4	5
18) My school rewards accounting faculty who serve the profession and the public through involvement in various professional activities.	1	2	3	4	5
19) At my school, the promotion and tenure decisions are based mainly on research.	1	2	3	4	5
20) Accounting research grants are awarded by my university, to support only theoretical research.	1	2	3	4	5
21) Senior faculty members should teach introductory accounting courses.	1	2	3	4	5
22) Introductory accounting courses should not be taught in sections larger than 40 students.	1	2	3	4	5
23) A student's ambition, work ethics, and leadership potential are derived from within, rather than taught.	1	2	3	4	5

24) To maintain quality, the accounting department/school should implement educational peer reviews of its programs by accounting faculty from other schools, and by practitioners. 1 2 3 4 5
25) Ultimately, only graduate programs in accounting should be subject to accreditation. 1 2 3 4 5
26) Our university should allow decentralization, giving accounting faculties more autonomy, regarding student admission and retention, budget and promotion. 1 2 3 4 5
27) The accounting profession is expanding, entering a new era with new functions within organizations and within society and with new expectations of those who enter it. 1 2 3 4 5

APPENDIX B
PRACTITIONER QUESTIONNAIRE

INTRODUCTION

This questionnaire is based on the American Accounting Association Committee report, "Future Accounting Education: Preparing for the Expanding Profession." Please return this questionnaire, after checking your choice on the described scale in the attached envelope.

Please circle your appropriate response:
I have been practicing accounting:
(a) less than 10 years (b) 10–20 years (c) more than 20 years
2) My present job is in:
(a) public accounting practice: ( ) national ( ) regional ( ) local
(b) industry
(c) nonprofit organization
( ) Federal ( ) State & local ( ) Other
3) My undergraduate degree was:
(a) accounting (b) in another area
4) I have read the AAA Committee report, "Future Accounting Education . . . ."
(a) yes (b) no
Please circle your choice using the following scale:

1	2	3	4	5
strongly agree	agree	not sure	disagree strongly	disagree

1) Accounting is a total information system of which financial reporting is a part. 1 2 3 4 5
2) Accounting should be viewed as a broad economic information development and distribution process based on the design, implementation and operation of multiple types of information systems. 1 2 3 4 5
3) It will be difficult to shift accounting practice from the traditional model of transaction recording to a broad economic information development model. 1 2 3 4 5
4) Accounting faculty should advise students that a rigorous general accounting education and the development of broad personal capacities and skills are preferable to premature specialization in accounting. 1 2 3 4 5
5) Accounting programs should encourage students to take liberal arts and science courses that aim to develop their capacities for analysis, synthesis, problems solving, and communication. 1 2 3 4 5

6) The content of accounting programs should induce students to develop higher levels of professionalism, leadership and work ethics. 1 2 3 4 5

7) The quality of an accounting program can be inferred from the percentage of its graduates passing the CPA exam on the first sitting. 1 2 3 4 5

8) In preparing students for the future, accounting faculty should rely on accounting practice and research, and on multidisciplinary research, in establishing curriculum content, rather than merely preparing them to qualify for current practice. 1 2 3 4 5

9) An accounting program should structure its undergraduate requirements to include humanities, arts and sciences (general education) and the general conceptual information development and reporting knowledge required of all accountants (general professional accounting education). 1 2 3 4 5

10) The undergraduate accounting program should emphasize the broad introductory knowledge and skills spanning the entire spectrum of the accounting discipline. 1 2 3 4 5

11) The undergraduate accounting program should not cover in depth the specialized accounting areas (i.e., Tax, Auditing, . . .). 1 2 3 4 5

12) Specialized professional accounting areas should be taught only at the graduate level. 1 2 3 4 5

13) A complete accounting curriculum covering all three levels of education (i.e., general education, general professional accounting education, and specialized professional accounting education) will require a minimum of five years. 1 2 3 4 5

14) Accounting faculty should design educational experiences for students that require them to be active, independent learners and problem solvers rather than passive recipients of information. 1 2 3 4 5

15) Accounting faculty should serve the profession and the public through involvement in various professional activities. 1 2 3 4 5

16) Accounting research grants should be awarded to support only applied research. 1 2 3 4 5

17) To maintain quality, the accounting department should implement educational peer reviews of its programs by accounting faculty from other schools, and by practitioners. 1 2 3 4 5

18) In the future, more students with graduate degrees will be recruited by my organization. 1 2 3 4 5

19) Students with an accounting specialty (e.g., Tax, MIS,...) will be more in demand. 1 2 3 4 5

20) Over the next five years, the numbers of undergraduate new appointments will decrease. 1 2 3 4 5

21) Future accounting graduates should possess more basic knowledge/skills in:
(a) Liberal arts and science (b) General Business
(c) General Accounting (d) Specialized Accounting 1 2 3 4 5

22) The accounting profession is expanding, entering a new era with new functions within organizations and within society and with new expectations of those who enter it. 1 2 3 4 5

23) Recent accounting graduates are equipped with the knowledge and skills needed for an expanding profession. 1 2 3 4 5

APPENDIX C
MATCH OF ACADEMICIAN QUESTIONNAIRE ITEMS TO BEDFORD COMMITTEE RECOMMENDATIONS

	Bedford Committee	Questionnaire Items
A. SCOPE & CONTENT	#1	#2
	#2	#3
	#3	#5
	#4	—
	#5	#7
	#6	—
	#7	#26
B. STRUCTURE		
	#8	#11, #12 , #13
	#9	#14, #15
	#10	(came into discussion at regional meetings)
C. FACULTY, ADMINISTRATIVE, AND PROFESSIONAL CONCERN		
1. Teaching Process		
	#11	#16
	#12	#17
	#13	—
2. Faculty Responsibilities		
	#14	—
	#15	#20 (some changes)
3. Administration		
	#16	#26 (some changes)
	#17	#21, #22
	#18	#17
	#19	#24
	#20	—
4. Accreditation/University		
	#21	—
	#22	—
	#23	#26
	#24	—
5. Professional Exams		
	#25	#10, #9
6. Economic Dimensions of Accounting Education		
	#26	—
	#27	—
	#28	#17-20 (could provide answer to these issues)

APPENDIX D
MATCH OF BEDFORD COMMITTEE TOPICS TO FACULTY AND PRACTITIONER QUESTIONNAIRE NUMBERS

	Questionnaire Numbers	
	Academicians	Practitioners
I. SCOPE		
A. Main objective	#27	#22
B. Accounting discipline nature	#1,2	#1,2
C. Implementation	#3	#3
II. STRUCTURE AND CONTENT		
A. Liberal Arts.....NOT random	#5	#5
B. Accounting versus. liberal arts (ratio, content)	#6,11,12	#9,10
C. Role of specialized courses	#13,14	#11,12
D. Time requirement - Fifth year	#15	#13
E. Role of CPA exams	#9,10	#7,8
III. STUDENT DEVELOPMENT		
A. Advising	#4	#4
B. Student personal capabilities	#8,23	#6
C. Learning method experience	#7,16	#14
D. Role of senior faculty and class size	#21,22	—
E. Impact of administrative policies on implementation	#17,18,19, 20,26	#15,16
IV. EVALUATION OF THE ACCOUNTING PROGRAM	#24, 25	#17
V. DEMAND		
A. For graduate degrees	—	#18,19
B. For undergraduate degrees	—	#20
VI. ASSESSMENT OF EXISTING PROGRAM OUTPUT		
A. As is today	—	#23
B. Areas to expand	—	#21 (A-D)

APPENDIX E
MATCH OF QUESTIONNAIRE NUMBERS BETWEEN FACULTY AND PRACTITIONER FORMS

Academicians	Practitioners
#1	#1
#2	#2
#3	#3
#4	#4
#5	#5
#6	—
#7	—
#8	#6
#9	#7
#10	#8
#11	#9
#12	#10

Academicians	Practitioners
#13	#11
#14	#12
#15	#13
#16	#14
#17	—
#18	#15
#19	—
#20	#16
#21	—
#22	—
#23	—
#24	#17
#25	—
#26	—
#27	#22

APPENDIX F
CLASSIFICATION OF FACULTY RESPONDENTS

		Private	Public	Total
1)	Number of respondents	247	572	819
2)	Responses by degree offered			
	Bachelor only	76	119	195
	Mix	150	444	594
	Graduate only	21	9	30
		247	572	819
3)	Responses for accredited business schools			
	Yes	166	464	630
	No	81	108	189
		247	572	819
4)	Responses for accredited accounting program			
	Yes	90	278	368
	No	157	294	451
		247	572	819
5)	Response by rank			
	Full Professor	70	221	291
	Associate Professor	91	145	236
	Assistant Professor	82	192	274
	Other	4	14	18
		247	572	819
6)	Response by primary teaching area			
	Financial	124	265	389
	Cost/Managerial	58	132	190
	Tax	26	77	103
	Auditing	24	53	77
	Systems	11	32	43
	Others	4	13	17
		247	572	819

APPENDIX G
THE PRACTITIONER GROUP

Years of service	
Less than 10	98
10–20	195
More than 20 years	395
	688
Type of work	
CPA practice	418
Industry	172
Nonprofit	98
	68

REFERENCES

Allyn, Robert G., "Accreditation of Accounting Curriculums," *The Accounting Review* (April 1966), pp. 303–311.

American Accounting Association (AAA), "Report of the Committees on Accreditation," *The Accounting Review* (supplement 1977), pp. 161–177.

———, Committee on the Future Structure, Content, and Scope of Accounting Education, "Future Accounting Education: Preparing for the Expanding Profession," *Issues in Accounting Education* (Spring 1986), pp. 168–190.

———, Committee on Changes in Accounting Education, unpublished report, 1987 (AAA, 1987A).

———, Committee on Future Structure, Content, and Scope of Accounting Education, unpublished report, 1987 (AAA, 1987B).

———, *Report on Supply and Demand for Accounting Professors* (Sarasota, Fla: American Accounting Association, 1987; AAA 1987C).

———, Committee on Contemporary Approaches to Teaching Accounting Information Systems, *Journal of Information Systems* (Spring 1987; AAA 1987D).

American Assembly of Collegiate Schools of Business (AACSB), *Membership Directory*, annual.

———, "Accreditation Council Policies, Procedures and Standards" (1986), pp. 43–45.

———, "Accredited Accounting Programs: Listing by State" (1986–87).

American Association of Fund-Raising Council, *Giving USA—Annual Report 1985* (American Association of Fund-Raising Council, 1986).

American Institute of Certified Public Accountants (AICPA), *Supply and Demand of Accounting Graduates*, annual publication.

———, *Accounting Education: A Statistical Survey 1972–73*, AICPA (1973).

———, *Accounting Education: A Statistical Survey 1977–78*, AICPA (1978).

———, *Accounting Education: A Statistical Survey 1982–83*, AICPA (1983).

———, "AACSB Accredits Six," *Journal of Accountancy* (July 1987), p. 50.

———, "AICPA Members 'Vote for Excellence,'" *The CPA Letter* (January 15, 1988).

——— and National Association of Schools of Business Administration, *Digest of State Accountancy Laws and State Board Regulations* (New York: AICPA and NASBA, 1987-88).

American Taxation Association, 1977–78 Committee on Undergraduate Tax Education," *The Accounting Review* (July 1981).

Arens, Alvin, and James Loebbecke, *Auditing, An Integrated Approach*, Prentice-Hall (1984).

Arthur Andersen & Co., Private Data from World Headquarters Office (Fall 1985).

———, Arthur Young, Coopers & Lybrand, Deloitte Haskins & Sells, Ernst & Whinney, Peat Marwick Mitchell & Co., Price Waterhouse, and Touche Ross,

Perspectives on Education: Capabilities for Success in the Accounting Profession (April, 1989).

Ball, R., and P. Brown, "An Empirical Evaluation of Accounting Income Numbers," *Journal of Accounting Research* (Autumn 1968), pp. 159-178.

Bausch, T. A., "Pressure on for Improved Faculty, Curriculum Reform," *AACSB Newsline* (October 1987), pp. 8–9.

Beaver, W. H., "The Information Content of Annual Earnings Announcements," *Journal of Accounting Research* (Supplement 1968), pp. 67–92.

Bedford, N. M., and W. G. Shenkir, "Reorienting Accounting Education," *Journal of Accountancy* (August 1987), pp. 84–91.Bloom, Robert, "The Development of Schools of Accounting and the Underlying Issues," *Journal of Accounting Education* (Spring 1986), pp. 7–29

Bloom, R., "Research: For Pedagogue or Practitioner?" *CA Magazine* (January 1986), pp. 66–68.

Board of Examiners of the American Institute of Certified Public Accountants, *Proposed Changes in the Uniform CPA Examination*, Exposure Draft (New York: American Institute of Certified Public Accountants, 1987).

Bok, D. C., *Higher Learning* (Cambridge, Mass.: Harvard University Press, 1986).

Boley, Richard, and Paul Danos, "Awareness and Usage of LEXIS by Accounting Educators," *The Accounting Review* (January 1980).

———, and Edmund Outslay, "Doctoral Programs with a Concentration in Taxation: An Examination of Recent Trends," *Journal of the American Taxation Association* (Fall 1986).

Boley, Richard, and Patrick J. Wilkie, "Practitioners' Views of the Common Body of Tax Knowledge for Persons Entering Public Accounting," *Journal of American Taxation Association* (Fall 1986). Bowen, H. R., and J. H. Schuster, *American Professors: A Natural Resource Imperiled* (New York: Oxford University Press, 1986).

Bowen, H. R., and J. H. Schuster, *American Professors: A Natural Resource Imperiled* (New York: Oxford University Press, 1986).

Boze, K. M., C. T. Cox, and L. Schwendig, "An Examination of Accounting Faculty's Actual and Preferred Use of Time," Working paper (1986).

Broden, Barry C., and Myron S. Lubell, "The Master's Degree in Taxation: An Assessment of its Growth and Future," *Journal of the American Taxation Association* (Summer 1979).

Brown, James F. Jr., and Thomas Balke, "Accounting Curriculum Comparison by Degree Program of Schools Intending to Seek AACSB Accreditation," *Issues in Accounting Education* (1983).

Bureau of Labor Statistics, U.S. Department of Labor, *Occupational Projections and Training Data* (Washington, D.C.: U.S. Government Printing Office, 1986).

Burdick, R. K., "Statement of Hypotheses in the Analysis of Variance," *Journal of Marketing Research* (August 1983), pp. 320–324.

Burton, John C., "The Evolutionary Revolution in Public Accounting," Abraham Pomerantz Lecture, Brooklyn Law School, October 21, 1985.

Campbell, David R., "Accreditation of Accounting Programs: Administrators' Perception of Proposed AACSB Standards," *Issues of Accounting Education* (1983).

———, J. Gaertner, and R. P. Vecchio, "Perceptions of Promotion and Tenure Criteria: A Survey of Accounting Educators," *Journal of Accounting Education* (Spring 1983), pp. 83–92.

Campbell, D. R., and R. G. Morgan, "Publication Activity of Promoted Accounting Faculty," *Issues in Accounting Education* (Spring 1987), pp. 28–43.

Campbell, T. L., and R. H. Hermanson, *Doctoral Programs in Accounting—1986* (Plans, Tex.: Business Publication, 1986).

———, "Doctoral Programs in Accounting: Trends and Estimated Output 1985–1987," Working paper (1987).

Cargile, B. R., and B. Bublitz, "Factors Contributing to Published Research by Accounting Faculties," *The Accounting Review* (January 1986), pp. 158–178.

Carnegie Foundation for the Advancement of Teaching, *College: The Undergraduate Experience in America* (Princeton, N.J.: Carnegie Foundation, 1987).

College Blue Book, The, annual (Macmillan Publishing Co.).

Commission on Auditor's Responsibility, *Report, Conclusions, and Recommendations* (New York, 1978).

Cooperative Institutional Research Program, University of California at Los Angeles and American Council on Education, *The American Freshman: National Norms for Fall 1971–1984* (Los Angeles: University of California at Los Angeles: Graduate School of Education, 1971–1984).

Daroca, F. P., and W. T. Lin, "Toward Accounting Education by the Year 2000," Working paper (1987).

Dyckman, Thomas R., "On the Investment Decision," *The Accounting Review* (April 1964), pp. 285 ff. (Dyckman, 1964A).

———, "The Effects of Alternative Accounting Techniques on Certain Management Decisions," *Journal of Accounting Research* (Spring 1964), pp. 91 ff. (Dyckman, 1964B).

Eichenseher, J. W., and P. Danos, "The Analysis of Industry—Specific Auditor Concentration: Towards an Explanatory Model," *The Accounting Review* (July 1981), pp. 479–492.

Elliott, R. K. "Auditing in the 1990s: Implication for Education and Research," *California Management Review* (Summer 1986), pp. 89–97.

Engle, Terry J., and Rick Elam, "The Status of Collegiate Auditing Education," *Issues in Accounting Education* (1985).

Ernst & Whinney, *Ernst & Whinney Guide to Graduate Tax Education* (1987).

Ernst & Whinney People (Summer 1986).

Fawcett, C., "Effective Education and Training for the 21st Century," *Accountancy* (September 1986), pp. 139–140.

Flaherty, Richard E., Personal Interview (June 30, 1989).

Frakes, Albert H., "Survey of Undergraduate Auditing Education," Working paper (1986).

Gardner, Deborah, Letter from Executive Office of the American Accounting Association (December 10, 1987).

Gordon, R.A., and J. E. Howell, *Higher Education in Business* (New York: Columbus University Press, 1959).

Greene, R., "Blood on the Ledger," *Forbes* (May 18, 1987), pp. 202–204.

Grinaker, Robert L., "The Auditing Curriculum—Is There a Need for a Change?"

Researching the Accounting Curriculum: Strategies for Change ,American Accounting Association (1975).

Hasselback, J. R., *Accounting Faculty Directory* (Engelwood Cliffs, N.J.: Prentice-Hall, 1974, 1986, and 1987).

Heller, Kenneth H. et. al., "Committee Report, American Taxation Association, 1979–1980 Committee on Undergraduate Tax Education (July 1980).

Higher Education Research Institute, University of California at Los Angeles and the American Council of Education, *The American Freshman: Twenty Year Trends, 1966–1985* (Los Angeles: University of California at Los Angeles: Graduate School of Education, 1985).

Howard, T. P., and L. A. Nikolai, "Attitude Measurement and Perceptions of Accounting Faculty Publication Outlets," *The Accounting Review* (October 1983), pp. 765–776.

Implementation Committees on Standards of Professional Conduct for Certified Public Accountants, *Plan to Restructure Professional Standards* (New York: American Institute of Certified Public Accountants, 1987).

Jackson, D. W., J. E. Keith, and R. K. Burdick, "Purchasing Agents' Perceptions of Industrial Buying Center Influence: A Situational Approach," *Journal of Marketing* (Fall 1984), pp. 75–83.

Jacobs, F.A., A. L. Hartgraves, and L. H. Beard, "Publication Productivity of Doctoral Alumni: A Time-Adjusted Model," *The Accounting Review* (January 1986), pp. 179–187.

Jacobs, F. A., and H. C. Herring, III, "Salary Compression in the Academic Marketplace: Some Empirical Evidence," *Issues in Accounting Education* (Fall, 1987), pp. 237–250.

Jensen, Daniel L., ed., *The Impact of Rule-Making on Intermediate Financial Accounting Textbooks*, Ohio State University (1982).

Kirk, Roger E., *Experimental Design: Procedures for the Behavioral Sciences* (Belmont, Calif.: Wadsworth Publishing Co., 1968).

Kneer, Dan C., "Master's Degree Programs in Accounting Information Systems/EDP Auditing," *The Journal of Information Systems* (Fall 1986).

Langenderfer, Harold Q., "Accounting Education's History- A 100 Year Search for Identity," *Journal of Accountancy* (May 1987), p. 302– 331.

Larson, R. E., "For the Members, By the Members," *Journal of Accountancy* (October, 1987), pp. 116–122.

Lewis, M. T., W. T. Lin, and D. Z. Williams, "The Economic Status of Accounting Educators: An Empirical Study," *Advances in Accounting* (1984), pp. 127–144.

Lubell, Myron S,. and Barry C. Broden, "The Master's Degree in Taxation: An Academic Survey," *The Accounting Review* (January 1975).

MacNeill, J. H., "Tomorrow Is Now," *Massachusetts CPA Review* (Spring 1987), reprinted in *Journal of Accountancy* (August 1987), pp. 132–133.

Marshall, Don C. et al., "Committee Report, American Taxation Association, 1985–86 Committee on Computer Assisted Tax Research" (February 1987).

Mautz, Robert and Hussein Sharaf, *A Philosophy of Auditing*, American Accounting Association (1961).Mednick, R., "Our Profession in the Year 2000: A Blueprint of the Future," *Journal of Accountancy* (August 1988), pp. 54–58.

Mednick, R., "Our Profession in the Year 2000: A Blueprint of the Future," *Journal of*

Accountancy (August 1988), pp. 54–58.

Mitchell, F., "School Accounting Qualifications and Student Performance in First Level University Accounting Examinations," *Accounting and Business Research* (Spring 1985), pp. 81–86.

Mueller, Gerhard, Memorandum to the American Accounting Association Executive Committee (January 9, 1989).

National Center for Education Statistics, Office of Educational Research and Improvement, U. S., Department of Education, *The Condition of Education*, 1985 Edition (Washington D.C.: U.S. Government Printing Office, 1985).

—, *Projections of Education Statistics to 1983–1984, 1992–1993* (Washington, D.C.: U.S. Government Printing Office, 1974, 1985).

National Commission on Excellence in Education, U. S. Department of Education, *A Nation at Risk: The Imperative for Educational Reform* (Washington, D.C.: U.S. Government Printing Office, 1983).

Palmrose, Z., "Litigation and Independent Auditors: The Role of Business Failures and Management Fraud," *Auditing: A Journal of Practice and Theory* (Spring 1987), pp. 90–103.

Peat, Marwick, Mitchell Foundation, *Peat Marwick Foundation Research Opportunities in Auditing Program, Interim Report 1986* (Peat, Marwick, Mitchell Foundation, 1986).

Pierce, J. L., "Controllership and Treasurership: Modern Definitions," *Financial Executive* (June 1964), pp. 49–52.

Pierce-Snyder, Speech at the American Accounting Association Annual Meeting, Reno, Nev., August, 1985.

Pierson, F. C., *The Education of American Businessmen* (New York: McGraw-Hill, 1959).

Practicing CPA (January 1985), pp. 3–5.

Raby, William L., *The Income Tax and Business Decisions*, Prentice-Hall (1964).

Reinstein, A., and R. G. Schroeder, "The Impact of Additional Quality Standards upon Future Accounting Faculty and the Accreditation Process," *Journal of Education for Business* (May 1986), pp. 348–353.

Robert, R., and J. MacNeill, *Horizons for a Profession* (New York: American Institute of Certified Public Accountants, 1967).

Robert Half's Prevailing Financial and Data Processing Starting Salaries 1987 (New York: Robert Half International, 1987).

SAS User's Guide: Basics, Version 5 Edition (Cary, N.C.: SAS Institute, Inc., 1985)

SAS User's Guide: Statistics, Version 5 Edition (Cary, N.C.: SAS Institute, Inc., 1985)

Schaffer, J. P., "The Analysis of Variance Mixed Model with Allocated Observations: Application to Repeated Measurement Designs," *Journal of the American Statistical Association* (September 1981), pp. 607–611.

Shimerda, Thomas A., and Tom D. Lewis, "Five-Year Accounting Programs and Professional Schools of Accountancy: A Report on their Current Status," *Georgia Journal of Accounting* (Spring 1983).

Skadden, Donald H. et. al., "Committee Report, American Accounting Association, 1961 Committee on Income Tax Instruction," *The Accounting Review* (July 1962).

Smith, Jay M., "The Advanced Financial Accounting Curriculum—Recent Developments

Practice in Courses Beyond the Introductory Level," *Researching the Accounting Curriculum—Strategies for Change*, American Accounting Association (1975).

———— ,"Audit Education for the 1980s," *The Accounting Review* (April 1978).

Sommerfeld, Ray M., "Taxation: Education's Orphan," *Journal of Accountancy* (December 1966).

———— , *Federal Taxes and Management Decisions*, Richard D. Irwin (1974).

———— , "The Taxation Curriculum— Is There a Need for a Change?" *Researching the Accounting Curriculum: Strategies for Change*, American Accounting Association (1975).

Special Committee on Standards of Professional Conduct for Certified Public Accountants, *Restructuring Professional Standards to Achieve Professional Excellence in a Changing Environment* (New York: American Institute of Certified Public Accountants, 1986).

Standish, P.E.M., "An Appraisal of the Teaching and Studying of Auditing," *The Accounting Review* (July 1964).

Stigler, G., *The Organization of Industry* (Homewood, Ill.: Irwin, 1968).

Stedry, Andrew C., *Budget Control and Cost Behavior*, The Ford Foundation Doctoral Dissertation Series, 1959 Award Winner (Englewood Cliffs, N.J.: Prentice-Hall, 1960), pp. xiii–161.

Thomashower, J. E., Personal Correspondence (June 2, 1989).

Timm, N. H., "Multivariate Analysis of Variance of Repeated Measures," in P. R. Krishnaiak (Ed.), *Handbook of Statistics*, vol. 1 (New York: North-Holland Publishing, 1980), pp. 41–87.

Touche Ross, *The Business of a Business Education* (New York: Touche Ross, 1986).

United States Bureau of the Census, *Statistical Abstract of the United States 1961–86* (Washington, D.C.: U.S. Government Printing Office, 1961–86).

United States Dept. of Education, National Center for Education statistics, Fall Enrollment in Higher Education.

Usry, Milton F., "Accounting Student Quality," *CPA Journal* (September 1987).

Vasarhelyi, M. A., D. H. Bao, and J. Berk, "Data Base of Six Accounting Journals" (Computer Disks, 1987).

White, Debra M. et al., "Committee Report American Taxation Association, 1984–85 Computer Usage Committee," *Journal of the American Taxation Association* (Spring 1987).

Williams, Doyle Z., *Accounting Education: A Statistical Survey 1967–68*, AICPA (1968).

———— , "Ten Years of Changes in Accounting Education," Working paper (University of Southern California, 1979).

———— , M. T. Lewis, and W. T. Lin, "Accounting Data Base: 1979–80, 1980–81, 1982–83, 1983–84, 1984–85, 1985–86, 1986–87" Administrators of Accounting Programs Group (Sarasota, Fla.: American Accounting Association, 1981–86).

Zeff, Stephen A., "Theory and 'Intermediate Accounting,'" *The Accounting Review* (July 1979).

———— , "'Intermediate' and 'Advanced' Accounting: The Role of Economic Consequences," *The Accounting Review* (October 1980).